Children of Peace

Taking its title from the religious sect examined, *Children of Peace* is a history of one of the most significant and least-studied religious sects in English-speaking Canada. John McIntyre paints a colourful picture of a group of individuals who tried to provide a model for a new church and a new society.

The Children of Peace, which existed from 1812 to 1890, was started by former Quakers from the United States who set up a utopian community near Toronto. With their propensity for fine architecture, music, and ritual, adherents to the sect attracted the attention of the religious, political, and social élites. Their leader and founder, David Willson, was one of the most prolific religious writers and theorists in Canada at the time. The Children of Peace sought to create a church where God spoke directly to all and where both Christians and Jews could find a home.

McIntyre looks at life in the community and places the sect within its broader historical contexts. His examination of the community's buildings and artefacts provides additional insights into the beliefs and behaviour of its adherents. *Children of Peace* makes an important contribution to the growing field of religious and cultural history in Canada.

W. JOHN McINTYRE is professor of liberal studies, Seneca College.

McGill-Queen's Studies in the History of Religion
G.A. Rawlyk, Editor

Volumes in this series have been supported by the Jackman Foundation of Toronto.

1 Small Differences
Irish Catholics and Irish Protestants, 1815–1922
An International Perspective
Donald Harman Akenson

2 Two Worlds
The Protestant Culture of Nineteenth-Century Ontario
William Westfall

3 An Evangelical Mind
Nathanael Burwash and the Methodist Tradition in Canada, 1839–1918
Marguerite Van Die

4 The Dévotes
Women and Church in Seventeenth-Century France
Elizabeth Rapley

5 The Evangelical Century
College and Creed in English Canada from the Great Revival to the Great Depression
Michael Gauvreau

6 The German Peasants' War and Anabaptist Community of Goods
James M. Stayer

7 A World Mission
Canadian Protestantism and the Quest for a New International Order, 1918–1939
Robert Wright

8 Serving the Present Age
Revivalism, Progressivism, and the Methodist Tradition in Canada
Phyllis D. Airhart

9 A Sensitive Independence
Canadian Methodist Women Missionaries in Canada and the Orient, 1881–1925
Rosemary R. Gagan

10 God's Peoples
Covenant and Land in South Africa, Israel, and Ulster
Donald Harman Akenson

11 Creed and Culture
The Place of English-Speaking Catholics in Canadian Society, 1750–1930
Terrence Murphy and Gerald Stortz, editors

12 Piety and Nationalism
Lay Voluntary Associations and the Creation of an Irish-Catholic Community in Toronto, 1850–1895
Brian P. Clarke

13 Amazing Grace
Studies in Evangelicalism in the United States, Canada, Britain, Australia, and Beyond
George Rawlyk and Mark A. Noll, editors

14 Children of Peace
W. John McIntyre

Children of Peace

W. JOHN McINTYRE

McGill-Queen's University Press
Montreal & Kingston • London • Buffalo

© McGill-Queen's University Press 1994
ISBN 0-7735-1195-4

Legal deposit third quarter 1994
Bibliothèque nationale du Québec

Printed in Canada on acid-free paper

This book has been published with the help of a grant from the Social Science Federation of Canada, using funds provided by the Social Sciences and Humanities Research Council of Canada. Publication has also been supported by the Canada Council through its block grant program.

Canadian Cataloguing in Publication Data

McIntyre, W. John (William John), 1951–
  Children of Peace
  (McGill-Queen's studies in the history of religion; 14)
  Includes bibliographical references and index.
  ISBN 0-7735-1195-4
  1. Children of Peace – History. 2. Christian communities – Ontario – Sharon – History – 19th century. 3. Ontario – Church history – 19th century. 4. Millenialism – Ontario – History – 19th century.
  I. Title. II. Series
  BX9999.S43M34 1994   289.9   C94-900316-6

This book was typeset by Typo Litho Composition Inc. in 10/12 Palatino.

To my grandparents

Contents

Figures and Tables ix

Preface xi

1 A Gathering of Friends 3

2 Meeting House and Camp Meeting 14

3 Visions 30

4 Meeting House and Temple 47

5 Doctrine, Worship, and Ritual 82

6 Life and Work in the Community 108

7 House and Home: The Ebenezer Doan House 140

8 Religion and Politics 151

9 The Last Years of the Children of Peace 178

10 The Children of Peace and the World Around Them 186

Notes 211

Bibliography 237

Index 253

Figures and Tables

FIGURES

1 Yonge Street Friends Meeting House 4

2 Portrait of David Willson 10

3 Bonnet from the Yonge Street Quaker community 22

4 Buckingham Friends Meeting House, Bucks County, Pennsylvania 23

5 Painted banner, attributed to Richard Coates 32

6 Painted banner, attributed to Richard Coates 34

7 First meeting house of the Children of Peace 50

8 Bank Meeting House, Philadelphia 53

9 Temple of the Children of Peace 58

10 Interior of the temple 59

11 Altar at the center of the temple 61

12 Desk made by John Doan 71

13 David Willson's study 75

14 Second meeting house of the Children of Peace 77

15 Interior of the second meeting house 79

16 Ebenezer Doan house   141
17 Hall/kitchen of the Ebenezer Doan house   147
18 Box made in prison by Charles Doan   168

TABLES

1 Members of the Children of Peace, 1851   133
2 Inventory of Jacob Lepard, 1850   137

Preface

What are we to make of a group of people who called themselves Children of Peace; were inspired by visions of men, women, and children in varying states of nakedness; and believed that they were called by God to build a temple and a community that would usher in the Christian millennium? They do not fit our national myths or stereotypes of pioneers, but to dismiss them merely as cranks or eccentrics would be to miss a fascinating story from the rich diversity of early Canadian life.

To begin to understand the Children of Peace, we must consider what they left behind – words and objects – and listen to what they said about themselves through that legacy. This is harder than it may at first appear, for, to do so, we need to step back into a world that placed great emphasis on faith and the supernatural. Certain aspects of the sect can be explained with reference to economic issues, political upheaval, and competing theories of social organization, but people pressed by secular concerns do not usually turn to temple-building. The Children of Peace may be understood only if we are willing to put religious conviction and secular concerns on an equal footing, to take the record of a vision as seriously as the record of a land transaction as evidence of why people behave the way they do, and to not overwhelm the spiritual with the temporal or vice versa.

While much of late-twentieth-century North American culture remains sceptical of too many references to faith and belief in explaining contemporary phenomena, there are strong undercurrents of Christian fundamentalism and New Age philosophy that take quite the opposite approach. Consider that in the summer of 1993 a Gallup poll found that nearly twenty per cent of Americans believed that recent floods in the midwest indicated God's judgment on the people of the United States for their sinful ways. Horoscopes continue to be published in important newspapers, and the sale of crystals, tarot cards, and objects linked with fortune-telling and nature worship continues to rise. Some schools of thought might regard the Children of Peace as New Age seekers born before their time.

The Children of Peace came into being in 1812 and existed as an independent religious organization until 1890. They numbered nearly three hundred members and lived in East Gwillimbury Township, Upper Canada (now Ontario), around the village of Sharon. Their founders were Quakers who had come from the United States in the early years of the nineteenth century. During their seventy-eight years of existence, the Children of Peace built buildings that symbolized their beliefs and helped establish their identity as a sect: these were among the most ambitious and unusual structures built in preconfederation Canada. The group also created a prosperous farming community that experimented with various forms of cooperative organization, mutual support, and charitable enterprise, which were described in many popular travellers' books of their day. They built schools for girls and boys, organized a band and choir, and had pipe organs built for use in worship. Their founder, David Willson, published books, pamphlets, hymns, and broadsides and was among the most prolific religious writers and theorists of early-nineteenth-century Canada. He and his followers played a conspicuous role in the political life of the colony, taking part in controversies that led to the Rebellion of 1837 and to the reform movements of the 1840s and 1850s.

Today the Children of Peace are remembered through their buildings, which are part of a museum begun by the York Pioneer and Historical Society in 1918 and now run by the Sharon Temple Museum Society. Many now know of the sect through the series, "*Music at Sharon*," broadcast nationally every year on radio in conjunction with an annual music festival of international renown. Their former territory, now known as the town of East Gwillimbury, is undergoing rapid change. Located about fifty kilometres north of Toronto, near Newmarket, the area is being transformed by housing developments, shopping centers, and industrial parks. Working farms are rapidly disappearing, replaced by modern subdivisions or divided into "country estates" for prosperous commuters.

As the land they settled has changed and their members have passed beyond living memory, the Children of Peace have become the subject of scholarly attention. The first analysis of their buildings was Charles E. McFaddin's unpublished master's thesis at the University of Toronto in 1953.[1] In it, McFaddin looked for architectural precedents and analysed the sect's buildings according to documentary information then available. All subsequent analyses, including my own, have benefited from his work; however, today many more archival resources are available. When the Children of Peace ceased to exist, their records were scattered or destroyed. Only in recent years have substantial portions of these records been rediscovered and added to public collections or microfilmed for public use.

In 1972, I first began working with these records while researching two papers: one on the early writings of founder David Willson, and the other on his interest in politics and social organization (both published by the York Pioneer and Historical Society).[2] Prior to that time, I had spent several summers as curator of the museum, although curatorial duties then involved cutting the grass, keeping the buildings in order, and giving tours more than anything else. Since those days, the archival materials I examined have been thoroughly catalogued by others, and many more manuscripts have come to light. In fact, even as I was revising this book, a substantial amount of manuscript material was discovered, stored in a compartment hidden inside the altar at the temple. Sadly, there are still many gaps in the records: of David Willson's personal and family life, for instance, we know very little.

During the late 1970s and 1980s, several important studies were completed on various aspects of the history of the Children of Peace, among them Carolyn Mann's genealogy of the Willson family, Jean McFall's documentation of the last days of the Children of Peace, Ann Schau's work on music at Sharon, Thomas Gerry's analysis of Willson's mystical beliefs, Janette Diceman's statistical study from 1851 to 1889, Matthew Cooper's questioning of the sect's communal organization, Kitch Hill's analysis of construction techniques, and Albert Schrauwers's work on the separation of the Children of Peace from the Quakers and on their meetings outside of East Gwillimbury. Recently, Schrauwers's research has expanded into book form, so one may wonder if another book, this one, is needed so soon. Certainly every future writer about the Children of Peace will be indebted to Schrauwers, particularly for his painstaking research into the ways in which economic concerns intersected with religion and for his gathering of genealogical detail. I have taken a different approach, however, placing greater emphasis on the mystical, spiritual side of this story and on bringing information together in narrative form.

My own research has taken me increasingly into the study of material culture, and the number of pages I devote in this book to analysing buildings, artifacts, and the stuff of everyday life also sets this study apart from others. As a graduate student in the master's program in Early American Culture at the Henry Francis du Pont Winterthur Museum and the University of Delaware, and subsequently in the PhD program in the History of American Civilization at the same institutions, I lived near those parts of the Delaware valley from which many of the founders of the Children of Peace, including master builder Ebenezer Doan, came. More and more, it seemed clear to me that any further study of the Children of Peace should include analysis of their material culture as an important component. I also became convinced that Quaker community life in the Delaware valley provided important background to this study. I came to believe that, despite their location across the Canadian border, the Children of Peace were part of "American Civilization" in its broad sense. This was not only because they shared the North American continent, but also because their original members came from the United States, and their story seemed to be part of the broader history of American religious communities. I felt that further research on the Children on Peace would be of interest, not only to Canadians, but also to Americans concerned with the study of religion and society in the nineteenth century. Too often, research projects stop at the international border,[3] even when the movement of people and ideas suggests that political boundaries do not always reflect social and cultural limits. This study may also be of interest, not only for the similarities it reveals between the material culture, ideas, and community organization of the Children of Peace and nineteenth-century sects elsewhere, but also for the differences it uncovers.

In defining "material culture," an important focus of this study, I have been influenced by anthropologist James Deetz's definition: "that sector of our physical environment that we modify through culturally determined behavior."[4] Thus, material culture includes all artifacts, from clothing to buildings; altered landscapes, including ploughed fields and village streets; physical motion, including ritual movements; many examples of food and drink; and even language and speech. (Deetz has said, "Words, after all, are air masses shaped by the speech apparatus according to culturally acquired rules."[5]) Earlier research on the Children of Peace has only occasionally been concerned with material culture. Charles McFaddin's 1953 thesis remains the exception, although it looks only at buildings and approaches them from the point of view of an art historian. In this study, material culture has a broader role to play, starting with the material culture of the Quaker community from which the Children of Peace sprang, and using clothing, household goods, farming practices, ritual, diet, and speech, as well as buildings, as texts for analysis. Objects, as well as written documents, can provide important clues to understanding the past. For example, two painted banners have been used in this study as starting points for understanding why the Children of Peace broke away from the Quakers, and the shapes and floor plans of meeting houses have been analysed to suggest changing patterns of belief. In other studies, material culture has served more as a backdrop to research based almost exclusively on written documents.

This study has also been influenced by the work of Dolores Hayden,[6] who has given full weight to the importance of buildings and the use of space in the religious communities she has studied. She has emphasized dialectical relationships between spatial layout and social organization, and between architectural forms and religious beliefs. Earlier writers such as Charles Nordhoff, who in 1875 published the first sophisticated comparative study of American religious communities,[7] described material culture in considerable detail and used it as evidence of the success of communal societies in increasing the prosperity and general well-being of their members. They did not go beyond that, however, and maintained an antiquarian's interest in much of what they saw. In the 1950s, Arthur Bestor, Jr and Mark Holloway wrote comparative studies drawing on techniques of sociology,[8] as did more recent historians such as Rosabeth Moss Kanter and Charles J. Erasmus in the 1970s.[9] As important as these studies were, they seldom used material culture as primary source material: it has remained in the background as illustration.

Along with Dolores Hayden's work, that of Richard Bauman has been particularly useful in establishing an approach to studying the Children of Peace.[10] Bauman's analysis of Quaker speech patterns and doctrines of plainness has opened the door to a better understanding of why the Children of Peace had such a successful leader and developed their own views of plainness. In analysing the sect's buildings and attempting to go beyond mere description and the search for architectural precedents, studies such as those of Henry Glassie,[11] strongly influenced by structural anthropology, were also important. Seeing material culture as evidence of complex structures of beliefs and ideas has been an important aspect of Glassie's work, which is now widely followed by analysts of vernacular architecture in both the United States and Canada.

Early on, however, it became apparent that material culture alone would not provide all the information necessary to understand the Children of Peace. Thus, an interdisciplinary approach emerged, drawing on published and unpublished writings of leader David Willson and, when available, on writings of other members of the sect, early newspaper articles, travellers' accounts, land records, census and assessment records, wills and probate inventories, and a merchant's account book. (When quoting directly from archival sources, I have retained their original spelling and punctuation, along with their use of both the decimal system and the English system of pounds, shillings, and pence.) Not to have used these sources would have left an important part of the story of the Children of Peace untold. In discussing the sect's involvement in politics, for example, or in recording the last years of the Children of Peace, these sources were invaluable. In other parts of this study, written documents have been used side by side with artifacts to shed light on important topics. The aim, then, is a partnership between material culture study and other approaches to social history, drawing on the strengths of each without claiming superiority for either words or objects.

The writings of three other scholars have influenced this interdisciplinary approach. James Lemon's study of the Delaware valley during the eighteenth century[12] and, more particularly, Barry Levy's recent analysis of Quaker family life in early southeastern Pennsylvania provided models for understanding the kind of society established by Quakers and Children of Peace in Upper Canada.[13] In addition, William Westfall's recent work on the "religion of order" and the "religion of experience" in nineteenth-century Upper Canada added to the conceptual framework for this study.[14] All three explored aspects of material culture and took an interdisciplinary approach to their subject.

I also gratefully acknowledge the advice and encouragement I received from Dr Richard L. Bushman of Columbia University (formerly Chairperson of the Department of History, University of Delaware) and Dr Bernard L. Herman of the Center for Historic Architecture and Engineering at the University of Delaware. Jacqueline Stuart, curator of the Aurora Museum, provided many useful comments along the way; I am indebted to her and to the Aurora and District Historical Society for access to word processing and printing facilities. Thanks are also expressed to Ruth Mahoney of the Sharon Temple Museum, Jane Zavitz Bond of Pickering College, and to Albert Schrauwers for providing access to archival materials and generously sharing their own knowledge and research. Joan Harcourt of McGill-Queen's University Press and editors Sandra Black and Curtis Fahey have also made important contributions.

Children of Peace

1 A Gathering of Friends

On the eve of the War of 1812, travellers could go north from York (later called Toronto), the tiny capital of the colony of Upper Canada, and for mile after mile see nothing but unbroken forest and a few scattered clearings. The road in front of them, named Yonge Street in honour of former British secretary of war, Sir George Yonge, was little more than a trail, muddy during much of the year. Here and there, another path led off to the side to avoid a creek or marsh, but the road was clearly intended to go due north, as straight as a surveyor's chain could make it. Alongside Yonge Street stretched plots of land, each 200 acres in size and surveyed as perfect rectangles; however, few were settled. Yonge Street was not a path worn by custom: it was a military road, opened to link York on Lake Ontario with the navigable waters of the Holland River, and so with Lake Simcoe and the upper Great Lakes.[1] It gave York a means of communication with the west should the Americans decide to blockade Lake Ontario. The straight line of Yonge Street, a symbol of the military mind, appeared logical when conveyed on paper, yet it ignored the centuries-old Indian trail nearby that followed a more natural path along heights of land to the west. Yonge Street's creators sought to master the landscape by geometry rather than work within the natural framework of hills, valleys, and waterways. Yet in 1812, this mastery was still more imagined than real.

Only after reaching the Oak Ridges, some twenty miles north of the capital, did the landscape change, and something closer to Simcoe's vision emerge. From there, after slowly climbing upward from York,

Figure 1 Yonge Street Friends Meeting House, built 1810–12, Newmarket, Ontario.

travellers would begin to descend toward the Holland River and the lakes beyond. Gradually, the clearings on either side of the road would become larger and neat farmlands with log houses and barns would appear. Amid them stood a meeting house (Fig. 1), built by the Yonge Street Meeting of the Society of Friends – the first place of worship the travellers would have encountered since leaving York. The Friends, or Quakers, of Yonge Street had come from the United States. Their neat settlement was in striking contrast with the wild and forested land to the south. Its presence in the midst of a vast wilderness often aroused the curiosity and comments of travellers. Robert Gourlay, in his *Statistical Account of Upper Canada, Compiled with a View to a Grand System of Emigration*, wrote: "Where Yonge Street is completely settled, it is well cultivated and thriving, particularly beyond what is called the Oak Hills or Ridges ... In this quarter, the land is excellent, and it is well occupied by industrious people, mostly Quakers."[2]

The founder of this community was Timothy Rogers, a Vermont Quaker who had heard of earlier Friends' settlements on the Bay of Quinte and Niagara peninsula and decided to explore Upper Canada's possibilities for himself. In 1800, he travelled to York and thence northward on Yonge Street until he came to the vacant but promising land north of Oak Ridges. Returning to York, he found the colonial government willing to sanction his scheme for attracting up to forty families to the area whereby each family would receive a grant of 200 acres of Crown land. Evidently, the government was impressed by the record of Quaker settlers. As early as 1792, Lieutenant-Governor Simcoe had issued an invitation to Quakers in the Philadelphia area, offering them free land as well as exemption from militia duty and taxation for military purposes. In return, they were to clear that land immediately, build houses upon it, and help open and maintain the road in front of it. Simcoe had served in the British army during the Revolutionary War and had spent considerable time in New Jersey and southeastern Pennsylvania. There he must have been impressed by neat Quaker farms no less than by the Quaker refusal to take up arms in support of the American cause. In the spring of 1792, Simcoe had written to Phineas Bond, British consul in Philadelphia, noting that: "[His Majesty's] interests will be essentially promoted by the speedy condensation of a numerous, virtuous, agricultural people in Upper Canada, and such, I have experience, are the inhabitants of Pennsylvania. I have only to add that should any Society wish to emigrate, I should be happy to see those persons who should be authorized under mutual confidence for that purpose, and to give my best assistance to promote their views and establishment."[3]

His arrangements made, Timothy Rogers returned to the United States and then largely fulfilled his promise to lead Quaker families back to the Yonge Street settlement. Not all came at once, however. Rogers's most important role may have been as an initiator and publicist: news of free land in the Yonge Street settlement spread quickly through the network of Quaker meetings to which he belonged. Already, two meetings had been established in Upper Canada, one at Adolphustown on the Bay of Quinte and the other at Pelham on the Niagara Peninsula. The Adolphustown Monthly Meeting met under the auspices of the New York Yearly Meeting, while the Pelham Monthly Meeting was under the jurisdiction of the Philadelphia Yearly Meeting. Representatives of Upper Canadian meetings would have been in regular contact with their supervisory bodies. Timothy Rogers is known to have travelled to Pelham just after he applied for patents for forty 200-acre farms on Yonge Street. News of his plans was likely conveyed to Philadelphia quickly since the Upper Canadian Friends were eager to add to their numbers. Of nearly equal importance were the contributions of Samuel Lundy and Isaac Phillips, two Friends from Muncy, Pennsylvania, who secured tracts of land for another twenty Quaker families, adjoining the lands selected by Rogers.[4]

As soon as the Quakers arrived, they began meeting in each other's homes for worship, at first in Timothy Rogers's own house and then at Rufus Rogers's. In 1804, the Yonge Street Preparative Meeting was granted official status under the direction of the Pelham Monthly Meeting. The smallest unit in the organizational framework of the Society of Friends, a preparative meeting was under the authority of a monthly meeting that had the power to receive or reject recruits and to discipline or disown members. The monthly meeting, in turn, was supervised by a Quarterly or Half Yearly Meeting that served as a court of appeal and received and summarized reports to inform the Yearly Meeting. The latter acted as the final court of appeal and arbiter of discipline, faith, and practice. In 1806, the Yonge Street Meeting became a monthly meeting in its own right, under the auspices of the New York Yearly Meeting. During this same decade, Friends who settled farther east of Yonge Street began meeting in each other's homes in communities now known as Pine Orchard, Uxbridge, Sharon, and Pickering. These informal gatherings eventually received official status as preparative meetings under the jurisdiction of the Yonge Street Meeting.[5]

When Friends transferred their membership from one monthly meeting to another, careful records were kept. A survey of transfers to the Yonge Street Monthly Meeting between 1803 and 1828 shows that, out of a total of 108 members, forty-four came from Pennsylvania. Of these, twenty-five came from the vicinity of Muncy or Catawissa near the Susquehanna River, and another ten came from the Buckingham Meeting in Bucks County. Sixteen were from Vermont, mostly from Monkton and Ferrisburg. Fourteen came from New York State, one from New Jersey, fifteen from other meetings in Upper Canada, and eighteen from overseas.[6] The American settlers who came to Yonge Street were on the northern fringe of the "Great Migration" that saw over twenty thousand Quakers move north and west beyond the Allegheny Mountains. This movement began once the Northwest Ordinance of 1787 opened United States lands north of the Ohio River to settlement, while guaranteeing freedom of religion and the prohibition of slavery, an institution the Quakers opposed. The government of Upper Canada also opened its lands to Americans and, after 1793, prohibited the importation of slaves. Quakers who moved from Pennsylvania to the Yonge Street settlement did so for several reasons. Loyalty to the British crown was seldom among them since Quakers eschewed political involvement, refused to swear oaths of allegiance, and had tried to stay aloof from conflict during the American Revolution. The lure of free or inexpensive farmland and the guarantee of religious freedom were more important, as was the

Friends' growing anti-slavery sentiment. By the end of the eighteenth century, leaders such as John Woolman, William Reckitt, Benjamin Ferris, and Norris Jones had begun to inspire Friends "to move away from the environment of slavery and to get entirely free from its depressing influences."[7]

In Lycoming and Columbia counties, from which the largest group of Pennsylvanian settlers came, land was expensive. Isaac Webb and his family, for example, rented land near Catawissa for sixteen years and saw little prospect of owning their own farm. Around 1803, Webb's daughter and her husband, Mary and John Hartman, moved to the Yonge Street settlement. In 1805, his brother, George, also moved his family there. Isaac's son, Job, went with him, and, when he had claimed 200 acres of land for himself, returned to Pennsylvania to tell others of his good fortune. The following spring, Isaac Webb himself decided to move, along with the rest of his family and about thirty neighbours. In later years, Webb's son, Clayton, recalled: "In the fore part of the fifth month, we started with quite a caravan, about 33 people and 4 wagons. Father had of his own: 2 wagons, 4 horses hitched to one wagon, two horses and a yoke of oxen to the other, one riding horse, and 7 cows. In the new country cows were scarce. There were: our family, Henry Rose's, Jonathan Gould's, John Hilborn's, and Jess Teats and wife."[8]

The story of Isaac Webb illustrates a repeated pattern: a neighbour or younger family member would set out for new territory, bring back a favourable report, and inspire others to follow. When they moved, settlers generally travelled in groups for safety, convenience, and, not least of all, company on the long journey. Those who made the trip could not have been the poorest. Perhaps Isaac Webb was exceptional with his two wagons, horses, and livestock (or perhaps his son's memory exaggerated the extent of his possessions), but only the foolhardy would have left without ample tools and supplies. Nor was their journey from Catawissa through uncharted territory. For a good part of the way, they would have followed the Williamson Road, laid out in 1792 from Northumberland, Pennsylvania, to Bath, New York. From there, they would have travelled northwest to the site of the present-day village of Avon on the Genesee River, and then moved west through Batavia to Tonawanda, crossing the Niagara River at Lewiston. From Queenston, on the Upper Canadian side of the river, they would have taken a schooner down Lake Ontario to York.

While the desire for land was probably their strongest reason for moving, two well-known incidents of the 1790s may also have played a role. In 1795, the "Whiskey Rebellion" broke out in the Pittsburgh area when the United States Congress attempted to impose a tax on domestically produced whiskey, a major source of income for local farmers. The rebellion was put down only after militia units numbering fifteen thousand men from four states had been called to the scene. Then in 1799 John Fries led a rebellion near Bethlehem, Pennsylvania, when Congress planned to levy taxes on houses and land.[9] Both the Whiskey Rebellion and Fries's Rebellion were instances of popular resistance to Congress's efforts at political centralization and strengthening the national economy. To many, these efforts seemed to threaten individual freedom and liberty. While the Quaker emigrants were largely apolitical, they were not unaffected by rumours that the government was out to pick their pockets.

In Bucks County, from which another large contingent of Yonge Street Quakers came, land prices increased ten-fold, farms became smaller, and crop yields declined during the last quarter of the eighteenth century.[10] Conditions improved in the 1790s, however, with the result that farmers and craftsmen could dispose of their property more easily and gather the resources needed to start afresh elsewhere.[11] Ebenezer Doan, for instance, purchased a farm of 79¾ acres in Solebury Township for £957 in 1801.[12] He later sold it and got a 200-acre grant of Crown land free in Upper Canada. That land was forested and had to be cleared, but the offer was worth the effort. Closely linked through strong religious and familial bonds, Quakers living in the Delaware valley of Pennsylvania placed great emphasis on buying, exchanging, and preserving land for their children. Indeed, the mid-Atlantic region was the first in North America to build a successful regional economy based on agricultural surpluses generated by family farms.[13] It is not surprising, then, that so many Quaker farmers claimed land in Upper Canada when farms in their native region became scarce and expensive, making their way to the new land in groups of extended families.

In fact, Upper Canada was just one of several destinations Quaker settlers might have chosen. In his narrative, Joseph Gould, who came to Upper Canada with the Webbs, recalled that his father and eldest brother were offered a grant of 600 acres between them, but were disappointed with what they saw and "did not like the country." They decided to move to Ohio, where the Goulds had relatives. To earn enough money to return to the United States, Gould's father spent two years farming and working as a teamster. His plans fell through, however, when one of his creditors went bankrupt. The Goulds were then left with no alternative but to stay and seek their fortune in Upper Canada.[14]

The political boundary between Upper Canada and the United States seemed less important to these people than the ties that linked them to family and friends back home. Such ties continued well into the second generation. In 1830 twenty-three-year-old Oliver Doan wrote to his cousin, Howard Paxson of Bucks County, "It is just as easy for thee to Come to Canada as it is to go to Philadelphia only it takes a little longer, ten days, that is not a very long time."[15] When he wrote these lines, Oliver Doan had just returned from a trip to Bucks County. His mother was to start out the next day for a visit, and he hoped his cousin might make the return journey with her. He spoke lightly of a journey that, despite the new canals and improved roads of 1830, still involved four hundred miles of difficult travel. Even though Oliver was scarcely a year old when his family left Pennsylvania, he, like his mother, maintained strong ties to the place.

Marriage patterns also suggest strong, continuing links among people of Pennsylvania background. Of the sixty-five Pennsylvanians married within the Yonge Street Meeting between 1804 and 1828, forty-five married other Pennsylvanians. Of the rest, fifteen married Vermonters, three married New Yorkers, and two married Upper Canadians.[16] These statistics are predictable, given the make-up of the community, but evidence also suggests that if a suitable marriage partner of Pennsylvania background was not found locally, a trip would be made or a letter sent back home to find one. During this early period, men outnumbered women in the community by roughly three to two,[17] resulting in a scarcity of prospective brides.

Within a few years, the Quaker settlement that grew around Yonge Street had become visibly prosperous and successful. It had moved quickly to establish religious institutions in its midst. Yet the Children of Peace would soon challenge the peace of the Quaker community. To understand the changes that were to come, it is important to examine the background of two individual community members: David Willson (Fig. 2), founder of the Children of Peace, and Ebenezer Doan, a master builder who oversaw the erection of buildings that embodied their beliefs.

David Willson (1778–1866) arrived in the community during its first year of settlement, 1801.[18] Unlike the majority of settlers, however, Willson came from New York state and was not of Quaker background, although his wife was. Perhaps for these reasons, Willson took up land on the eastern fringes of the community, on what was to be called Queen Street (today's Leslie Street) in East Gwillimbury Township. Willson's ancestors had been involved in the linen trade in Carrickfergus, County Antrim, Ireland. His father and uncle were both well-educated men. David's uncle, Hugh, had been destined for the Presbyterian ministry, but the economic disruptions of the Seven Years' War (1756–1763) had led to a downturn in family fortunes and

Figure 2 Portrait of David Willson, possibly by Richard Coates, oil on canvas, c.1825. (Private collection, North York, Ontario)

put an end to Hugh's schooling. David's father, John, may have been a more adventurous character. In 1768 John Willson came to America, leaving a pregnant wife behind in his parents' care. To secure a brighter future for himself and his family, many a young man set out from Ireland at that time, leaving wives and children behind until they could establish a place for them in the New World. However, John's wife died before she could join him, leaving a young son. Willson remarried and took up farming, renting land in the vicinity of Nine Partners, near Poughkeepsie, in New York's Hudson River valley. During the Revolution, he supported the Loyalist cause and was fined and imprisoned several times for his activities. In 1775, Hugh Willson followed his brother to America, bringing with him John's son, Hugh Jr, who went to live with his father and stepmother. John's second wife, Catherine, bore at least four children: David; John Jr; Mary; and Ann. When John died around 1793, Hugh Jr took responsibility for the family and their rented farm. Even though the Willsons were of Presbyterian background, Quaker influence on them must have been strong. Nine Partners was at the centre of an important Quaker community to which they were linked when Hugh, Jr married Mary Titus, eldest daughter of Austin Titus, a prominent Quaker preacher. Evidently, by the time of his marriage, Hugh Jr had become a Quaker, since there is no mention in the records of Mary being disowned by the Nine Partners Meeting, which she surely would have been had she married a non-Quaker. Phebe Titus, on the other hand, *was* disowned when she was courted by Hugh Jr's stepbrother, David Willson, who was then working at least part-time as a carpenter.

Hugh Jr supplemented his farming income through trips on a sailing ship that carried flour, pork, horses, and agricultural commodities to the West Indies. In 1798, he moved his family to New York City, where he invested in the sloop, *The Farmer*, and pursued West Indian trade full-time. His stepbrother, David, also participated in this venture. The year 1798 was not, however, a good year to become involved with sailing ships: in July the United States Congress repealed its treaties with France, launching an undeclared naval war between the two countries that lasted two years. The same summer, Congress passed its controversial Alien and Sedition Acts, which sharpened hostility against people of foreign birth and severely restricted political opposition. Hugh Jr soon sold his shares in *The Farmer* and made plans to leave the dangers of the sea and the turmoil of New York City behind him. He and his family moved to Upper Canada in 1800, settling just west of Kingston. For several years, he taught school and worked on the farm of Joseph Ferris, an old acquaintance from the Nine Partners area. In 1801, David Willson joined Hugh Jr, bringing with him his wife, Phebe, and two sons, John and Israel. Once there, they heard of the new settlement Timothy Rogers was planning on Yonge Street and set off for the town of York by boat. Family tradition tells that just as they neared their destination, they were shipwrecked. Having lost everything but David's money belt and the clothes they were wearing, they managed to swim ashore with their two young sons clinging to the spokes of Phebe's spinning wheel. From York, they walked to their land east of Yonge Street. Shortly afterwards,

Willson's mother, brother, and two sisters joined them. In 1810, Hugh Jr brought *his* family to the community, too.

Although David Willson was not a member of the Society of Friends when he first arrived in Upper Canada, he soon joined the activities of the Quaker community and became a full member in 1805. He served on numerous important committees of the Yonge Street Monthly Meeting and in 1809 gave a corner of his farm as the site for a meeting house for the new Queen Street Preparative Meeting.[19] By 1812, David Willson appeared to be fully integrated into the Quaker community. However, there were important differences between Willson and his neighbours: he was not a Quaker of long standing; he came from a Loyalist family; he was probably better educated than most of his neighbors; and, while raised on a farm, he had once lived in New York City and sailed the seas to the West Indies, so he had seen more of the world. Furthermore, his safe arrival among them may have seemed providential, saved as he was from shipwreck and near disaster.

Ebenezer Doan's links with Quaker history were stronger than David Willson's, and his roots in North America ran much deeper. An ancestor, Deacon John Doan (or Doane), a "gentleman tailor," had been among the early settlers at Plymouth, Massachusetts, and was a founder of the community of Eastham on Cape Cod.[20] John's son, Daniel (c.1636–1712), became a carpenter, as would many of his descendants after him. Daniel's son, also named Daniel (d. 1743), was influenced by early Quaker missionaries on Cape Cod to join the Society of Friends. Feeling persecuted there, Daniel Jr moved to Newtown in Bucks County, already a sizable Quaker settlement, in 1695 and followed in his father's footsteps as a carpenter.[21] Daniel Jr's son, Joseph (b. 1697), continued the family tradition of carpentry and eventually purchased land in Wrightstown, Bucks County. One of *his* sons, Ebenezer (1733–1818), took up land near Brownsburg, Bucks County, and fathered our subject, Ebenezer Doan (1772–1866). Young Ebenezer and his brother John (1768–1852) trained as carpenters under their considerably older brother, Jonathan (1755/6–1818). John wrote the following verse during their apprenticeship; it refers to an accident and subsequent temper tantrum in the shop:

> See poor Eben get a chip
>   See him hang his under lip –
> See his tow head fumbled o'er –
>   See his red cap on the floor
> Tink de Lawdle Tink de law
>   Eben's broke the compas saw.[22]

Ebenezer and John were trained under no ordinary carpenter. Their elder brother, Jonathan, superintended various building projects for the state of New Jersey throughout the 1790s. These included the first New Jersey State House in Trenton, across the Delaware River from Bucks County, in 1791–92 and the New Jersey State Prison in 1797–99. In the records pertaining to these projects, Jonathan is listed as an agent, undertaker, or master carpenter, fulfilling a role similar to that of a general contractor today.[23] Ebenezer may have worked with Jonathan in New Jersey as part of his apprenticeship, being only nineteen when work on the State House began. Perhaps he was anxious to set out on his own, away from the shadow of his older brother. By January 1795, he had moved to Savannah, Georgia, where he married a woman named Sabra Fray. By 1801, however, he returned to Bucks County. After his first wife died, he married Elizabeth Paxson and purchased land in Solebury Township, close to other members of his family. At twenty-nine years old, Ebenezer Doan owned one of the largest farms in the area.[24] Most Bucks County farmers were not as fortunate: their farms were small and, though the local economy was improving, few could hope to add to their holdings. The neighbouring farm owned by Ebenezer's brother, John, was only half as large.

Perhaps that was why John set his sights on moving to Upper Canada, a destination other local farmers and craftsmen had chosen since as early as 1786.[25] John and Ebenezer's sister and her husband, Martha and Amos Armitage, had moved to the Yonge Street Quaker settlement in 1804.[26] John and his family followed in 1807. They must have sent back favourable reports because in 1808 Ebenezer joined them, along with his wife and three children, his father, brother Mahlon and family, brothers William and Joseph, and his sister Mary. The Doans came as an extended family to the Yonge Street settlement. They brought with them certificates from the Buckingham Monthly Meeting in Bucks County and were immediately accepted as full members of the Yonge Street Meeting.[27] Yet one factor set Ebenezer Doan and his brother, John, apart from most settlers on Yonge Street: the Doan brothers had been trained by one of the leading builders of the mid-Atlantic states. In time, both would be called to use their special skills in a task much more challenging than the construction of houses, barns, and Quaker meeting houses.

2 Meeting House and Camp Meeting

The religious life and beliefs of the Quaker community may be found written in the fabric of their Yonge Street meeting house. It stood as a symbol, yet was more than a symbol: its structure, floor plan, furnishings, and detail embodied the beliefs of the Friends. It spoke to the faithful of their roots, their traditions, and their beliefs, and it preached those beliefs to the unconverted. Anthropologist Robert Plant Armstrong has used the term, "the affecting presence," to describe that aspect of a work of art or artifact that embodies emotion, thought, or values and goes beyond symbolism.[1] By its treatment and location of doors, windows, partitions, and furnishings, or by the height of its ceiling and the length and breadth of its interior spaces, a meeting house, like a cathedral, can impose on its users certain patterns of behavior and decorum. By its facilities for providing light, heat, and ventilation, it will not only achieve a certain level of physical comfort, but will also evoke a particular mood or atmosphere. These patterns of use and atmospheric qualities are active, influential forces that sprang from the beliefs of the meeting house builders and designers. Analysis of the "affecting presence" of the meeting house can be important, not only in uncovering more about the thought and beliefs of the Yonge Street Quaker community, but also in suggesting differences between them and the Children of Peace, who broke away in 1812.

Written documents alone cannot give the entire picture: the minutes of the Yonge Street Meeting are generally terse and businesslike. Regarding the building of the meeting house, they list the names of those who oversaw the work, the amount of money subscribed for construction, the acquisition of a site, the overall dimensions, and other information of a general nature. For example, on 15 December 1808, they recorded: "that this meeting is united in the work going forward, & Appoints Isaac Phillips, John Doan, Thomas Linvill, Reuben Burr & Amos Armitage to have the management and oversight thereof, fix on the Spot, provide Materials and Carry on the work ..."[2] This minute not only lists the original committee members charged with supervising construction, but in its opening phrase, "that this meeting is united," it recalls the Quaker practice of coming to consensus over important issues. Concerns would be discussed until agreement was reached, and the "sense of the meeting," rather than a recorded vote, determined the direction to take. The minutes generally do not record details of the discussions that led to these decisions or the reasons why specific plans or shapes were chosen. This is to be expected since those attending a meeting would come with certain common expectations that did not need to be put into words. The meeting house itself, then, provides another part of the story. As a three-dimensional embodiment of the unspoken beliefs and assumptions of the Yonge Street Friends, it may be read like a text to better understand the religious life of their community.

The Yonge Street meeting house, still in regular use, is said to survive today "in virtually the same condition as when it was built in 1810–12."[3] On the exterior, however, its original horizontal clapboards were replaced many years ago by vertical board-and-batten siding, a sheathing material that did not come into vogue until the mid-nineteenth century. A long covered porch on the south side, almost certainly another addition of the Victorian era, is said to have been remodelled once[4] and may not have existed at all when the building first opened. In its place, there may have been projecting "pent eaves," like those shown in an early photograph of the Pine Orchard Preparative meeting house, built about five miles to the east in 1821. Pent eaves, a shallow extension of the eaves along a gable wall, were a common feature of Pennsylvania architecture,[5] and may well have been used on the Yonge Street meeting house. More changes occurred in the 1970s, when a full basement with a meeting room, kitchen, washrooms, and utility rooms was added, but these facilities are invisible from outside. Despite these alterations, much of the early meeting house has survived intact.

The building's site was significant. Since the Quaker settlement grew along a straight, government-built road, it lacked a true village square of the kind Timothy Rogers would have known in New England. Still, the site chosen for the meeting house was as close to the centre of the Yonge Street settlement as was practical. Symbolically, the community's spiritual centre was located at its geographic centre. The general layout of the community resembled a rural village in Bucks or Lycoming counties, rather than a New England village with a central common.[6] In the Delaware and Susquehanna valleys, from which many of the Yonge Street Friends had come, most Quaker communities consisted of long, narrow rows of farms, houses, and shops. There, as on Yonge Street, community ties were maintained through common religious beliefs and complicated networks of kinship, tangibly expressed by the meeting house, rather than by corporate squares or commons.[7]

The settlers erected a log meeting house on the site of the present building once they had outgrown the practice of gathering in members' houses (probably in 1804 or 1805).[8] In October 1807, less than four months after the arrival of John Doan, a committee was formed to investigate building a more durable structure. No doubt Doan and his brother-in-law, carpenter Amos Armitage, were included because of their knowledge of the practical details of construction. By the end of 1808, the committee recommended building a one-storey frame structure, thirty-five feet wide by seventy feet long. They had taken over a year to formulate this recommendation, being perhaps preoccupied with land clearing and house building. Once their decision was made, $1,600 was subscribed in less than a month.[9] The year 1809 brought another delay, however, as a mysterious sickness spread through the community, killing thirty people, including seven members of Timothy Rogers's family.[10] In January 1810, renewed efforts were made, though the building size was reduced to thirty by sixty feet.[11] On its completion in 1812, it was still the only house of worship on Yonge Street north of York.

Oriented with its shorter sides parallel to Yonge Street, the meeting house consists of two thirty-foot squares, set side by side. Inside, an adjustable partition divides the two squares, separating the men's meeting on the east side from the women's on the west. The partition was opened for First Day (Sunday) and Fourth Day (Wednesday) meetings for worship. It was closed when men and women needed to meet separately to discuss discipline or business concerns. Since the late 1660s, when Quaker founder George Fox (1624–1691) first developed the organizational pattern of preparative, monthly, quarterly, and yearly meetings, Friends had been urged to establish women's business meetings parallel to men's meetings at each level. Controversy arose over this directive: since Quakers believed in the essential equality of men and women in the eyes of God, some wondered why they should conduct business separately. On the other hand, some Quaker men objected to the amount of power given to women's meetings, set apart from the watchful eye of men. Particularly worrisome to these objectors was the women's meetings' authority to oversee the first steps in preparing a young couple for marriage. This authority went against the tradition of patriarchal leadership within the family and suggests that many early Quakers were interested, not only in religious reform, but in social change and the rights of women as well.

In North America, the role of women's business meetings grew stronger as time went on. In Britain, however, they tended to decline by the late seventeenth century, as conservative Friends borrowed increasingly from the Puritan concept of male authority in the church, government, and home.[12] Thus, some English meeting houses were built without partition walls to accommodate separate business meetings, while most North American meetings houses were divided in this way. A sense of modesty and decorum also provided a rationale for the separation of men's and women's business meetings. As George Fox declared in 1675, "There is some dark spirits that would have no women's meetings, but as men should meet with them, which women cannot for civility sake and modesty sake speak amongst men of women's matters, neither can modest men desire it and none but ranters will desire to look into women's matters."[13] In the social context of the times, separate spaces for women's business meetings gave women both power and freedom, which they could not have had otherwise.

The partition was opened when Friends met for worship. Then, both women and men were allowed to speak and address the worshipping assembly as the "Inner Light" moved them. Most Christians took literally St Paul's belief that it was shameful for women to teach or speak during worship (1 *Timothy* 2:9–12): the Friends, respecting the talents and ministry of women, challenged this doctrine. By providing men's and women's seating areas of equal proportions and layout, they gave tangible expression to their belief in equality. Quakers stressed the importance of the Inner Light, which their English founder believed was available to all, male or female.[14] That Inner Light, representing the spirit of God, led to speech and action as well as to belief. Quaker insistence on the right of women to preach and to address mixed assemblies scandalized many of their early opponents and led to both persecution and slander.[15]

The two thirty-foot-square halves of the Yonge Street meeting house were identical, suggesting the equality of those who worshipped there. Each half could be entered by a double door on the long, south face of the building or by a door on either end wall. Each half was lit by six windows, symmetrically placed in relation to the door openings. Light from these windows reflected off the light-coloured walls and ceiling inside, giving a bright and airy effect. The lightness, balance, and symmetry of the meeting house were linked to the prevailing Georgian and neoclassical styles of the time, but this does not diminish the building's role as a purveyor of Quaker beliefs and values. As part of an Atlantic culture as well as a distinctive religious sect, Quakers were inevitably influenced by the prevailing trends of their day.[16]

Builders living in the Yonge Street community worked in the broad context of Georgian and neoclassical architecture. Reuben Burr, for instance, was a skilled craftsman on the original building committee. On his arrival in 1805 from Catawissa, Pennsylvania, he was designated a joiner when he obtained a deed for twenty-five acres of land.[17] Burr possessed a first edition copy of Owen Biddle's *The Young Carpenter's Assistant*, published in Philadelphia that same year, which he used in training apprentices Eleazar Lewis from 1809 to 1813.[18] *The Young Carpenter's Assistant* was a very conservative work. As architectural historian, Talbot Hamlin, wrote: "Its designs, much more restrained and austere than those shown in Asher Benjamin's plates, are all in the dignified Georgian style of the late Philadelphia Colonial. Although occasionally they show some of the delicate attenuation of the New England work, generally they have that kind of quiet correctness so typical of the Philadelphia region. Of the newer classical feeling championed by Jefferson there is scarcely a trace; of even the delicate creative modifications of the Adam spirit that characterized the work of New England, New Jersey, and New York there is little sign."[19] The conservative, restrained style of Biddle's plates may have appealed to Quaker taste for plainness and simplicity. Ownership of such a recent publication suggests that Burr's conservatism was not the result of some backwoods aesthetic or cultural lag, but a reflection of the general conservatism of many Pennsylvania-born builders at the time.

Inside each half of the meeting house were rows of long benches divided by a centre aisle. Six benches faced north; three south. That meant that when the meeting house was in use, members sat facing each other. This arrangement allowed a sense of intimacy within the worshipping community. Facing each other in meetings was the physical equivalent of the Quaker linguistic practice of addressing all people by the familiar and personal *thee*, rather than the formal, originally plural *you*. As Richard Bauman has shown, Quakers consciously developed new habits of speaking in order to set themselves apart from others; their exclusive use of the familiar *thee* stressed their belief in the equality of all people.[20] For similar reasons, Quakers avoided the usual seating arrangements of churches, with their rows of pews or benches focusing on an altar or pulpit. They distrusted not only the liturgical worship of Roman Catholics, Anglicans, and Episcopalians but also the prepared sermons, prayers, and Biblical commentaries of evangelicals.

Robert Barclay, whose books were widely read by Quakers and could be found in the small library of the Yonge Street Friends, declared that worship should be prompted by the Spirit: "All other worship, then, both Praises, Prayers and Preachings, which man sets about in his own will, and at his own appointment, which he can both begin and end at his pleasure, do or leave undone, as himself sees meet; whether they be a prescribed Form, as a liturgy, or Prayers conceived extemporarily, by the natural strength and Faculty of the Mind, they are all but Superstitions, Will-worship, and abominable Idolatry in the sight of God, which are to be denied, rejected, and separated from, in this Day of Spiritual Arising ..."[21] Barclay's words did not mean that the Quakers were antinomians – that is, believing in no authority except that given to them directly by the spirit of God. They believed, as Barclay himself put it, that divine revelations "neither do nor can ever contradict the outward Testimony of the Scriptures, or right and sound Reason."[22] One of the greatest fears of Barclay, of George Fox, and of William Penn, who established the Friends on a firm footing in America, was that Scripture and church authority would be perverted by a "hireling ministry" whose teachings and discipline were prompted by a desire for monetary gain and power rather than by God.

Thus, the meeting house had no one obvious focal point where one member of the meeting might stand to preach, pray, sing, or perform any liturgical act or sacrament. Instead, the benches on the north side, fewer than those on the south, were arranged in three tiers to accommodate the elders, overseers, and those who were felt to have special gifts of ministry. Quakers were mystics who emphasized God's direct revelation to the souls of men and women, but the arrangement of the benches in the meeting house shows them to have been practical mystics, acknowledging the importance of order and authority in their community. The Friends met on the first and fourth days of the week to wait on the Lord, feel the prompting of the Spirit, and give voice to their Inner Light. They did not expect that those promptings would lead to disorder. William Penn and other Quaker writers told of intense, spiritual awakenings, but laid equal stress on "plain, sound and practical knowledge to be felt by those that are in any measure restored to the Exercises of the Spiritual Senses."[23] Early nineteenth-century Quakers saw no contradiction in this mixture of mysticism and practicality. Their meeting houses, blending authority and equality in three-dimensional form, also expressed this harmonious duality.

Raised benches for ministers, elders, and overseers symbolized the evolution of Quakerism from its charismatic beginnings to its status in the early nineteenth century as a mature religious organization, complete with its own discipline, order, and hierarchical structure. Even by the late seventeenth century, Friends had lost some of their initial zeal, when all would stand to speak in a meeting, and had begun to defer to those who were believed to have special gifts of ministry and spirituality. This "routinization of charisma," as it has been called, is a common phenomenon in the evolution of religious organizations. After a period of inspiration, zeal, and growth comes a period when rule and order are emphasized to consolidate the gains that have been made, ensure the stability of the organization, and check any disruptions or challenges to the organization's continuance.[24]

Because of the Quakers' dual emphasis on community order and the inner life of individuals, they felt uncomfortable with displays of personal wealth or extravagance. Such displays could range from overly decorative clothing to drunkenness, including anything that could arouse the envy or ill will of a neighbour or suggest that the spiritual life of an individual was neglected or at risk. Quakers also emphasized plainness in order to set themselves apart from the rest of the world. One meeting directed, "Great mouldings one above another ... ought to be avoided, only what is decent according to Truth." Committees were set up to inspect houses, causing an early Friend to write, "Our wainscots or woodwork we had painted of one plain colour, large mouldings or finishings of panelling, &c.; our swelling chimney-pieces, curiously twisted banisters, we took down, and replaced with useful plain wood-work &c ..."[25] Quakers met in such houses before they had the resources or the legal right to build meeting houses. Belief and practice did not always coincide, however. As early as 1698, the Yearly Meeting of Women Friends in Philadelphia warned against the use of superfluous household furniture and curtains. Throughout the eighteenth century, others gave similar warnings, climaxing in a great purge of luxury items at the time of the Revolution, complete with visitation committees and disownments.[26]

Yet a survey of high-style Chippendale furniture owned by Philadelphia Quakers before and during the American Revolution has shown that some of the most elaborately ornamented pieces were owned by devout, active Quakers. Disciplinary measures were rarely taken against the owners of these objects because of the objects *per se*. Rather, measures were aimed at correcting more serious problems concerning immoral behavior, marrying without the consent of the meeting, or buying and selling slaves, for example. Considerable latitude prevailed regarding personal possessions. When ownership of a highly decorative object became a stumbling block to faithfulness or a distraction from more important obligations to the meeting or to one's family and community, then disciplinary actions might be taken. Otherwise, they were not. Quaker theology could bear directly on members' perceptions of material objects without dictating their appearance.[27]

In the Yonge Street community, excessive indulgence in ornament was not an issue, since most members lived in simple log houses while clearing the land and taking on the back-breaking business of farming. Few could afford luxury. One excess a pioneer could, and did, indulge in was drunkenness, made possible by home-distilled liquor. In 1807, a committee was set up by the monthly meeting "to treat with such of our Members as are concerned in the practice of Distilling or Retailing ... and also to advise to true moderation on the use thereof in Every Respect."[28] In the Yonge Street community, as in every community, there was a gap between an ideal standard of behavior and reality.

The meeting house gives evidence of that complicated dialectic between what was necessary for efficiency and function and what lay beyond necessity. Its interior may be described as plain only in relative terms – in contrast with the popular modern definition of the word *church*, for example, with its suggestions of stained glass, colourful hangings, organ pipes, and so on. When it was first built, the interior of the meeting house was scarcely more plain than the original St James Church in York, which was shared by Anglicans and Presbyterians.[29] By the early nineteenth century, Quaker plainness, originally a reaction against seventeenth-century excess, was close to the mainstream of fashion, which had come under the influence of austere neoclassicism.

Examination of the boards covering the ceiling and interior walls shows delicate beaded edges in the neoclassical manner. Moulding planes were run along one edge of each board for purely aesthetic reasons. Similarly, the doors, exterior shutters, and parts of the interior partition wall are carefully panelled, not plain. The ends of the benches are made to look lighter than they actually are by means of graceful curves only partly determined by the need for armrests. The meeting house stove, an early addition, displays many elements of the neoclassical style – garlands, ovals, and delicately cast borders –

22 Children of Peace

Figure 3 Bonnet from the Yonge Street Quaker community, black and white silk, 12" × 9.5" × 8.5", mid-nineteenth century. (Aurora Museum acc.no. X72.9.9)

and stands on four paw feet. Even the exterior colour of the meeting house, yellow, puts the lie to the sometimes exaggerated image of Quaker austerity. Before paint analysis was done in the 1970s, the Yonge Street meeting house was painted grey and white in keeping with what its twentieth-century congregation thought was appropriate. Research, however, showed traces of the original yellow, which has now been restored. A study of New England meeting houses built by the Puritans, another group whose "plainness" is often misunderstood, shows that yellow was the most common meeting house colour at the time.[30]

Aside from the meeting house, relatively few artifacts linked to the early settlers on Yonge Street have survived. One of them, a bonnet (Fig. 3), may be considered here in context with the meeting house. The bonnet complied with Quaker aesthetics in its relative simplicity and lack of elaborate applied ornament or colourful pattern. Yet, it was made of black silk, an expensive imported material, and its broad

23 Meeting House and Camp Meeting

Figure 4 Buckingham Friends Meeting House, built 1768, Bucks County, Pennsylvania.

brim may have had as much to do with fashion as with Quaker modesty. Thus, in the bonnet, as in the meeting house, there is a subtle blending of simplicity and worldliness, a rejection of fashion and an acceptance of it. Such blending is not the stuff of hypocrisy or mere accommodation. It is, rather, a symbol of the way Yonge Street Quakers held themselves apart from the world through the mystical emphases of their religion, but still participated in worldly affairs as efficient and ultimately prosperous settlers. They no doubt saw God's hand at work in their prosperity as well as in their inner revelations.

The design of their meeting house sprang from the beliefs of the Yonge Street Quakers, but its links with widespread Quaker practice and prevailing architectural taste meant that it was not entirely original or unique. A comparison with the Buckingham meeting house (Fig. 4), built in 1768 in Bucks County, Pennsylvania, is revealing. From this meeting house came the certificates of removal presented by the Doan family to the Yonge Street Friends.[31] Many of those who witnessed the marriage of Ebenezer Doan and Elizabeth Paxson in this setting later became their neighbours once again on Yonge Street.[32] The Buckingham Friends' meeting house was larger, older, and built of stone, the preferred local building material. Like other meeting houses of the time, it was divided into two equal parts, each with symmetrically arranged window and door openings, panelled shutters, and facing rows of benches. A mental picture or template of this building would have been carried in the mind of Bucks County Quakers such as John Doan, who played an important role on the Yonge Street Friends' building committee. Thus, the Yonge Street meeting house provides an example of the diffusion of vernacular building forms across the North American continent. That diffusion was not so much a matter of details as of "organic wholes wherein style, aesthetic conventions, social organization, and religion are structurally related," as anthropologist Claude Lévi-Strauss put it.[33] The two meeting houses owe their similarities not only to their builders' common geographic origins, but also to their common and deeply rooted understanding of style, aesthetics, community, and belief.

During the first decade of the nineteenth century, Methodists provided the only real challenge to Quaker hegemony in the Yonge Street settlement. Officially, the colony of Upper Canada had an established church, which most assumed was Anglican; however, the Constitutional Act of 1791, which had divided Upper from Lower Canada, had not been specific about this. The Anglican Church remained weak, with relatively few clergy and adherents and little interest in evangelizing on Yonge Street. The Methodists, in contrast, set out with enthusiasm to take their particular brand of frontier religion to the farthest corners of the colony. They were Americans, like the majority of Upper Canada's settlers at the time. Even by 1812, only seven of the Methodists' seventy-six missionaries in Canada were Canadian-born; the vast majority were from the United States.[34] To the Quakers, the Methodists brought not only similar backgrounds, but also similar beliefs and approaches to worship.

Many Methodist statements regarding worship could easily have been written by Quakers. For example: "In considering the public worship of the Methodists, the first characteristic which strikes our attention is its *primitive and scriptural simplicity and purity* ... In all this there are no needless and cumbrous rites; no ceremonies which are learned and observed with difficulty. But there is a striking similarity to the mode of worship which obtained in the early stages of Christianity."[35] The early Methodists, like the Quakers, emphasized personal and family devotions as well as weekday meetings, and generally separated men and women in worship. The Methodists also shared the Quaker emphasis on a deeply felt inner experience of God's presence: "Other denominations have trusted chiefly to the effect of doctrinal and ethical disquisitions, without seeking to stimulate their hearers to the exercise of faith and love by direct exhortation and personal persuasion. Methodism does both. It unfolds the truth. It also habitually enforces with tears, entreaties, exhortations."[36] Like the Quakers, the Methodists rejected Calvinist doctrines of predestination, which had influenced the Puritans and Reformation-era Christians. Instead, they believed that all could be brought to salvation through conversion and faith.

Unlike the Quakers, however, Methodists emphasized the doctrine of original sin and stressed the importance of Christ's sacrifice on the cross in bringing mankind to salvation. They avoided the more universalist tendencies of Quaker thought and would have considered heretical Robert Barclay's proposition that even non-Christians could be saved "if they receive and resist not that Grace, *A Manifestation Whereof is given to every Man to profit withall.*"[37] The Methodists also followed different patterns of worship that included Bible readings, sermons, hymns, prayers, quarterly fasts, quarterly love feasts, and the sacraments of baptism and the Lord's Supper. They did not share the Quaker emphasis on mysticism or the Inner Light. While believing that the Holy Spirit could move the hearts of men and women, they emphasized the power of scripture, sermons, and hymns to guide and heal. Their sermons and hymns drew on the power of carefully chosen words, vivid narratives, climactic rhetoric, and the rhythms of music to reinforce their teachings. These gave a Methodist meeting a decidedly more theatrical quality than a Quaker one. Methodism was more populist in tone and approach, relying less on mystic introspection and more on techniques from the theatre for its success. Methodist meeting houses had pulpits and space for movable communion tables; otherwise, they were much like Quaker meeting houses in their simplicity, plainness, and squarish shape.[38]

In dress, also, early Methodists resembled the Quakers. An early biographer of Nathan Bangs, one of the first Methodist preachers to reach the Yonge Street settlement, recorded: "He [Bangs] conformed himself to the severest customs of the Methodists. He had prided himself on his fine personal appearance, and had dressed in the full fashion of the times, with ruffled shirt, and long hair in a queue. He now ordered his laundress to take off his ruffles; his long hair shared the same fate ..."[39] Bangs, like the Quakers, saw plain clothing and short hair as emblems of humility and simplicity of spirit. Whenever individuals present themselves and their actions to others, they attempt to guide or control the impressions others have of them. Consciously or unconsciously, they use techniques similar to those of an actor presenting a character to an audience.[40] Bangs wished to present his conversion to Methodism in tangible form, so he radically altered his personal appearance. His transformation made it easier for him to be accepted into the pioneer mission field of Upper Canada: it made him look more like his audience.

To a Methodist or a Quaker, long hair and a ruffled shirt suggested that too much time was spent on caring for one's personal appearance – time that could have been devoted to prayer, meditation, reading scripture, or doing good works. In that way, long hair and ruffled shirts became metaphors for things that could keep a person from salvation and godliness. They also stood as metaphors for the ruling elite of the period, and so represented wealth and status, since only the very prosperous could afford the time and resources to keep a ruffled shirt and queue in good order. Thus, when a Methodist minister removed his ruffles and queue, he made both a religious and a political statement. He declared that tangible earthly concerns were less important than spiritual matters and less worthy of his time and attention. He could appear as a highly spiritual individual, unconcerned with material rewards. Politically, he declared that he wished to have nothing in common with men of wealth, prestige, and power, thereby attracting those who might feel burdened and oppressed by secular government or authority. In these ways, costume enhanced the popular appeal of Methodism and, like rhetoric and music, served as a theatrical technique designed to gather and influence an audience. Clothing and the way it is worn can be of great importance in communication. A Quaker's refusal to remove his hat, for example, could constitute an important metaphoric gesture in the presence of someone of high social standing. It would signify a Quaker's belief in the equality of all people, regardless of rank, and show his refusal to submit to worldly authority. To cite another example, some early Quakers in England even went through the streets naked to preach the gospel, much to the scandal of their neighbours. By doing so, they sought to emphasize humanity's helpless condition in the eyes of God. In these ways, clothing, or the lack of clothing, was transformed into an important medium of communication. Early Methodists as well as Quakers knew and used the language of clothing in spreading their message to the world.[41]

The Yonge Street Methodist itinerant, Nathan Bangs, was born in Connecticut in 1778 and lived in New York State from 1791. In 1799, he moved with his brother-in-law's extended family to the Niagara area and joined the Methodists. From 1802 until 1808 Bangs served the New York Conference of the Methodist Episcopal Church as an itinerant preacher in Upper Canada. He was generally well-received by the Quakers of Yonge Street, however suspicious they sometimes were of his status as a "hireling" minister. They attended his meetings and often rose to give favourable testimonies after his sermons. Bangs returned the compliment by reading the works of Fox, Barclay, and Penn and attending Quaker meetings. He is said to have found much good in the writings of the Quakers, but believed that the Friends did not pay enough attention to the teachings of the Bible.[42] Bangs's criticism foreshadowed later controversy over scriptural authority – controversy that would come from within the meeting itself. Other of his observations also seem to have foretold future troubles. Bangs noted that few people rose to speak in the Quaker meetings he visited in Upper Canada and found the Friends lacking in spiritual energy. "He felt deeply interested for them, and perceiving that they were losing their spiritual life in this distant region, he endeavored to recall them to the best teachings of their own founders, as well as to the better teachings of Holy Scripture."[43] Bangs's observations were made at a time when Friends' meetings were becoming increasingly decorous and controlled. The Society of Friends had originally been known for its often agitated style of worship, when the word *Quaker* was an accurate description of a member's actions when under the power of the Inner Light. Times had changed, however, and now order and authority were more in evidence, as indicated by such tangible signs as partitions between men's and women's sections of meeting houses and raised benches for those considered to have special gifts for ministry or leadership. Bangs, an outsider, noticed something that the Children of Peace would oppose in 1812, and which the broader Orthodox/Hicksite schism of 1828 would challenge as well.

In contrast with the more restrained indoor meetings of the Quakers, Methodist meetings were often held in the open air, in a meadow or forest clearing. To bring their message to the backwoods of Upper Canada, American Methodist preachers emulated the camp meetings first held on the Kentucky frontier, whose material culture was short-lived but immensely powerful. As Bangs's early biographer described, "Some brought tents, some erected booths of trees and shrubs. The scene circled with these temporary but picturesque shelters, in the midst of a primeval forest, illuminated at night by pine torches ... varied by a daily succession of sermons, of prayer-meetings, of hymns, which sometimes resounded for miles through the wooded solitudes, presented a poetic and indescribable impression to the powerful, though rude, eloquence of the frontier preachers."[44] The scene was sensual and rife with metaphor. At night within the circle of tents and shelters, all was in motion through the flickering, unsteady light of the torches. People, unaccustomed to crowds, sat or stood in close proximity. Beyond the circle was the echoing darkness of the forest. Some, overcome by emotion, shouted, sobbed, fell to their knees, or thrashed about on the ground.

The forest clearing was in striking contrast with the churches of the establishment *and* with the meeting houses of the Society of Friends. By nature transient, it was a place where social order and constraints need not be observed too closely since all signs of human habitation would soon be packed up and gone. In such an atmosphere was freedom. Neighbours today would be strangers tomorrow. Here was a place to let down one's guard, to throw off restraint. The camp meeting site showed little sign of human skill and craft: it was close to nature, with grass and earth underfoot, trees or fields around, and the sky above. In such a place, a preacher could expound on God's handiwork since the significance of human effort seemed small in comparison. To it came crowds of people who rarely saw crowds. The crowds themselves added an extra sense of excitement and tension to the camp meeting scene. The physical contortions of those who were moved by the words of the Methodist preachers or by the volatile atmosphere of the forest clearing were known as "the jerks." They had first been described at early camp meetings in the American midwest and the Mississippi Valley: "Hearers, hundreds of hearers would fall as dead men to the earth under a single sermon. The extraordinary scenes called the "jerks" began at one of these meetings. They were rapid, jerking contortions, which seemed to be always the effect, direct or indirect, of religious causes, yet affected not only the religious, but often the most irreligious minds."[45]

In time, Methodist meetings, like those of the Quakers, became much more orderly and subdued. Their spontaneity was tempered by method and control – yet another instance of the "routinization of charisma." But in the early years of the nineteenth century, Methodist meetings must have conjured up for the Quakers an image of what once had been theirs. The camp meeting, like the Quaker meeting, had two zones to accommodate its participants. Just as a place in the meeting house was reserved for members with special spiritual gifts or authority, at the camp meeting logs were set out in front of the preaching stand for those who were termed the "people of God." That left the "crowd" standing or seated on the ground in a large semicircle around the logs. As the meeting progressed, the distinction between the "people of God" and the "crowd" grew as "the circle of spectators unconsciously fell back, step by step, until quite a space was opened between them and those who were seated."[46]

Both the Quakers and the Methodists emphasized the importance of intense, individual experience of the power and presence of God. To Quakers, this experience came through the Inner Light. To Methodists, it came more through exhortation, sermons, hymns, the reading of scripture, and the emotionally charged atmosphere of the camp meeting. But the goal of each was essentially the same. Their "religion of experience" was quite different from the "religion of order" espoused by the colony's Anglican elite and led to different views of society and social change. The opposing "religion of order" was more rational and systematic, looking at the order of nature as a metaphor to explain the nature of God, people, and the universe. The natural order was compared with the order of clockwork, pointing to the existence of a sort of divine clockmaker, whose orderly creation could be reflected and advanced by civil government and an established church. The purpose of this orderly creation and orderly society was to promote human happiness. In the "religion of order," prophecy and revelation were used to convince believers that their happiness was not only of this world, but of a world to come. Thus, by regulating their conduct in the hope of a better life in future, they made present social and economic inequalities seem more bearable. "The religion of experience" gave less importance to reason and order and more to a personal experience of salvation. Its emphasis on the equality of all believers meant that it was much more likely to lead to social radicalism than its tamer Anglican counterpart.[47] "The religion of experience" would come to play a major role in the evolution of the Children of Peace, both as a religious sect and as a group intent on social reform.

3 Visions

In 1812, religious controversy shook the Yonge Street settlement as a new sect, the Children of Peace, came into being. Part of this story may be traced in the records of the Yonge Street Meeting, in the writings of leader David Willson, and in a study of the secular conflicts – social, economic, and military – of that troubled year. Of equal importance, however, are two painted banners (Figs. 5 and 6) made and used by the Children of Peace. Objects such as these are often considered only as "folk art," prized by antiquarians, but shunned by social historians, except when used as quaint illustrations to enliven accounts based solely on written sources. Since three-dimensional objects can also provide insights into human belief and action, these banners deserve to be considered on their own merits. They can provide a starting point for understanding why the Children of Peace became a separate religious sect and how their beliefs differed from the Quakers. The fact that these banners were used in processions, not merely hung in a building or locked in a member's private chamber, gave them special significance as corporate symbols of belief and identity.

The banners are attributed to Richard Coates, a retired military bandmaster, who emigrated from England in 1817 and took up residence in York. Coates came to the Children of Peace as a music teacher and organ builder, then turned his artistic talents toward the painting of banners under the direction of David Willson.[1] Banners had long been used in church processions and also in the marches and gatherings of fraternal organizations, political movements, trade and craft associations, and numerous other groups throughout history. Carried aloft, they provided a focal point for group identity and lent a ceremonial quality to public occasions. The Children of Peace used banners when they processed to their meeting house. As a visitor from New York wrote in 1825, "They go in procession to their place of worship, the females taking the lead, being preceded by banners and two of their number playing on the flute."[2] Members also carried banners when they held services or meetings outside their own community.[3] The use of banners, processions, and instrumental music set the Children of Peace apart from the Quakers. One of the driving forces behind the creation of this sect was a love of music, colour, and pageantry that Quakers could not condone.

Both banners reveal many of David Willson's religious beliefs and, by extension, his reasons for breaking away from the Quakers. Referring specifically to them, the *Colonial Advocate*, published in York on 18 September 1833, announced a procession of the Children of Peace, "bearing representations of one Church nursing the two dispensations, by presenting a woman with two children, and of Moses and the Saviour in Communion in an infant state of life."

On the first banner (Fig. 5), the central figure is a long-haired woman dressed in red. Her breasts are bare, but a golden belt holds her flowing robe in place. The woman wears a plain, gold wedding band on her left hand and a more ornamental ring on her right index finger. In each arm, she holds a child dressed in a long white robe. Her right arm holds aloft a red, gold, and black flag on a golden pole capped by an arrow-like finial. On the flag is a stylized sun surrounding an open eye placed beside the word *PEACE*. The woman appears to be standing on the waves of a wide sea, while in the background, the colours of dawn lighten the sky.

This image was inspired by a vision David Willson had on 21 June 1812. In later years, he was careful to point out that he had witnessed this vision, not with his eyes, but with his mind and soul. He wrote, "Although I never saw a vision or spirit with my natural eyes, yet they gave light to my soul, and understanding to my mind."[4] Within the context of Quaker belief, Willson's vision could be interpreted as a manifestation of the Inner Light. In recording this vision, identified as a "description of the Church of Christ," Willson declared that he saw the red-robed woman coming from the east, her breasts bare, her face "like the sun," her countenance "sharper than steel," and the words of her mouth "sharper than a two-edged sword to the defence of her children." Her robe, Willson wrote, was stained red with the blood of Christian martyrs, while the girdle about her waist was of pure gold, symbolizing faith in God. Around her, beasts lay in wait

Figure 5 Painted banner, attributed to Richard Coates, oil on canvas, 48" × 54", c.1825. (Collection of Sharon Temple Museum)

to devour her children as soon as they were born. Willson heard a voice commanding him to bear the woman on his shoulders and set her upon the sea, where the beasts could not go.[5] The painted banner shows the rescued woman, standing on the sea with her children in her arms, safe under a flag that represents peace and the all-seeing eye of God. The open eye depicted on the flag, brings to mind a symbol commonly used by the Masons. Here, however, the eye is contained within a sun, rather than a Masonic pyramid, perhaps a play on the concept of the Son of God. It also suggests a link with the "woman clothed with the sun" in Revelation 12, who like the woman in Willson's vision, had also been surrounded by beasts who lay in wait to devour her children. Willson wrote that he could not interpret this vision until he saw one of the woman's children walking naked in a stream of pure water flowing from the east. This stream, he concluded, stood for the restoration of ancient wisdom to the world, while the naked child walked in the stream "back to ancient simplicity." According to his interpretation, the stream also represented the sea of glass that stood before the throne of God in Revelation 4 and symbolized "the end of a Church that is established by the grace of God."[6] In David Willson's vision, water had a two-fold meaning, recalling both ancient wisdom and the coming apocalypse. The two children on the painted banner represented "the two dispensations": Jewish law and Christianity.

Interpreting the banner from a secular twentieth-century perspective, the children could also have been modelled after David Willson's own sons, and the woman after his wife. Willson's sons were named Israel and John, suggesting that their father had an interest in ancient Israel and in the biblical book of Revelation, written by St John the Divine, long before his visions began. Israel and John were common enough names among Quaker children at the time; still, a man deeply concerned with symbols, as David Willson undoubtedly was, may have made the connection. He also may have linked his own name with David of the Old Testament, the giant-killer and leader of ancient Israel. He may even have known that his wife's name, Phebe (a variant of Phoebe), was the female form of Phoebus, the Greek god of the sun. In Willson's vision, the red-robed woman had a face "like the sun," while on the banner, she carried a flag with a picture of the sun painted on it. Willson's vision and the banner itself must have brought to mind the shipwreck that he, his wife, and his two sons experienced on their arrival in Upper Canada – an incident in which Willson was, in a literal sense, a rescuer. Conversely, the memory of their shipwreck and his wife and sons' rescue may unconsciously lie behind both the vision and the banner.

The second banner (Fig. 6) also shows two children. The naked child on the right points to the text of a large book that covers his lap. The child on the left wears a loose robe over his right arm and lap and has a loosely folded robe of darker colour under his feet. On his lap is a large book closed with a seal that he is holding. His right hand points upward to a dove that is descending from a cloud, carrying a scroll in its mouth. Another scroll lies at the child's feet, bearing the inscription, *PEACE*. To the left are two lambs: one standing and looking backwards, the other lying down and facing forward. In the background, a stream appears on the left, with mountains in the distance. The message of this banner seems more readily accessible since it uses more conventional imagery to make its points. It is not directly related to David Willson's visions, although it does borrow from them. According to the 1833 description from the *Colonial Advocate*, the children represented Moses and Christ. The child pointing to the open book in all likelihood was intended to represent Moses and the revelation of scripture and the law. The child holding the sealed book, then, represents Christ and direct revelation from God. He points to

Figure 6 Painted banner, attributed to Richard Coates, oil on canvas, 48" × 54", c.1825. (Collection of Sharon Temple Museum)

a descending dove, which brings to mind the descent of the Holy Spirit in the form of a dove following Christ's baptism. The two lambs may also represent the old and new dispensations: one looking away, representing the ritual lamb of the Jewish Passover; the other looking ahead, representing Christ, the symbolic, sacrificial lamb of God. In the distance, the stream may, like Willson's visionary stream, stand for the restoration of ancient wisdom to the world. At the heart of this banner's symbolism is the concept that divine wisdom is open to all – to a child even more than to a learned academic or theologian. That concept was fully in keeping with Quaker belief and with an anti-intellectualism that runs through prophetic movements generally. It became a common theme in the writings of David Willson, who declared, "The simplicity of my mental abilities cannot be conceived or known by the regular educated in schools, seminaries, academies, and colleges because they are quite in a different sphere of action from my simple and uneducated life."[7]

However we may explain or interpret his visions today, David Willson felt he was called to play a special role in the Christian church. However, when he made his views known to his fellow Quakers, he was censured and rebuked. Willson described the scene in this way: "I began to speak something of my knowledge of God, or a Divine Being in the heart, soul or mind of man, all which signifies the same to my understanding; but my language was offensive, my spirit was abhorred, my person was disdained, my company was forsaken by my brethren and sisters."[8] His dispute with the Quakers came after a period of intense spiritual turmoil that had begun, according to Willson's own account, in 1807. It was then that he turned to the Bible for help, but soon felt he was called to "put up the book" since God "should alone be trusted in." In August 1811, Willson confided in Rachel Lundy, a prominent member of the Yonge Street meeting. By September of that year, he was able to tell her that "a New and Glorious Dispensation was about to break forth in the world, And that it would be more bright than any had been since the days of Jesus Christ." On 15 September 1811, Willson declared in a meeting "that Jesus Christ was not God (As some believe him to be) But a man Endued with Divine power." He went on to say "that there was a day at the first, when there was no Scripture, no prophet, no Mediator between God and man, and that the Church must travel to that state again, from which she fell."[9]

The minutes of the Yonge Street Monthly Meeting provide additional details. On 13 August 1812, they record that a report had been received from the Queen Street Preparative Meeting, where Willson was a regular attender and first made his views known. The report stated that he had refused discipline and, several weeks earlier, had announced his intention to hold meetings in his own home every Sunday and Thursday. Furthermore, it was noted that several others had left the Queen Street meeting to follow him.[10] Willson himself was more specific, declaring that the Friends had accused him of blasphemy: "*Blasphemy* hath been your speech, – *denying of Jesus Christ* hath been your common sayings ... and that I denied and condemned the scriptures, hath been your byword from day to day, to almost every one you did chance to meet."[11] The Yonge Street meeting appointed a committee to try to bring about a reconciliation, but found Willson unyielding and no longer expecting that the Friends would tolerate him. On 17 September 1812, the meeting decided that he should be disowned.[12] Before the year was out, proceedings were taken against fifteen other members as well.[13]

On 15 March 1813, another vision came to David Willson – a vision which may also relate to the imagery of the two banners. Again he saw a child in a stream flowing from the east. This time, perhaps symbolizing Willson's own growing sense of persecution, the child swam against a current and encountered many obstacles in its path. When Willson asked what he might do to help the child, he was told to "dress the child and keep it clean." He followed the child for three days and three nights until they came to a calm sea. There the child turned into a beautiful virgin, her breasts naked, and the rest of her body clad in a white garment with a golden band around the waist. She sang praises to God and promised Willson that she would teach him her songs and that, after his death, he would return to her and partake of her glory.[14] Like the banners, Willson's descriptions of his visions are steeped in Biblical imagery. They recall two passages from the book of Revelation. Chapter one describes "one like unto the Son of Man, clothed with a garment down to the foot, and girt about the paps with a golden girdle ... His eyes were as a flame of fire ... And he had in his right hand seven stars: and out of his mouth went a sharp two edged sword: and his countenance was as the sun shineth in his strength." Chapter twelve tells of "a woman clothed with the sun, and the moon under her feet, and upon her head a crown of twelve stars: And she being with child cried, travailing in birth, and pained to be delivered ... and the dragon stood before the woman which was ready to be delivered, for to devour her child as soon as it was born." According to Carl Jung, the child-bearing woman of Revelation was Sophia, or Wisdom, the original consort of Jahweh, God of Israel. Jung believed that she represented the feminine, the "anima," coming to consciousness in the mind of John, the author of Revelation.[15] Jung defined the anima as the female element in the male unconscious, "a personification of all feminine psychological tendencies in a man's psyche, such as vague feelings and moods, prophetic hunches, receptiveness to the irrational, capacity for personal love, feeling for nature, and – last but not least – his relation to the unconscious."[16] He noted that in art and literature men are frequently depicted as heroes fighting monsters to rescue "damsels in distress" who symbolize their anima.[17] Willson saw himself in the role of rescuer (and once actually *had* rescued his wife and sons from drowning) and may unconsciously have projected his own anima in the two female figures of his visions.

Willson's anima – to continue a Jungian interpretation – came to consciousness at a time of great crisis for the Yonge Street community. In 1812, the year of Willson's first vision, war broke out between the United States and Canada. President James Madison declared war on Britain and her colonies on 18 June; Willson's first vision occurred on 21 June. The Quakers were pacifists and had thought that their views would be respected in Upper Canada; however, in return for exemption from militia or military duty, members of the Society of Friends were forced to pay a fee of twenty shillings a year in times of peace and five pounds a year in times of war. If they refused, they were fined or imprisoned. In 1810 the Yonge Street meeting reported that £243 11s 6½d in goods had been confiscated from members who refused to pay, and that eight members had been imprisoned for a period of one month.[18] Once war broke out, the Quakers' position was made even more difficult. Not only were they pacifists, but they were American pacifists with family and friends across the border and formal ties with the New York Yearly Meeting. To make matters even worse, they were located on or near Upper Canada's major north-south transportation route, a road that had been originally designed for military purposes. During the war years, members of the Quaker community were continually harassed and persecuted. Clayton Webb recalled that his older brothers were drafted for militia duty, despite their Quaker beliefs. Two of his brothers took refuge in the woods along with several others, while one brother was imprisoned. Webb's brother-in-law was forced to drive his team of horses to Fort George with a load of supplies, caught a cold on the journey, and died a week later.[19] Willson's own sufferings at this time have not been documented; however, it is known that he lost some property[20] and must have been concerned about the fate of his older son, John, who would have been just the right age for military service. Hardships continued even after the War. The harvests of 1815 were poor, and the following year virtually all crops failed. Snow fell in June, and temperatures remained unusually cold until well into the next year.[21]

Conditions such as these led to a psychic or spiritual crisis for Willson and other members of the Yonge Street community. They must have seriously questioned the effectiveness of the Quakers' peace testimony and the ability of their leaders, when all around them was constant fear of fines, imprisonment, confiscation, hunger, and forced military duty. For David Willson, visions arose to help resolve this crisis, offering powerful images of safety, rescue, peace, innocence, and comfort. Willson's testimony was undoubtedly effective: in 1812, fifteen members of the Yonge Street meeting were disciplined and/or disowned for following him; in 1813, a further thirteen; in 1814, five; and in 1817, two – a total of thirty-five people. These included some of the meeting's most active members, two former clerks and three of its five elders.[22] As someone who knew him wrote, David Willson "was endowed with that rare magnetism that made him a ruler of others and his power over his members was almost absolute, which he used for the good of his Society."[23] Willson's visions provided hope, an attractive alternative to the difficult situation facing the Quaker settlement.

David Willson was a prolific writer of verses, and images of children and sensual, nurturing women appear in some of his earliest poetry as well. The following verse, dated 15 June 1816, is entitled "A Song of the Church sung to the Nations in the Name of the Children of Peace described by a Woman Showing forth her Glory in the Midst of her Children":

> Behold my breasts how fair they shine
> With wisdom over flow
> Containing Milk and precious wine
> To feed these babes I show ...
>
> My face appears like stars at night
> Amidst the state of sin
> My speech declares my ways are right
> As soft as silks my skin ...
>
> And all the nations may partake
> As my sweet breasts doth give
> I suffer for the Gospels sake
> To help the dead to live ...
>
> If you would hear a damsel sing
> Or Church that God's set free
> Cast off your pride and offerings bring
> Rest with my babes and me.[24]

The links between this poem and the imagery of the first banner are unmistakable. Here Willson says that all his listeners, like the children the woman holds in her arms, may find rest, new life, and nourishment in her. In a poem dated 2 February 1817, Willson saw a woman as the builder of a new temple. The poem is entitled "The Vale of the Inner Temple described – the house of God finished and the builder Entring into rest – the inward paradise regaind, the land of Canaan set free from the External law, and Zions mount to Ever reign."

> The woman did disern his [Christ's] End
> Her substance did she freely spend
> Pourd forth upon a Saviours feet
> The same henceforth the temple build
> With more compassion was she filld
> Than men that sat with him at meat

See where the woman has begun
The lowest state beneath the sun
The same the foundations doth lay
The same the pillars of the work
That the designs of men hath broke
Regardless what the wise doth say ...

When masons works are tumbling down
Each stone lay scatterd on the ground
Will Christ the inner temple build
By her that did his feet anoint
The same my father did appoint
Her second cup shall be fulfilled.[25]

These three verses, from a much longer poem, creatively combine elements from the Gospels of Matthew, Luke, and John in the New Testament. They show David Willson's free and highly original use of Scripture. The same mixing, reordering, and altering of scriptural images is found in Willson's descriptions of his visions and in the painted images of the banners. All are biblical in origin and came from the mind of a man steeped in religious imagery. His use of the Bible, however, was a far cry from orthodox Protestantism's emphasis on careful translation and scholarly exegesis. Willson's approach was more in keeping with that of early Quakers, who had stressed so strongly the importance of the Inner Light above and beyond scriptural authority. Willson saw himself as heir to the early traditions of the Quakers at a time when more and more Friends were demanding a greater degree of creedal and scriptural orthodoxy. In 1819, Quaker itinerant Mathias Hutchinson of Newtown, Bucks County, wrote in his journal that Willson had told his followers that he "had taken up the Principle where George Fox left it and was going on to Perfection."[26] Willson himself wrote, "As David laid a foundation, And Solomon built thereon, So George Fox laid a foundation, and I would build thereon."[27]

Hoping to see his disownment from the Yonge Street Friends overturned, Willson appealed to the broader North American Quaker community. His first published pamphlet, *The Rights of Christ*, was printed in Philadelphia in 1815 and put his case before American Quakers.[28] In a second pamphlet, *An Address to the Professors of Religion*, published in New York in 1817, Willson sought to clarify his views and, in so doing, linked them to the apocalyptic imagery that had characterized his visions. In the pamphlet, he belittled a "scripture knowledge of God" and stated that "while Christ did abide in the flesh ... he was a man, and opened not the book of life unto any."

Willson believed that the *spirit* of Christ, much like the Quaker Inner Light, had the power to open the human heart to God. He saw the apocalypse itself as a personal experience, wherein an individual could experience the Second Coming of Christ in a spiritual sense: "We may expect that the second coming of Christ is at hand, yea, even at the door of the heart, where he is kept too long knocking for entrance to us." Willson wrote that Revelation should be read as a book about the regeneration of the soul, rather than as a description of a climactic end to the world. Recalling his own experience, he wrote of St John's vision, "It was *spirits* that John saw, rather than *flesh*, described unto us by outward things, that we thereby might know the power of spirits in the soul ..." In his second pamphlet, Willson looked forward to a time when Jews as well as Christians would find unity with God, hoping for the establishment of a new kingdom "where God and the lamb abideth in the midst thereof, a state of mind in which kings and priests rule no more ..."[29]

Willson's defence and the arguments presented in his Philadelphia and New York pamphlets placed him within a broader controversy that ultimately led to the Orthodox/Hicksite schism of 1828. "Orthodox" Quakers sought to move the Society of Friends toward the mainstream of American Protestantism by emphasizing the divinity of Christ and the authority of scripture. They were evangelicals who, in their attempts to add members in competition with the rapid growth of Methodists and Presbyterians, found a need to define their beliefs more precisely. While never denying the importance of the Inner Light, they saw in it a potentially dangerous tendency toward "free thought" and disunity. In Philadelphia in 1805, Orthodox Quakers tried to introduce a Uniform Discipline, which would govern all the American yearly meetings. This move was opposed by a group who would later be known as "Hicksites," after one of their outstanding spokesmen, Elias Hicks of Long Island. Hicks was a self-educated Quaker preacher who had visited Upper Canada as an itinerant in 1803.[30] Like Willson, he put little emphasis on the sacrificial role of Christ in bringing salvation and gave the Bible secondary importance in comparison with the Inner Light. Hicks wrote, "The best outward ... help, either from reading the scriptures or hearing the gospel preached ... can do for any man, is to lead the minds of the children of men home to this divine inward principle manifested in their own hearts and minds."[31] Such emphasis drew heavily on old Quaker traditions of mysticism and on the seventeenth-century writings of Robert Barclay. It recalls Willson's own statement regarding the Children of Peace: "They accept of no theory, or articles of faith, as a distinguishing mark of religion, but will accept of practice only."[32]

When Hicksite theology took artistic form – as it did in the paintings of Edward Hicks, Elias Hicks's cousin – it did so in a way reminiscent of Richard Coates's banners for the Children of Peace. Hicks's famous *Peaceable Kingdom* paintings recall Coates's painting of the two children and lambs, set against a backdrop of landscape and water.[33] No direct link is suggested (although Edward Hicks, a native of Bucks County, did visit several Quaker meetings in the Yonge Street area in 1819);[34] however, the paintings do provide further evidence of a common outlook held by the two groups.

The introspective nature of Hicksite teaching led to a tendency to withdraw from the world. On the other hand, Orthodox belief, which tried to define and codify doctrine, left the door open for greater separation between belief and behavior, allowing Orthodox Friends to play a greater role in worldly affairs. Thus, the Orthodox/Hicksite dispute was not only theological in nature. It was also influenced by social and economic divisions within the Society of Friends: the Orthodox tended to be involved in business, politics, and community affairs, while the poorer Hicksites were alienated from positions of power or prestige.[35] This dispute recalled mid-eighteenth century controversies that divided the Quakers of Pennsylvania over their proper role in worldly affairs: urban Quakers favoured compromise in business and political matters, while rural Friends sought a return to rigorous Quaker principles and practice.[36] The schism of 1812 between the Quakers and Children of Peace was also linked to differing outlooks on social and economic issues. Albert Schrauwers has argued that members of the Children of Peace broke with the Society of Friends to preserve a traditional "moral economy" in the face of encroachments by competitive urban capitalism and intrusions by secular authorities.[37] Certainly during the war years, there were very real threats to the Yonge Street Quakers' prosperity and peace; however, as Schrauwers would agree, economic motivation by itself cannot explain the formation of a new religious sect.

David Willson's visions and the banners of the Children of Peace offered a glimpse of another world that was free from war and strife. All the visions had happy endings and were in striking contrast with the earthly troubles and tensions his community faced during and after the War of 1812. By naming their new sect "The Children of Peace," David Willson and his followers confirmed their opposition to what was happening in the world around them. They considered themselves not only *people* of peace, but *children* of peace, suggesting purity and innocence as well as peacefulness. When Richard Coates translated elements from David Willson's visions onto canvas with his paints and brushes, he too was careful to incorporate children amidst symbols of peace. The visions and banners symbolized a spiritual world, which Quakers accustomed to the Inner Light and divine revelation might enter. To the secular mind, this could seem like mere escapism. To many Quakers, it marked a dangerous assault on unity and discipline, but to those who joined the Children of Peace, it seemed a perfectly acceptable extension of Quaker mysticism. In the spiritual world evoked by the visions and banners, the sacrifice of Christ and the authority of Scripture became things of the past. Christ and the Scriptures had helped open the way to this new world, but once there, the spirit could find unity with God and all else could be abandoned.

Willson believed that this new spiritual state marked a sort of personal apocalypse.[38] Thus, his thought may be linked with widespread interest in the nature and timing of the Christian millennium. Christians had long debated whether the millennium, the thousand-year reign of Christ on earth, would precede or follow the Last Judgment. They also debated whether mankind could help bring on the millennium of peace and justice, or whether it had to be preceded by a literal return of Christ to the world. However they defined it, there was a great upsurge of interest in the millennium in the late eighteenth and early nineteenth centuries. Beyond Upper Canada, this was a time of international crisis, anxiety, and insecurity. Britain and Europe were engulfed in the Napoleonic Wars in the wake of the French Revolution, which itself seemed to challenge all political and social norms. The climactic events of the period and their challenge to Papal authority were widely linked to the prophecies of Revelation 13 and Daniel 7. In England, Richard Brothers claimed to have had a series of visions beginning in 1790, foretelling the arrival of the millennium; his writings were published in Britain, France, and America. Joanna Southcott of Devon was also visited by a series of prophetic visions foretelling the last days of the world; she wrote sixty-five pamphlets between the years 1792 and 1814.[39]

Tied to interest in the millennium was a fascination with the Jews. Richard Brothers believed that he was descended from King David and had been called to lead the return of the Jews to the Holy Land, where he would direct the rebuilding of Jerusalem. Brothers believed that a large part of the British population was of Hebrew descent and shared this interest in the restoration of the Jews with many other Britons of his time. Some claimed that the Garden of Eden had been located in the British Isles, that the Druids had followed the religion of Abraham, and that Christ himself might once have trod on British soil. Poet William Blake explored these ideas in verse, but they were also a deeply ingrained part of popular culture.[40]

In the United States, interest in the millennium was evoked by the New England Puritans with their strong sense of mission and divine guidance, by the success of the American Revolution, by the sense of great potential embodied in the settling of a new continent, and by the widespread belief that the natives of North America were descendants of the ten lost tribes of Israel.[41] From Central Europe came Protestant groups such as the Moravians, who were strongly influenced by the belief that the Second Coming of Christ could be hastened by human effort. Like the Ephrata Cloister and the Harmony Society, both centred in Pennsylvania, they set themselves apart in cooperative communities following biblical models. In 1793 Moravians came to Upper Canada, establishing a mission at Fairfield in the southwestern part of the colony.[42]

Of all the groups influenced by millennial thinking at that time, the Shakers, the community of the Publick Universal Friend, and the followers of Joanna Southcott seem to have had most in common with the Children of Peace. The same traveller, who in 1825 described the processions of the Children of Peace, declared the sect to be "something like the Shakers."[43] The Shakers established their first settlement in North America at Niskayuna, near Albany, in 1776. Their founder, "Mother" Ann Lee, had arrived in New York from England two years earlier along with eight followers. They believed that she was the female counterpart of Christ, ordained to found a new church in America. In England, Ann Lee had belonged to a dissident sect, which had broken away from the Society of Friends. Because of their agitated style of praise and worship, members had come to be known as the Shaking Quakers. With them she had found solace following the deaths of her four children. In America, her new church, known as the Millennial Church or the United Society of Believers in Christ's Second Appearing, asserted that the millennium had now arrived. Believing their mission to be the slow, progressive redemption of the world from sin and evil, her successors had founded twenty-five Shaker communities from Maine to the Ohio frontier by 1826. The largest was at Mount Lebanon, New York, only sixty miles away from David Willson's birthplace.[44] The story of Mother Ann Lee – the female counterpart of Christ, the woman who was to found a new church and usher in the millennium, the mother whose children had been taken from her – brings to mind the woman of Revelation 12, David Willson's vision, and the red-robed woman of the banner. Mother Ann, like David Willson, was the leader of a sect that had broken away from the Quakers.

Jemima Wilkinson, the Publick Universal Friend, shared many things with Mother Ann. She too came from Quaker tradition, and the same millennial emphasis was present in her teaching. While never laying claim to divinity, she did declare that after a vision in 1776, a new spirit had inherited her body. That spirit was a messenger from

Christ who preached "News of Salvation to all that would Repent and believe the Gospel." She led a community similar to those of the Shakers, first at Seneca Lake and later in New Jerusalem Township, near Keuka Lake, New York, from 1788 until she "left time" in 1819.[45]

The English prophetess, Joanna Southcott, claimed twenty thousand followers by the time of her death in 1814. She believed that "as woman tempted man at first, so at the last she is to bring his deliverance." Deliverance was to come after she had given birth at age sixty-four to a son conceived by God's power. She died, amidst great controversy, about the time the baby was expected. Historian J.F.C. Harrison has observed that, like members of other contemporary social and religious movements, Joanna Southcott's followers were largely artisans, small tradesmen, and servants. They were active members of existing churches and sects that emphasized some sort of "inner light" experience and were deeply dissatisfied with conditions around them.[46]

David Willson must have known of the existence of Mother Ann Lee and Jemima Wilkinson and may have heard of Joanna Southcott. He could have been influenced by them; however other, less direct, links are more important. All four sects – the Shakers, the community of the Publick Universal Friend, the followers of Joanna Southcott, and the Children of Peace – grew out of the same social and religious background. With their emphasis on the Inner Light, mysticism, and social and sexual equality, these four independent movements shared common ground, which nurtured their leaders and followers. All four had their genesis during wartime: the American Shakers and the community of the Publick Universal Friend during the Revolutionary War, the followers of Joanna Southcott during the Napoleonic Wars, and the Children of Peace during the War of 1812. All four held the belief that the millennium was at hand and could be furthered by members of a new church. All four, to some degree, believed that a woman would usher in the new age. Mother Ann, Jemima Wilkinson, Joanna Southcott and David Willson's visionary woman stood in opposition to the injustice and turmoil of the warring world around them, offering their followers alluring symbols of comfort, hope, and peace.

The Society of Friends, unlike any other major religious group in North America at the time, offered women positions of leadership and authority. Within Quaker families, women played important roles in decision-making and childrearing. In their maternal authority, Quaker women were decidedly "modern" and considerably stronger and more independent than their Puritan counterparts in New England.[47] Quaker women could preach in public and participated fully in the affairs of their meetings, where they held positions beyond those of almost any other women of their day. During his 1819 visit to the Yonge Street area, Quaker Edward Hicks wrote the following after preaching to a group of Methodists: "I was led to speak of the rights of women – that they were one in Christ with men, and entitled to equal privileges, and that I had heard the Gospel preached by them in greater sweetness and power than I had ever heard from the lips of men. There was a precious silence covered the meeting, which seemed only interrupted by the suppressed weeping of some of the women. After the meeting ended, our kind Methodist friend took me by the hand and said in substance, 'Dear brother, you ought to preach that sermon a dozen times over. Why, we have been contending with our women about their right to preach.'"[48]

What Friends took for granted – women preaching the gospel – members of other denominations resisted. Quaker women also played an important role as writers and diarists, sharing in print their views on moral and religious issues. It is not surprising, then, that several of the earliest leaders of the women's rights movement in North America were born or "convinced" Quakers: Lucretia Mott, a founder and secretary of the Philadelphia Female Reform Society; suffragist and reformer, Susan B. Anthony; feminist Abby Kelley Foster; and Sarah and Angelina Grimké, crusaders for women's rights and the abolition of slavery.[49] Sarah Grimké urged American women to read and interpret the Bible for themselves. "Until we read all the precepts of the Bible as addressed to women as well as to man, and lose ... the consciousness of sex, we shall never fulfil the end of our existence," she declared.[50] In time, some of these strong women would leave the Society of Friends, often to explore spiritualism or join with the Universalists. Nevertheless, their Quaker background undoubtedly influenced their work as outspoken moral and social reformers. By the mid-nineteenth century, women from other Protestant backgrounds joined them – some equally radical, but many, such as New England Congregationalist Catherine Beecher, arguing for an enhanced spiritual role for women within their traditional sphere of home and motherhood.[51] Clearly, Quaker initiatives had spurred the rights of women: their influence on several generations of North Americans was substantial.

The Shakers, the community of the Publick Universal Friend, the followers of Joanna Southcott, and the Children of Peace emerged as forerunners of other broadly based religious, social, and reform movements of the nineteenth century. However, since all four sects challenged some of the traditional roles of women, their leaders and members were often accused of moral and sexual deviance. Mother

Ann and some of her early followers were killed in a brawl, Jemima Wilkinson was slandered and accused of bearing an illegitimate child, Joanna Southcott became a target for ridicule and derision, and David Willson was plagued by rumours of sexual misconduct throughout his ministry.

The first scandal Willson had to face was a charge of adultery with Rachel Lundy, his spiritual confidante. Rachel's husband, Israel Lundy, became jealous and informed some of his Quaker friends of his feelings. At first, Willson made light of this episode and penned a humorous account of the incident that is preserved today in a manuscript book begun late in 1814.[52] Things must have been settled amicably, since the following year Rachel accompanied David Willson and William Reid on a trip to New York and Philadelphia to plead their case for reconciliation with Quakers there.[53] Following this trip, however, charges of impropriety were renewed, leading Willson to write, "To the Celect Meeting of the Children of Peace," assuring them of the good conduct of both himself and Rachel Lundy, so that "their lives or the remaining part of them May be a witness of peace and friendship on Earth or as a soul and body redeemd from the tender love of this world to remain together forever as the soul and spirit thereof ..."[54] Willson's cryptic assertion of the platonic nature of their relationship seems to have satisfied most of his followers, without divulging the details of his and Rachel Lundy's attraction to each other. Of the thirty-five members who had left the Yonge Street Meeting, only four returned because of this incident.[55] Both Israel and Rachel Lundy remained active members of the Children of Peace, as did David Willson's wife, Phebe.

However, some of the Yonge Street Quakers, no doubt bitter over the departure of so many of their members, continued to spread rumours against Willson. Mathias Hutchinson, a traveller and diarist from Bucks County, wrote in 1819, "Some time ago there were reports circulated which were prejudicial to his moral character and some facts proved against him, whereupon the better part of his society left him and return'd to Friends."[56] Four members were hardly "the better part of his society"; nonetheless, stories of this scandal circulated for years. The David Willson/Rachel Lundy affair had its counterpart in stories told against the Shakers, the Publick Universal Friend, and Joanna Southcott. By pointing the finger at alleged improprieties, detractors attempted to discredit their beliefs and trivialize anything they might have had to say against the status quo. Having prevailed against early cricitism, Willson and his followers could now set out to build a new world through their own unique organization, ritual, and architecture.

4 Meeting House and Temple

After their disownment by the Yonge Street Quakers, David Willson and his followers set about their mission to rescue and purify the Christian church. In 1812 they began holding meetings in Willson's farmhouse on Queen Street, East Gwillimbury Township,[1] and in the carpentry shop of Amos Armitage, south of the Yonge Street meeting house.[2] These were difficult times. War continued until late in 1814 and, with it, continuing harrassment and persecution. Following the war, three years of bad weather led to crop failures, scarcity, and high prices for food.[3] Against this backdrop, Willson condemned both those who made a profit at the expense of others and those who opposed him on theological grounds. In his mind, they were often one and the same: "Quakers ... are a remarkable injenious sharp dealing people, and are as capable of extending their bounds beyond the seas, as any people on the Continent of America ... How think ye that religious people ... spend their time, when they are contending with their neighbour, or brother about the price of things; why, I should almost say that they loved the world and the love of God was not in them ..."[4] Nevertheless, Willson continued to try to resolve his differences with the Quakers, appealing to Friends at Pelham and at West Lake, near the Bay of Quinte. He also appealed to the Methodists for support, but early in 1815 found himself embroiled in a dispute with itinerant preacher Peter Conger. Though he was accused of being an "offender of the laws of the British Government, either religious or civil,"[5] the grounds for Conger's charge are not recorded. Because of their American origins, Methodists were viewed with considerable suspicion by the colonial government during and immediately after the War of 1812 and may have attempted to display their own loyalty by casting doubts on Willson's.

Appeals were also made to Quakers in Philadelphia and New York. In Pennsylvania, Willson published four pamphlets: *The Rights of Christ* (1815), *A Lesson of Instruction* (1816), *A Testimony to the People Called Quakers* (1816), and *A Present to the Teachers and Rulers of Society* (1821). In New York City, he published *An Address to the Professors of Religion* (1817). In all five of these pamphlets, Willson expanded on the beliefs that had led to his disownment from the Society of Friends. He condemned those who emphasized the authority of scripture and the divine nature and sacrifice of Christ, rather than the direct experience of God's presence. The pamphlets proclaimed the importance of good works as evidence of God's presence and chastized those who touted their orthodox beliefs while persecuting others or profiting while others lived in poverty. From the beginning, Willson linked theological disputes with the need for social and economic change – a strategy bound to appeal to those who lived under economic and political persecution, in the Yonge Street area as well as farther afield. Willson also used these early pamphlets to expand on his belief that a new age, the Christian millennium, was at hand, if only mankind would let it begin: "We may expect that the second coming of Christ is at hand, yea, even at the door of the heart, where he is kept too long knocking for entrance to us."[6] Here too lay a call for social and economic change since, in Willson's view, the millennium could be hastened by human action. While he believed in the power of the Inner Light to offer guidance and direction, Willson also recognized the importance of human action in bringing about a new era of peace and happiness.

Even as Willson defined his mission to others, dissent spread within the ranks of the Children of Peace. First came the scandal that arose over Willson's relationship with Rachel Lundy. Then he faced problems with some of his followers who had broken away from the Uxbridge Preparative Meeting, about twenty-five miles to the east.[7] He also seems to have encountered opposition from within the Youths Meeting of the Children of Peace.[8] The records of these disputes are fragmentary, consisting only of a few transcripts of Willson's letters, prose, and poetry copied into a notebook. In his responses to this dissension, Willson seems to have modelled himself after the Apostle Paul, who in his epistles to the early Christian churches, urged unity, reconciliation, and understanding, without providing details about the exact nature of the troubles themselves.

Another early concern was the establishment of a school on Yonge Street, which opened at least as early as 1817. Again, records are fragmentary, but they indicate that this was a boarding school. William Reid, one of Willson's earliest followers, was appointed teacher, while David Willson's brother, John, was appointed "Judg of Play and Caretaker for the boarding scholars and hous."[9] It would appear that both boys and girls attended this school, which was possibly modelled on the co-educational boarding school founded in 1796 at Nine Partners.[10] The founding of a school within five years of the founding of the Children of Peace, before the sect had even erected its own building for worship, suggests how important education was to them. It relates closely to Willson's emphasis on the practical, as well as mystical, components of his religion. It also recalls his visions and the imagery of the banners, in which children played important roles. The establishment of the boarding school may also have been in response to, and in competition with, plans of the Yonge Street Quakers to build their own schoolhouse. The Friends had established a school in their community in 1806, with one of Timothy Rogers's sons as its first teacher, but that school met in the homes of Quaker families and did not have a building of its own until 1817.[11] The Children of Peace no doubt saw their school on Yonge Street as necessary to ensure the future survival of their organization and essential for the preparation of children who would later become members and leaders.

Soon after the establishment of the Yonge Street school, however, David Willson began to focus the attention of his followers farther away from the site of the Yonge Street Friends meeting house. This decision may have been forced on him when Amos Armitage, in whose Yonge Street carpentry shop the Children of Peace had begun to meet, returned to the Quakers following the scandal over Rachel Lundy.[12] Since Willson's own farm was located some five miles east of Yonge Street, it was only logical that his followers would begin to congregate there. A few years earlier, while still a member of the Society of Friends, Willson had given land from his farm on Queen Street, East Gwillimbury Township, for the site of the Queen Street Preparative Meeting. Now he offered land to the Children of Peace for the erection of their own meeting house. The community Willson and his followers founded came to be known as "Hope," a fitting name for a place to start anew.

The meeting house that the Children of Peace constructed (Fig. 7) symbolized their desire to return to some of the founding principles of the Society of Friends. Built in 1819 and demolished in 1893, the building related to some of the earliest meeting house designs

Figure 7 First meeting house of the Children of Peace, built 1819/demolished 1893, Sharon, Ontario. (Photograph courtesy Sharon Temple Museum)

in North America. It was forty feet square with walls sixteen feet high,[13] capped by a hipped roof with a low square cupola at the top. Its square plan was similar to that of meeting houses built by Puritans, Quakers, and other dissenting groups in seventeenth and early-eighteenth-century America. Square plans were chosen in order to contrast with the rectangular plans of mainline and state-supported churches of their day. Square plans were also better suited accoustically to the dissenters' form of worship, which placed great emphasis on preaching and Bible reading, rather than on the mysteries of the Eucharist. In a square building, a congregation could be grouped around a pulpit in such a way that all could hear and see much more readily than if they faced toward a pulpit at the narrow end of a rectangular building, as in Roman Catholic and Anglican tradition.

Square meeting houses were first built by the Puritans of New England. Claiming English and European precedents for their designs, Anthony N.B. Garvan wrote:

When, in 1630, the Great Migration to New England began, its ships carried not only Puritan settlers and Puritan theology but also a full-fledged

Protestant aesthetic. The meeting houses of New England were not haphazard or accidental responses to the demand of the American forest. The nonliturgical floor plan, ... the low ceiling, the elaborate pulpit, all were known to Protestant builders who, by 1630, had striven for almost a century to create a Plain Style of church architecture ... In each, space was closely defined, linear and well lighted; ornamentation was constrained and abstract; and construction direct, simple and apparent. Here was a lucid shelter within which the rational, literate Protestant might reach his god.[14]

More recent scholars have argued against Garvan's thesis, one declaring that the Puritan meeting house "had no known counterpart in English church history, and it may be viewed as the only original architectural invention of the English colonies."[15] Probably the truth lies somewhere in between. Before the passage of the Toleration Act of 1689, English dissenters were forbidden to build their own places of worship and had made do with "reforming" existing church or secular buildings. This situation left little opportunity to develop "a fullfledged Protestant aesthetic." Inspiration for British and American meeting houses may have come from late medieval market halls, where dissenting Protestants once met for worship.[16] Since Puritan meeting houses had secular as well as religious functions, the market hall model may have seemed appropriate. Clearly, square buildings suited the Protestant form of worship better than rectangular buildings did. In a symbolic sense, they set dissenting Protestant groups apart from Roman Catholics and Anglicans. In practical terms, they allowed sermons and Bible readings, focal points in Protestant worship, to be delivered in the most effective way possible. Thus, square meeting houses became popular among New England Puritans. The only surviving example today is the Old Ship Meeting House in Hingham, Massachusetts, built in 1681 and greatly altered since then. Other examples included the first (1646) and second (1670) meeting houses in New Haven, and those at Salem (1670), Woburn (1672), Bristol (1684), Deerfield (1696), and West Springfield (1702).[17] The square shape, with all sides equal, suggested the equality of all believers, an important tenet of seventeenth-century dissenters reacting against more hierarchical church organizations.

It has been suggested that New England Quakers, though at first persecuted by the Puritans, based their meeting houses on early foursquare Puritan meeting house models. Certainly, the 1699 Friends Meeting House at Newport, Rhode Island – two-storey, square, and topped by a hipped roof and cupola – brings to mind the Puritans' Old Ship Meeting House in Massachusetts.[18] Rhode Island, like Pennsylvania, was an early haven of religious tolerance in North

America; however, it seems unlikely that Newport Quakers would simply have copied a shape or form used by the Puritans. Yet, it is not unusual to see familiar architectural forms reappearing over widely scattered geographic areas. As people migrated from place to place, they took familiar building forms or "templates" with them.[19] More importantly, these recurring forms were the products of similar cultures and responses to similar needs. In a foursquare Friends' meeting house, the four equal sides conveyed the Quaker idea that the Inner Light was available equally to all people. The square shape precluded the axial focus common to rectangular structures. The only focal point for people gathered in a square building is the centre, just as the focus for a Quaker at worship is supposed to be the centre of his being, his soul. "Centreing down" is a phrase still used by Friends at worship to describe the process of overcoming the distractions of the world and focusing on the inner life of the soul.

Another early, square meeting house built by Quakers was the The Bank Meeting House (Fig. 8) in Philadelphia, begun about 1685 on North Front Street on a bank above the Delaware. It was a square structure with a double-hipped roof and doors on at least two sides.[20] Sufficiently unlike the foursquare meeting houses of the New England Puritans, it suggests how the Quakers used the square form to meet their own purposes. The Bank Meeting House was one of two structures that accommodated the Philadelphia Yearly Meeting. The other was a six-sided meeting house at Burlington, New Jersey, for which plans were first made in 1682.[21] Its hexagonal shape shows that early Quakers were not wedded to only one particular meeting house shape. Their most important design considerations were: to make their places of worship look different from the churches of their day, and to provide a worship space that would complement their religious beliefs. For both purposes, a hexagon answered equally as well as a square. So too did the shape of a Greek cross, which was used for the Merion meeting house built in 1695.[22] The square, the hexagon, and the Greek cross all avoided the long central axis of rectangular churches and focused the attention of a worshipping congregation inwardly upon itself.

Further use of the square plan in early American meeting house design may be found in the work of Huguenot builders in the Hudson River valley. The foursquare Huguenot meeting house at New Paltz, New York, is near the Nine Partners area where David Willson was born. It too shows the Protestant use of the square shape to symbolize separation from churchly ways and to suit a form of worship in which speakers had to be both heard and understood. Willson could have been inspired directly by either the Huguenot meeting houses of the

53 Meeting House and Temple

Figure 8 Bank Meeting House, Philadelphia, Pennsylvania, from an eighteenth-century engraving. (Courtesy Quaker Collection, Haverford College Library)

Hudson River valley or the Quaker meeting houses of the mid-Atlantic region. The first meeting house of the Children of Peace may be considered within this broader context of meeting house design; however, it is also important to consider why that design was appropriate for Willson and his sect in 1819.

The meeting house of the Children of Peace, like that of the Yonge Street Friends, had an "affecting presence" that both embodied and inspired the beliefs of its designers, builders, and users.[23] Its square shape and four equal sides conveyed the notion of equality, which Willson had already begun to express in his prose and poetry. In fact, the first meeting house surpassed the designs of Puritans, Quakers, and Huguenots in its emphasis on equality by including, not just one or two doors, but a door on each of its four sides. Not all were necessary, but they enabled the congregation to enter from all sides and ensured that the only possible focal point would be at the centre of the gathering. The square shape, with four doors opening into it, meant that men and women could not be separated by a partition, as at the meeting house on Yonge Street. Nor could a space be easily set aside for elders, ministers, and overseers. Willson's square design thus recalled, not only early Quaker meeting houses, but also the ways of the earliest Friends. Just as his theology reflected early Quaker emphasis on the importance of the Inner Light, his architecture reflected early Quaker worship practice. The lack of a physical barrier between men and women and the absence of raised benches for those in authority both suggest relatively loose forms of organization. This was appropriate for a group that emphasized the importance of divine revelation through direct, personal experience of the presence of God.

Another feature that set the meeting house of the Children of Peace apart from that of the Yonge Street Quakers was the absence of pews or benches. Instead, movable wooden chairs were used, again embodying the sense of individualism apparent in David Willson's theology. Colour, absent from the interior of the Friends' meeting house on Yonge Street, was used on columns that were painted green to contrast with the light-coloured walls and ceiling. Also prominent, after 1820, was a barrel organ capable of playing twenty hymn tunes. It was built by Richard Coates and is believed to be the first pipe organ constructed in Upper Canada.[24] Its pine case was grained to suggest dark mahogany or rosewood and was highlighted by a row of small gilded false pipes inset toward the top. This organ alone would have told a casual visitor that this was not a Quaker meeting house. Quakers eschewed instrumental music, considering it a distraction from, rather than a complement to, true worship. David Willson, however, had not grown up with Quaker plainness and interpreted afresh the needs of worship. The organ was placed on a high platform surrounded by a railing at the very centre of the meeting house. According to a visitor in the mid-1830s, a brass candlestick stood at each corner of this railing. Also at each corner was a short, black staff that projected horizontally and carried a small, black velvet flag with fringed edges. Surrounding the platform, described as being about five feet high and supported by four simple columns, was a railed area for musicians. Here another four brass candlesticks stood at the four corners, while four more were placed on a table below the platform.[25]

Colour was added by banners, which were brought to the meeting house at least as early as 1825.[26] The sketches upon which the banners were based were described in a poem that David Willson wrote in April 1832, recalling his visions of twenty years before:

The Interpretation of A few pencil drawings that
now remain in the house of the Lord, at Hope East
Gwilliams Buary, Uppercanada. April 11th 1832

    A mournful mother first I saw
      With painful beasts around

Amidst two mountains clothed with snow
    They laid upon the ground
With weeping eyes alone she stood
    Her voice to me did cry
Her mantels were as red as blood
    Amidst a morning sky
The eastern sun around her shone
    With rays most bright and clear
This mournful Mother stood alone
    Nor friends nor kindred near ...
Two darling babes designed to bring
    And Pregnant to full size
She mourn'd that was des'gn'd to sing
    And long repeat her cries
These beasts were clothed with deceit
    As wicked sinners lie
Like adders coild around her feet
    That her two babes might die
She constantly did mourn alone
    Nor friend nor parent near
I own'd this darling for mine own
    A kindred mother dear
I bow'd my face to Earth and wept
    To see this fair one stand
Amidst such beasts they scarcely slept
    A stranger in the land
I gave my heart for her abode
    And bid her enter there
Mine hands wrote the mysterious road
    And she came in by prayer
The beasts grew angry and despis'd
    Her lonesome place of rest
And as these truths were realized
    Threw arrows at my breast.

Behold her babes how bright they stand
    Beneath a rising sun
King Jesus is in her right hand
    Wiser than Solomon
Moses doth lean upon her breast
    Where once he lean'd before
The blood of Jesus is her rest
    She's come to him restore

> Behold her twins like shepherds rise
>   On little banks compos'd
> Two quiet lambs before them lies
>   To every storm expos'd
> These babes are to enjoy the land
>   Beneath the vine and tree
> Both have the bible in their hand
>   Their mother gave to me
> The dove descends with hovering wings
>   The cloud she hath pass'd through
> Truth from the throne of God she brings
>   And tidings for the year ...[27]

Besides the two banners described in these poems, which remain today in the collection of the Sharon Temple Museum, there were two others that have long since disappeared. One, showing Eve trampling the serpent underfoot, was noted by printer and political reformer William Lyon Mackenzie on a visit to the Children of Peace in 1828. Willson described it in poetry:

> Eve stands alone most dazzling sight
>   For ages to behold
> Behold she's plac'd her feet aright
>   On honor and on Gold
> Temptation lies beneath her feet
>   Nor in her name shall rise
> Bright angels come her heart to meet
>   Two spirits in the skies ...[28]

A fourth banner depicting the "son of Eve" restored to Eden inspired Willson to write:

> Behold Her son in king's estate
>   And children offerings bring
> What God in eden did create
>   Is for the priest and king
> His spouse found wisdom in his breast
>   Amidst this fruitful ground
> Parents and children are at rest
>   Where every fruit abound.[29]

Whether inspired by David Willson's visions of 1812 or by victorious images of Eve and the "son of Eve" restored to paradise, these banners offered images of hope for the people of Hope. Their impact on worshippers must have been strong, since they stood out vividly against the light-coloured walls of the meeting house. Their effect would have been increased by the fact that paintings and drawings of all kinds were frowned upon when shown in private homes. In 1832, the same year he described the pictures in poetry, Willson wrote, "Keep from splendid houses – and ornamented walls; from fine drawings of all kinds (for these belong not to the house of the Lord) lest they will be to us images of old to Israel if we delight in them ..."[30] Recalling Old Testament images of the Israelites tempted to worship idols, Willson disapproved of "fine drawings" unless they were used in the context of worship. In the meeting house, they could be interpreted as corporate symbols that had meaning within the group life of the Children of Peace. In a private home, however, they could represent individual or family pride and status and thus could be disruptive to the unity of the community.

While visiting the Children of Peace in October 1820, Philadelphia Quaker Jacob Albertson wrote home to his wife, Mary: "Well, the dissenting Quakers go farther and farther from friends. this David Wilson calls themselves friends of peace. they have got so far as to get an organ in their meeting ... Well, we have agreed to try David Wilson if he will encourage his hearers to meet with us at his meeting house which is near to friends meeting. in Queen Street is so near that from one house to the other that they can hear each other."[31] The Queen Street Preparative Meeting struggled along for more than ten years after the defection of David Willson and his followers. Like the new meeting house built by the Children of Peace, their building was located near the eastern edge of David Willson's farm. One can only imagine how annoying it must have been for the Quakers, meeting in silence, to have their worship interrupted by the sounds of an organ and congregational singing only a few hundred feet away.

The same traveller noted something even more significant when he wrote, "he [David Willson] is purposing to build a great house to commense in the year 25 and to compleat it in the year 32." This is the earliest known reference to the building that came to be called the "temple" (Fig. 9). As documented in Albertson's letter, it was planned to take seven years to build, as did Solomon's temple, described in I Kings 6. To Willson, the building of the temple fulfilled part of his divinely appointed mission. In his visions of 1812 and 1813, he had seen a new church carrying in her arms children that represented both Christ and Moses. Inspired by Solomon's Temple, Willson gave three-dimensional form to his vision of a new church by incorporating features that would deliberately reflect both Christian and ancient Jewish tradition.

Figure 9 Temple of the Children of Peace, built 1825–31, Sharon, Ontario, from a damaged glass plate negative, c.1860. (Aurora Museum acc.no. X81.36.18) View from the northeast. The fence no longer survives.

The temple built by David Willson and the Children of Peace is three storeys tall and measures sixty feet square by seventy-five feet high. It was designed symmetrically, with tall double doors in the middle of each of its four sides on the ground floor. On either side of each door are three tall, sliding-sash windows, making twenty-four windows in all. The second storey is lit by twelve more windows; the third, by four. The upper two storeys are stepped back from the first, much like the layers on a wedding cake. At each of the building's twelve corners is a square lantern surmounted by four green finials. From the four lanterns at the top hangs a golden ball, which once had the word *Peace* painted on it.

The building is of timber frame construction, held together by pegged mortice-and-tenon joints, and stands on a foundation of uncoursed fieldstone. Each wall of the first storey is made up of seven separate sections, clad in horizontal boards with decorative beaded edges. These sections are said to have been made elsewhere and then brought together to the site to be assembled. As a traveller wrote in 1825: "They have recently commenced the building of a Temple, which, like that of Solomon, is to be seven years in building. The frame is 60 feet square, and was prepared at a distance and brought and put together without 'the sound of an hammer or an axe being

Figure 10 Interior of the temple, from a photograph probably taken in the 1890s. (Photograph courtesy Sharon Temple Museum)

heard.'"[32] This last phrase recalled Solomon's Temple, built of material "made ready before it was brought thither: so that there was neither hammer nor axe nor any tool of iron heard in the house, while it was in the building" (I Kings 6:7). Each painted, white wall section is set off visually from the rest by a recessed vertical board painted green. This configuration is echoed in the second storey, where each wall consists of three separate sections. The four corners of each storey are lightened by tall, reeded quarter columns. A reeded frieze caps each storey just below the eaves. Each of the four reeded, double-leaf doors is likewise framed by a pair of reeded half columns supporting a delicately reeded frieze and simple projecting cornice.

The interior of the temple (Fig. 10) presents an open, spacious appearance, filled with light from twenty-four tall windows. The main floor of the temple consists of three distinct levels: the highest one close to the perimeter walls, then a slightly lower level, then a lower level still, surrounding the altar and leading toward it from the four double doors. There is approximately a six-inch difference between each of these three levels. Around the perimeter are benches fixed to the wall, backed by a high dado that extends up past the level of the window sills. The benches and dado are painted pale yellow, the window sills and frames are green, and the window sash is white. The vertical green strips that mark off the separate sections of timber framing on the outside of the building are repeated inside, rising amid whitewashed plaster walls to a reeded frieze and coved plaster ceiling.

At the very centre of the building is a large cabinet (Fig. 11), called the "altar," set on a low platform. Echoing the design of the temple itself, it too has four doors flanked by tall windows. The following description was published in 1861: "The roof of the cabinet rises in gentle curves, not unlike a Chinese temple, culminating in a sharp point in the centre, which is surmounted by a handsome spirit lamp with ground glass shade. On the four corners are lamps of the same description. A small table stands in the centre of the cabinet, it is covered with black velvet and hung with crimson merino and fringe ..."[33] The lamps have long since disappeared, as have the cabinet's original doors and window sash. Near the four corners of the cabinet are four doric columns, painted green, rising from pale yellow plinths. On the four columns are the words *Faith, Hope, Love,* and *Charity*. From the tops of these columns spring four rounded arches. Above them is a musicians' gallery reached by a narrow, curving staircase located close to the east door. Above the gallery is a cupola that allows light to flood down upon the altar and into the centre of the main floor, adding to the light coming in from all four sides. Between the four columns surrounding the altar and the four perimeter walls is a second grouping of doric columns. Also painted green with pale yellow plinths, they support twelve round arches. On the shaft of each column is the name of one of the twelve apostles.

Willson planned the construction and symbolism of the temple carefully, beginning several years before actual work on the building began. In a poem entitled *The Lord's Celebration*, dated 1822 and printed as a broadside many years later, he declared:

In peace I write this structure The Lord to gratify,
And raise to him an altar built for his name alone,
That when he comes descending he'll make with me his home.

In Eighteen Hundred Twenty with five this date I'll pen,
We'll fasten the four corners and lay the bottom stone;
United with my Brothers we'll build this house alone.

Hewn stone is the foundation well beaten into square,
And then we'll raise the pillars aloft the work shall go,
Plan'd by the Architecture that formed this globe below.

Figure 11 Altar at the centre of the temple, from a pencil sketch, c.1890[?], by Owen Staples (1866–1949). (John Ross Robertson Collection, Metropolitan Toronto Reference Library)

We'll ring it round with columns their number Twelve shall be,
To mind us of apostles that once the earth hath trod;
We'll try to follow after and build a throne to God.

In the midst of these columns we'll raise the royal square;
We'll never bow to Masons nor ask them of their art;
The skillfull Architecture is Grace within the heart.

We'll raise our semicircles and spring our arches high;
He is the executor that gives to me the plan,
He'll show the art to Woman that's bone of bone to man.

We'll chain the globe by quarters it on the top shall hang,
Like gold it shall be gilded and union testify,
High hanging by four spires to please the seeing eye.

Its length shall be feet sixty its breadth be equal square,
To North and South be facing to East and West the same;
The union of best timber shall build this royal frame.

We'll clothe it with white colours with green spread on the brow,
Its height to plates be twenty with adding number one
In twenty-five begin it in thirty-two get done.

An altar to all nations a standing pillar here,
With forty-eight bright windows no darkness there shall hide
With bars and gates surrounded to keep it clean inside.

On Ararat we'll place it and Peace its name shall be,
A house of lasting blessings where grace is multiplied,
A rest for every nature and God is the inside.

Its ornaments and gilding no architect can tell,
Its weights are without number its scales were never known,
And endless is its measures like mercies of the Throne.[34]

This poem provides important insights into Willson's thinking regarding the temple, its construction, its meaning, and its relationship to other aspects of his work. The first line, "In peace I write this structure," makes the temple itself a literary work, like one of his poems or pamphlets. This building was to communicate as words do. Willson's image of writing a building echoes key passages from the Old and New Testaments. In the creation story (Genesis 1), God was depicted as speaking the world into existence: "And God said, Let there be light: and there was light ... And God said, Let there be a firmament in the midst of the waters, and let it divide the waters from the waters ... And God said, Let the waters under the heaven be gathered together unto one place, and let the dry land appear: and it was so." Thus the story went, until all had been created. The writer of St John's gospel picked up this powerful metaphor: "In the beginning was the Word, and the Word was with God, and the Word was God. The same was in the beginning with God. All things were made by him; and without him was not anything made that was made" (John 1: 1–3).

As Richard Bauman has pointed out, Quakers placed great importance on the symbolism of speech: "By making the speaking of God within man the core religious experience of their movement, the Quakers elevated speaking and silence to an especially high degree of symbolic centrality and importance."[35] Speaking and silence were also given symbolic meaning throughout the Bible. When Willson sat down to "write this structure" into existence, he was following an established biblical model of expression, while also drawing on his Quaker heritage.

The structure that Willson "wrote" was intended to be more than just a three-dimensional object. Because he believed the temple's design was inspired by God, Willson linked its architecture to creation itself, "Plan'd by the Architecture that formed this globe below." It was not only a manifestation of "the Word" of John's gospel, but also of the "Inner Light" of the Quakers. Several phrases in the poem build on this theme: "the skillfull Architecture is Grace within the heart," and "A house of lasting blessings where grace is multiplied, / A rest for every nature and God is the inside," and "Its ornaments and gilding no architect can tell, / Its weights are without number its scales were never known, / And endless is its measures like mercies of the Throne."

In *The Lord's Celebration*, Willson sees a woman playing a vital role in the creation of this new, symbolic structure: "He is the executor that gives to me the plan, / He'll show the art to Woman that's bone of bone to man." These lines recall a verse in *The Vale of the Inner Temple*, quoted in chapter three:

See where the woman has begun
The lowest state beneath the sun
The same the foundations doth lay
The same the pillars of the work
That the designs of men hath broke
Regardless what the wise doth say ...[36]

These lines, in turn, recall the women of David Willson's visions, who represented the church that he was called to rescue.

Just as Willson's visionary women were inspired, in part, by the woman "clothed with the sun" in the book of Revelation, the temple too was linked to the imagery of the Apocalypse. In *The Lord's Celebration*, Willson saw the temple as a place to welcome the Lord, "Built for his name alone, / That when he comes descending he'll make with me his home." He even applied apocalyptic imagery to the exterior decoration of the temple, inspiring William Lyon Mackenzie to write in 1828, "Mr. David Willson is now erecting an elegant and fanciful building, on two sides of which are the representation of a setting sun, below which is inscribed the word 'Armageddon.' "[37] Armageddon was the site of the final battle before the end of the world, described in the book of Revelation. No trace of the painting remains today; however, one early photograph of the temple (Fig. 9) appears to show the outline of clouds painted across the upper portion of the east side of the first storey. Its presence would have been in keeping with Willson's interest in the Apocalypse, expressed not only in his poems, but also in his visions.

More subtle links with the book of Revelation are found in Willson's temple. Like the heavenly Jerusalem described in Revelation 21, the temple is square. This in itself sets it apart from Solomon's temple, which was rectangular – three times longer than it was wide (I Kings 6:2). Also like the heavenly Jerusalem, Willson's temple has entrances on all four sides, supports that bear the names of the twelve apostles, and an abundance of windows that made it seem "like unto clear glass." These windows were the one feature that Willson changed when the temple was actually constructed. *The Lord's Celebration* declared that it would have "forty-eight bright windows"; in fact, there are forty, suggesting that Willson's plans were modified over time.

The temple's apocalyptic imagery and its links with Armageddon and the heavenly Jerusalem should all be seen in the context of what David Willson believed the apocalypse to be. He was among those early-nineteenth-century Christians who believed that the Second Coming of Christ, hastened by human action, was essentially a symbolic, personal experience rather than a cataclysmic prelude to the end of the world.[38] Thus, when he wrote in *The Lord's Celebration*, "the skillfull Architecture is Grace within the heart," a link was made with the Second Coming of Christ. Through the many aspects of his design that recall biblical descriptions of the Apocalypse, Willson took an abstract theological concept and expressed it in three-dimensional form.

The Lord's Celebration was not the only poem Willson wrote describing the building of the temple. Several others survive from the time the building was actually under construction. They add to the sense that the temple was meant to be a three-dimensional metaphor, which not only contained symbolism, but had to be built in a symbolic way. For example, "A bill of timber for the house of the Lord, Jacob's God and Israel's name," dated 28 October 1829, is not merely a list of materials, but a cryptic and complicated poetic summary of what Willson believed were God's instructions for building:

> Two lengthy sills of royal Oak
> That we must soon prepare
> It is my sense Jehovah spoke
> Should be nine inches square
> From End to End full Eighty four
> With adding number one
> Two added on to half a score
> Across the sills to run
> Five added on to three times ten
> Or fifteen to a score
> We have the full dimensions then
> For Columns and for floor
> In equal parts we'll then divide
> To the small number three
> Eleven feet eight from the outside
> The Columns feet shall be ...
> And when we do this bill complete
> The lord will give us more
> This is the boddy of the frame
> Thats built in squares below
> The tops misterious and plain
> The measures none doth know.[39]

This poem set Willson's design in the context of classical architectural values such as rhythm, symmetry, balance, and geometry. His values were not based on the humanistic concepts of the Renaissance, however: they were more in keeping with the metaphysical bases of the Gothic style. Here classical values were expressed in terms of Christian spirituality.[40] The dimensions given in this poem did not coincide with the temple as it was actually built. The discrepancies in *The Lord's Celebration* make sense, since the poem was written in 1822, before building began. "A bill of timber," however, was written late in 1829, well after construction had started. Why are the measurements different? As built, the temple is sixty feet square; however, "A bill of timber" calls for sills – those parts of the timber frame that rested directly on top of the stone foundation – eighty-five feet long.

Also, the poem calls for only two sills, whereas four would be needed to build the building. Clearly, "A bill of timber" was not intended as a literal description of the building process.

Willson himself was trained as a carpenter and knew the ins and outs of building. Following a visit in 1833, the Reverend H.H. O'Neill wrote of Willson, "Being a good mechanic he constructed with the help of his followers, who style themselves 'Children of Peace,' a beautiful frame building which has received the imposing name of 'Temple of Peace'."[41] At that time, the word *mechanic* referred to a skilled workman and had much broader meaning than it does today. Further documentation of Willson's practical knowledge of building and design may be found in a postscript to his 1835 pamphlet, *A Friend to Britain*. In a statement signed by John and Ebenezer Doan, among others, the following credit is given: "He [Willson] has given gratis to his brethren his services as a builder, also the ground whereon our three buildings of worship stand. And although he is a man not versed in science, yet his pattern for building will stand the test of the most strict scrutiny, and we can say the house (which he designed) for our monthly sacrifice [the temple] has obtained the character of being a modern structure for chasteness of design unsurpassed."[42]

The Doan brothers had worked under one of the best master carpenters of the mid-Atlantic states. Their praise for Willson's contributions to the Children of Peace as a builder and designer should not be taken lightly. Interestingly, they characterized the temple as a "modern structure for chasteness of design unsurpassed." This simple description is surprising, given Willson's own thoughts about the elaborate symbolism of the temple. It suggests that at least some members of the Children of Peace saw the temple first and foremost as a building of clean, simple, and beautiful lines. Its perfect symmetry and its masterful interior, filled with columns, arches, and the light from forty windows, may have been testimony enough to the legitimacy of David Willson's leadership.

Willson's own words about his background as a carpenter provide another key to understanding *his* views about the construction of the temple. He wrote that after the age of fourteen he "inclined to mechanical business in joining timber one part unto another."[43] He could have said simply that he worked as a joiner. Instead, he used the phrase, "joining timber one part unto another," which has an archaic, poetic ring to it, reminiscent of the rhythms and phrasing of the King James Bible. Words and phrasing were of utmost importance to Willson. He used language not only to record facts about himself and his activities but also to evoke certain responses in the minds of his listeners. By speaking of "joining timber one part unto another," he set his craft in the context of religious history and tradition, giving it an importance above and beyond the mundane concerns of daily living in the early nineteenth century. By writing his "Bill of timber" in poetic form, he gave a similar sense of religious significance to the mundane task of dressing wood. The fact that measurements noted in the poem did not exactly coincide with the dimensions of the temple was of little importance in that context. When asked by traveller Patrick Shirreff if the design of the temple was his own, Willson replied that it was "the work of the mind."[44] This illustrates Willson's way of understanding of the building of the temple. It was never merely a three-dimensional structure of wood, glass, stone, and iron nails, but was rather a manifestation of ideas and belief.

Sometimes Willson's sense of himself as spiritual leader and guide to the builders of the temple went beyond the role of prophet and mediator. From time to time, his writings suggest that he saw the Children of Peace as modern-day Israelites wandering in the wilderness: he styled himself as a modern-day King David. In November 1830 Willson wrote a sermon based on the opening three verses of Psalm 16, "to the memory of the character of David Israel's King when we were preparing timber for the house of the Lord Armageddon In the desert wilderness of upper Canada." In that sermon, Willson declared that "David was a chosen servant of the Lord. When we fix our eyes upon him, we see whom the Lord hath chosen, and anointed, for his own."[45] There can be little doubt that David Willson intended his listeners to think of his own leadership in light of King David's. Like his poetry, this sermon combines mixed biblical images. Building a temple, wandering in the wilderness, and God's anointment of King David were all key events described in the Old Testament. Yet all were separate events: the Israelites did not build a temple while wandering in the wilderness or under the direction of King David. All three stories were familiar to Willson's hearers through their knowledge of the Bible. More importantly, all three could be understood by the Children of Peace through their own recent experience. They were in the process of building a temple, had lived in what could still be considered a wilderness, and followed a leader named David. As former Quakers, they were used to forms of religious thought and experience that de-emphasized biblical literalism, but stressed the importance of divine revelation. Thus, Willson's mixed metaphors would not have seemed unusual or inappropriate to them, nor would his mixing of visual metaphors in the temple. The combination of features reminiscent of both Solomon's temple and the heavenly Jerusalem can be understood in this context.

In the surviving records of the Children of Peace, even the names of the temple builders took on symbolic significance. A list dated 9 May 1831 includes "Builders names with Wives and Children," suggesting that even if women and children did not actually participate in construction, they were linked to it in some way. In fact, the list of builders is really a membership list of the Children of Peace. Over time, certain names were crossed out and other names added as membership changed. (Additions were made on payment of £1 for men, 10s for women, and 5s for children.[46]) The whole community was credited with building the temple. In this way, the temple became a metaphor for the community itself – a spiritual family that Willson believed God had called together. Just as the New Testament word *church* meant a gathering of faithful believers, so Willson considered his temple to represent a community as well as a physical structure.

Of the day-to-day details of the construction process, little is known. As a carpenter or joiner, David Willson must have been closely involved with many practical details. Tradition maintains, however, that Ebenezer Doan was the master builder, overseeing the work much like a contractor or construction supervisor would today. Doan was among David Willson's earliest followers. He broke with the Quakers soon after Willson was disowned, sold his farm near the Yonge Street meeting house, and took up land closer to Willson's on Queen Street in East Gwillimbury Township. Undoubtedly, Doan had picked up some of his older brother Jonathan's expertise in directing numerous workmen constructing large, complex buildings. It was one of his tasks to see that the temple was finished according to David Willson's prophetic timetable, beginning in 1825 and ending in 1832. Because the workmen earned their livelihood farming, construction could not take place during the busiest times of year, namely, the spring planting or the fall harvest seasons. Some work could have been done in mid-summer, when work on the farms slowed for a while, but the best time for building was during the winter. When leaves were off the trees, work in the forests was easier; when the ground was frozen hard, men, oxen, and horses could drag heavy logs across the forest floor and fields to be hewn into squared timber for building a frame. When David Willson wrote in *The Lord's Celebration*, "In twenty-five begin it, in thirty-two get done," he must have had winter construction seasons in mind. In order for the period from 1825 to 1832 to add up to seven years, the time it took to complete Solomon's temple, Willson must have considered the first construction period to be the winter of 1825–26 and the last the winter of 1831–32. Otherwise, this period would add up to eight years.

To keep construction noise to a minimum, as in the building of Solomon's temple, it was necessary to construct sections of the building at a distance. Like the framed bents of a house or barn, these were then raised and joined together on site. If it is true that, like Solomon's, the temple of the Children of Peace was built without the sound of a hammer striking an iron nail, then these sections would have been covered with wooden siding nailed to their frames before they were brought to the construction site. Window frames and interior features, such as the high dado and lath for receiving plaster, would also have been added at a distance. The nailed flooring inside may have been prepared in sections in the same way. Without dismantling the building, or large parts of it, there is no way of telling how much nailing took place on the site. Certainly, the roof would have required thousands of nails to secure its pine shingles and tin-plated flashing, discovered during recent restoration. It can be said, however, that frame construction methods of the time would have kept nailing to a minimum. Rachel Syllindia Willson (b. 1837), David Willson's great-grand niece, described the process:

the Temple had been built in sections, all three storeys of it, each section containing the frame for a window or a door. The sections were built on surrounding farms with sons and neighbours assisting in the work. When all was completed a great "Bee" was held, with the people coming from far and near. Sleigh runners were joined together to make a bed long enough for the long lower sections, and all were brought with great rejoicing to the site, where a dry-stone foundation had been prepared the fall before. Here the sections were left carefully covered till spring, when another great "Bee" and celebration was held for the raising. The sections were raised and joined together with hand-carved wooden screws, pegs and bolts at which whittlers, old and young had been busy for several years.[47]

Some details of this event, which took place before Rachel Willson was born, are open to question. In essence, however, she describes many of the most common features of a "bee" – a work gathering common to almost every pioneer community. Joseph Gould (1808–1886), whose family came from Pennsylvania as part of the early Quaker migration to Upper Canada, recalled: "Sparse and scattered as the settlers were – some of them living at as great a distance as six or seven miles apart – they assisted one another in blazing and "brushing" roads and cutting pathways through the woods and swamps, and over and around the hills, and at 'logging bees,' and otherwise in exchanging work from one clearing to another. Their helpful sympathies were awakened toward each other, and Quakers, or Friends, as they mostly all were, composing one little community, their offices of good neighbourhood were extended to each other in constant acts of brotherly kindness."[48] Bees were affirmations of community and kinship. They were acts of kindness, but also of necessity. In building a timber frame structure, the separate bents could not have been raised into place without the physical strength of a large number of workmen. John Rempel has described this process as follows:

The sills were laid first, either dry or in a bed of mortar, and were properly secured by a pinned joint at the corners. If heavy floor beams were required they were framed into the sills at this time. The bents – i.e., parts of a frame that were fitted and raised as a unit – were then assembled with hookpins, and placed so that when they were elevated the bottom tenon would slip into its mortise in the sill. The elevation of these bents was the reason behind the customary "raising bees": their weight and bulk was such that an immense amount of physical effort was required to lift them into position. The first bent erected did not have any lateral support and so was temporarily braced. After the second bent was raised, lateral braces or cross-ties were sprung into place and temporarily secured with hookpins between it and the first. These two bents now formed a self-supporting unit, and no further temporary bracing was required. The hookpins were knocked out when the joints had been checked and were then replaced with permanent pins. Once the frame was secure, unskilled help was dismissed (with the usual liquid refreshment) and the carpenters and joiners completed the building.[49]

Skilled supervision was necessary to make sure that all parts of the building fit together properly and that all joints were secure. Ebenezer Doan would have fulfilled this function as master builder. With the assistance of other skilled woodworkers, such as David Willson or his own brothers, John and Mahlon, Doan also completed the interior finishing and added such fine details as the corner lanterns and reeded double doors. Did Ebenezer Doan play any role in designing the temple? The building itself suggests that he, or his brothers, did. The use of finely reeded quarter columns at the four corners of the building suggests the Doan brothers' familiarity with cabinet-making traditions of the Delaware valley. These are most unusual in architecture, where their delicate detail is overwhelmed by the great bulk of the building, but they are often found on high-quality case pieces made by Delaware valley craftsmen in the late eighteenth and early nineteenth centuries. Indeed, they are found on pieces of furniture attributed to the Doans themselves (Fig. 12).

71 Meeting House and Temple

Figure 12 Desk made by John Doan, maple and pine, 40.5" × 23" × 44", c.1830. (Private collection, Sarnia, Ontario) The bookcase top is a twentieth-century addition. This is one of several similar desks made by Doan.

Evidently, much of the temple was completed as early as the summer of 1828, only three years after construction had begun. It was then that William Lyon Mackenzie commented on the "elegant and fanciful" building that the Children of Peace were erecting. The temple was used for worship as early as June 1831, although the first service was not officially held there until the last Saturday of October 1831. In a poem entitled *For the house of peace on the Jewish Sabbath in the afternoon*, and dated 13 June 1831, David Willson described the interior of the temple:

With spreading circles o'er our head
   Our walls adorn'd with green
The little flock Jehovah fed
   Within our walls are seen
Then walls did for thy glory rise
   That gave to us the plan

And here we'll come and sacrifice
With love of God to man ...[50]

The temple was not intended to replace the meeting house as a location for Sunday meetings. After it came into regular use in September 1831, the temple was used only fifteen times a year: on the last Saturday of each month; on the first Friday night in September, when its windows were illuminated with candles; on the following day, before the feast of the "first fruits"; and on the first Saturday in June, in honour of David Willson's birthday.[51]

The temple was not considered complete until the installation of the altar, built by John Doan. Tradition has it that the altar took exactly 365 days to construct.[52] In practical terms, this length of time would not have been necessary. To the Children of Peace, not only were three-dimensional objects symbolic, but so were the ways they were made. By taking 365 days to complete the altar, probably working on it only a short time each day, John Doan linked his cabinet-making to time itself. The altar thus represented a year, while the temple represented seven years. Seven stood for the number of days in a week, a reference to the time God took to create the world and rest, according to the creation story in Genesis 1.

In Revelation, there were seven churches to whom St John's prophecy was addressed (Revelation 1:4), seven golden candlesticks (Revelation 1:12), seven spirits of God (Revelation 3:1), as well as seven angels and seven last plagues (Revelation 15:1). For the Children of Peace, knowledge of the Bible, numerology, and astrology were deeply imbedded aspects of folk culture. Placing the completion of the altar within the broad context of biblical time, Willson wrote, "Our Altar was finished by the hands of John Doan and raised on twelve golden pillars in memory of the twelve apostles of Jesus Christ – on the 28th day of September in the year since the birth of Christ 1832."[53] Thus, Willson related the installation of the altar to the fundamental event in the Christian concept of time: the birth of Christ. The symbolic importance of the altar was heightened further by its use as a "time capsule." In a recent discovery, the pedestal that supports the Bible inside the altar was found to contain a large number of manuscript sermons and hymns as well as an account of the beginnings of the Children of Peace, evidently deposited there at the time of the altar's dedication.

These references to time and to the symbolism of numbers confirm that David Willson saw himself and his followers as acting under divine guidance to create something of great significance. They were not merely building a structure with symbolically significant component parts. They were players in a great drama. They were like the builders of Solomon's temple, the Israelites wandering in the wilderness, the followers of King David, acting within the context of universal time. They were building a structure linked symbolically to the beginning of time as well as to the end of time. Their work, as well as the product of their work, had great importance. After the completion of the altar, Wilson wrote:

> Oh Lord we've seen the great designs
>   Accomplish'd by thy will
> Thou gave the plan and drew the lines
>   And then thou did fulfill ...[54]

The altar has been changed over time and no longer has its original doors, windows, or lamps. When Willson recorded the installation of the altar, he said it was "raised on twelve golden pillars in memory of the twelve apostles of Jesus Christ." Only a few originals remain, their original gilding reproduced.[55] Yet the altar echoes many features of the temple and likewise shows its builder's Delaware valley origins. Both altar and temple are square, with a door centred on each side, flanked by equal numbers of windows. As in Philadelphia and Delaware valley cabinetry, both are lightened at the corners by quarter columns.[56] Each is also embellished with a fine reeded frieze. Inside the altar are two levels, reminiscent of the different floor levels inside the temple.

At the inner centre of the altar is a low platform supporting a Bible open to the Ten Commandments. Because of the symbolic presence of the Ten Commandments, the altar has come to be known as the *ark*. In a Jewish temple, an ark contains the Ten Commandments to recall the Ark of the Covenant, in which the ancient Israelites carried the stone tablets of the law given by God to Moses. In Jewish tradition, however, the ark was placed against the east wall, not in the centre of the building.[57] In Old Testament descriptions, the Ark of the Covenant was rectangular, not square, and designed to be carried, not left permanently in one place (Exodus 37:1–5). Thus, while Willson was inspired by the Ark of the Covenant in creating an appropriate focal point for his temple, he did not follow Jewish custom precisely, either as it existed in the synagogues of his time or as it was described in the Old Testament. This is another example of Willson's free and creative use of biblical imagery. He intended to remind his followers of their Judaeo-Christian heritage, not to duplicate any one specific tradition or design. The original placement of the ark on twelve pillars representing the twelve apostles of Christ is a striking instance of the blending of Jewish and Christian imagery. Subtler, perhaps, was Willson's use of twelve columns, inscribed with the apostles' names, surrounding the altar. These may have played on the Sephardic tradition of using twelve columns in a synagogue to represent the twelve tribes of Israel.

The question arises: had David Willson ever seen a Jewish synagogue before he designed the temple? None existed in Upper Canada at that time. However, New York City, where Willson had lived from 1798 to 1801, was the site of North America's oldest continuing Jewish community. The first group of Jews arrived there in 1654 from Curaçao and were Sephardic, of Dutch, Spanish, and Portuguese origin.[58] Among the earliest stockholders of the Dutch West India Company, for many years they continued to trade with the West Indies, a venture that also attracted David Willson and his stepbrother, Hugh. The New York Jewish community established a synagogue named *Shearith Israel*, "Remnant of Israel," by 1695. Although the evidence is entirely circumstantial, David Willson likely came into contact with Sephardic Jews during his brief period in business in New York City.

The only existing synagogue in the United States that dates to Willson's time there is the Touro Synagogue, built by Sephardic Jews in Newport, Rhode Island, between 1759 and 1763. Like David Willson's temple, it is plain and box-like on the outside, but rich with classical detail on the interior. Like the temple, it has seating around the perimeter, and its interior is dominated by classical columns. There is an ark against the east wall and a pulpit for reading the law at the centre. Its seating arrangements, the location of its ark and pulpit, and the columns that represent the twelve tribes of Israel were dictated by Sephardic tradition; however, the Touro Synagogue is otherwise a light and elegant essay in Georgian architecture. Its architect, Peter Harrison, drew freely and skilfully on several English design books of his time. No direct connection can be made with Willson's temple, yet both show how successfully Jewish tradition could be expressed through architectural trends of their day. Willson's temple, built sixty years later, was designed at a time when ideals of balance and symmetry and classical detail were still deeply rooted in architectural practice.

In this chapter, the term *temple* has been used to describe the building built by the Children of Peace between 1825 and 1832. Yet when visiting traveller Patrick Shirreff spoke of the temple in the early 1830s, David Willson said in response, "We did not wish to raise a temple, it is only a meeting house."[59] In November 1831, records of the Children of Peace note the completion of a meeting house,[60] not

Figure 13 David Willson's study, built 1829, Sharon, Ontario.

a temple. Elsewhere, Willson described it as "the house of peace," "the house of the Lord Armageddon," or simply as "the house of the Lord."[61] The word *house* has long been used in Protestant tradition to differentiate the meeting places of dissenters from the churches of Roman Catholics. Protestant sects that emphasized plainness – the early Puritans, Quakers, and Methodists, for example – continued to use the term *meeting house* well into the nineteenth century. They used the term *Church* to denote the people of Christ who met within the meeting house, not the worship space itself. As heirs of this tradition, Willson and the Children of Peace preferred to call their new building a house. However, in 1831 when Willson declared, "We have built a house for the purpose of off'ring to God *Israelite fashion*,"[62] and planned to hold services there on Saturdays, the Jewish Sabbath, many began calling the building a temple. That name has remained in use to this day.

Even while the temple was under construction, the Children of Peace began erecting yet another building – a study for David Willson's own use (Fig. 13). It was completed and opened in September 1829.[63] Measuring only sixteen feet long by eight feet wide, it has windows on all four sides and doors on the east and west, recalling the designs of both the 1819 meeting house and the temple. In a way, the study is like the temple turned inside out: around the perimeter is a colonnade much like the one inside the temple. Ten simple columns give support to a series of round arches, creating a continuous covered verandah, with a coved, plaster ceiling extending around all four sides of the building. Like the temple, the study has doors embellished with reeded panels and is painted white with green trim. Its gable roof is ornamented with twelve lanterns, similar to those on the temple. A brick chimney serves a small stove inside. (The present lanterns and chimney are modern reproductions that may not exactly duplicate the originals.) An observer in 1861 declared that "inside is a good organ, a bed in which no one ever slept, a table, chairs, books, &c., and here Mr. Willson writes and studies, quite secluded from the outer world"[64] – all this in a space measuring eight by sixteen feet! The barrel organ, similar to the one in the 1819 meeting house, was built by Richard Coates. In contrast with the meeting house organ, it played secular tunes and ballads, having ten pinned onto each of three interchangeable barrels. Women members of the sect made white muslin curtains trimmed with blue ribbon to drape the study's organ. The room's windows, also hung with white muslin, were highlighted by bright scarlet valances.[65]

Even when filled with a stove, bed, table, chairs, books, organ, and curtains, the study maintained a surprisingly open and airy appearance due to its many windows and high, barrel-vaulted plaster ceiling. It must have inspired Willson, for it was there that he wrote his longest book, the 270-page *Impressions of the Mind*, along with numerous shorter works, hymns, poems, sermons, and broadsides. The study may also have been where business transactions took place, and where accounts involving the sect's financial resources and expenditures were kept. This is suggested by traveller Patrick Shirreff's reference to the building as "the counting room" in the early 1830s.[66]

The sprightly and imaginative design of the study can be placed in context with summerhouses and fashionable garden pavilions of the early nineteenth century. It is light and playful in the manner of a Regency cottage.[67] Its specific design precedents may never be known. Perhaps Willson glimpsed the garden structures of the wealthy on his many trips into York. Whatever its background, the study picked up on designs already explored inside the temple – the colonnade, rounded arches, and coved ceiling – as if in preparation for yet another building project. In fact, the study worked out on a small scale the design of the second meeting house of the Children of Peace (Fig. 14), begun in 1834 and completed in 1842. This new build-

77 Meeting House and Temple

Figure 14 Second meeting house of the Children of Peace, built 1834–42/demolished 1912, Sharon, Ontario. (Photograph courtesy Sharon Temple Museum)

ing was needed as the sect outgrew its 1819 meeting house. It was also needed to house the twice-yearly feasts of the Children of Peace that had previously been held in the open air.[68] These feasts were, in a sense, the equivalent of Holy Communion services, so the second meeting house was sometimes called the "Communion House."[69]

Following a visit to the Children of Peace in 1836, the Reverend H.H. O'Neill recorded that, in addition to the temple, David Willson "has two meeting houses, an old one where the services of the sabbath are conducted and a new one of a larger and greater scale, not yet finished, all three on his own land."[70] This second meeting house, one hundred feet long by fifty feet wide,[71] was three times larger than the 1819 building. Some members of the sect were skeptical that such a large building was needed and that such a major project should be undertaken even before the temple was completed. In July 1834 Willson responded to his critics by declaring: "Your house that is now preparing is neither too large nor unnecessary, it is appointed the place of your solemn feasting, when I shall see you no more. Never the less, I trust our feast in the next ensuing year will be accomplished there."[72] Feasts may have been held in the uncompleted building; however, it was not until 1842, eight years later, that the building was finished. Willson struck a worrisome note when he wrote, "It looks dreadful to me to see so soon a want of care about our own precious buildings that the Lord hath given. Nevertheless, it is a sure token of the want of devotion." After little more than twenty years of existence, there were signs that the enthusiasm of the Children of Peace was beginning to decline.

On 19 September 1832, plans for erecting the new building were submitted by the elders to the monthly meeting of the Children of Peace. Probably following a pattern established during the building of the temple, the elders advised, and the congregation approved the designation of "publick days when all labour together" free of charge. They also agreed that those who worked on the building at other times, while their neighbors saw to their farms and businesses, should receive a small recompense. Contributions of money were to be put into the hands of David Willson "to be at his disposal."[73] At first, contributions both of money and work were slow to come in. Willson was the major contributor at first, donating labour valued at £10.5s.6d in 1834. His sons, John and Israel, each contributed £5 worth of labour. Ebenezer Doan gave £2.6s.6d. How the value of their contributions was calculated is not known, but it appears to have been recorded with considerable care. David Willson was also paid for some of his work. An undated account for $96.25, signed by Ebenezer Doan, John Doan, and Samuel Hughes, records that Willson split fifty-five thousand shingles, turned sixty-six columns, and spent eleven days "getting timber." By the time the building was finished in 1842, a total of £423.12s.3d had been contributed, plus "Twenty five pounds to Saml. Hughes for sawing." The most generous contributor was John Doan (£43.5s), followed by Murdoch McLeod (£32.10s), Charles Doan (£26.12s.6d), Israel Lundy (£21.10s), and David Willson himself (£20.12s.6d). At a meeting held on 30 July 1842, it was decided that all those who had contributed would become "the legal owners" of the building "and have votes in the disposal thereof, and their families as they become of age." While the second meeting house was under construction, however, two prominent members, Samuel Hughes and Ebenezer Doan, left the Children of Peace to rejoin the Quakers. To deal with this situation and any other defections that might follow, the meeting decided that "these that have separated from us shall have the privilege of the House, and vote after three years constancy therein, and their families." They also granted the option to "sell their right to another." Once these others had fulfilled a three-year probation period, they too would be admitted to full privileges.[74]

On the outside, the second meeting house closely resembled the study: it was painted white with green trim and had columns with rounded arches on all four sides, supporting an overhanging gable

79 Meeting House and Temple

Figure 15   Interior of the second meeting house, from a pen-and-ink sketch, c.1909[?], by Bernard Joseph Gloster (1878–1948). (John Ross Robertson Collection, Metropolitan Toronto Reference Library)

roof. According to a description of the interior (Fig. 15) published in 1846: "The ground floor is twenty feet high, the ceiling is arched, and is supported by three rows of pillars, on which are inscribed in letters of gold, the names – David, Ezekiel, Jeremiah, Moses, Jacob, Abraham, Solomon, David (with a harp), Judah, Reuben, Samuel, Levi, Isaac, Benjamin, Aaron, Joseph, and 'Our Lord is one God'."[75] A newspaper account from 1861 adds the following information: "Two large organs stand on one side of the area – in front of which a slightly raised platform serves Mr. Willson as a pulpit. In the centre of the floor stands a long table, round which the band and choir are ranged, while further on, opposite the organ, a spiral staircase ascends to a large hall in the upper storey. The building, as I have said before, is the common place of worship of the society, and here the tables are spread when they hold their 'feasts'."[76]

The "two large organs" may have included Richard Coates's 1820 barrel organ, moved from the first meeting house, as well as a keyboard organ built by Coates in 1848.[77] Those organs and the platform that Willson used as a pulpit were among the few items salvaged when the second meeting house was demolished in 1914. They are currently displayed in the temple. Also on display is a long, narrow table with sloping sides, which may be the "long table, round which the band and choir are ranged" from the meeting house. For many years, museum guides interpreted this as a table for holding men's hats during temple services; however, its sloping sides with projecting lips would have served a group of musicians very well for holding music. It resembles other tables used for this purpose in the early nineteenth century.[78]

The shape of this building differed significantly from both the 1819 meeting house and from the temple itself. It was rectangular, rather than square. In a square building with four doors, worshippers sat facing each other to emphasize that the Inner Light was available to all. The 1819 meeting house and the temple, by their very design, preserved this important characteristic of Quaker worship and theology. By choosing not to follow a square plan for the 1842 meeting house, David Willson and the Children of Peace set the course for a new type of worship. Twice as long as it was wide, the new rectangular building took the proportions of a church. Since it no longer exists, and documentary evidence is fragmentary, it is hard to picture the exact layout of the interior. The only interior photograph known shows Richard Coates's 1848 pipe organ with a lectern in front of it, placed against one of the narrow end walls.[79] This follows church practice and suggests that the worshipping congregation may have sat facing in one direction. In practical terms, this permitted one individual to dominate and lead a worship service more completely. Members of the congregation would have seen less of each other as their attention was drawn to one end of the room, where the pulpit and organ stood.

The transition from meeting house to church was not complete, however, since a long table for the band and choir stood "in the centre of the floor." This complicates the picture and indicates that, although the Children of Peace changed their patterns of worship over time, they did not adopt all aspects of church layout. Singers and musicians were not placed at one end of the building, but in the midst of the congregation. Descriptions of the interior of the second meeting house are so vague that it is hard to imagine exactly how this would have worked, but they do make clear the fact that even though the Children of Peace were making significant changes in the way they worshipped, they had not embraced churchly forms entirely. Also, the congregation continued to use chairs, as they had in the 1819 meeting house and in the temple,[80] rather than fixed benches or pews. This allowed great flexibility and suggests that interior seating arrangements may have changed frequently. Perhaps the table for the choir and the band was not always in the centre. At least twice a year, everything would have been moved around when the Children of Peace held their feasts there.

Recent archaeological investigations on the site of the second meeting house have revealed another significant feature: the building appears to have been built without stone foundations.[81] Its wooden sills, unlike those of the temple, may have been placed directly on the ground. This was an unsound building practice that would have led to rot and deterioration in a relatively short time. In fact, photographs taken around the turn of the century show the second meeting house leaning ominously to one side. The lack of care taken in laying the foundations is as important as the building's axial layout in suggesting that major changes were underway within the sect by the time the second meeting house was erected. These changes, related to political turmoil in the 1830s, weakened the foundations of the Children of Peace just as dramatically as inadequate construction weakened the stability of their second meeting house.

5 Doctrine, Worship, and Ritual

> What their creed is I cannot understand.
> Captain Thomas Sibbald, c.1839[1]

> He [David Willson] never speaks of doctrine or discipline but something new appears, and we ever find our selves at a distance from the things needful.
> Elders of the Children of Peace, 1831[2]

> Among the many sects which have taken root in the soil of Upper Canada, a new order of Christians has within a few years, arisen and become conspicuous (even to our legislature) less by the peculiarity of their doctrines (for they have no written creed) than for the outward form of their worship, which is very splendid.
> William Lyon Mackenzie, 1828[3]

These words summarize the thoughts of many nineteenth-century writers who tried to describe the doctrine of David Willson and the Children of Peace. Captain Thomas Sibbald, a member of a prominent Anglican family, looked in vain for a neat summary of Willson's beliefs – a counterpart, perhaps, to the Apostles' Creed, which was inscribed on the walls of Anglican churches of his day.[4] While Captain Sibbald's dilemma is understandable, more surprising is the statement by several elders of the Children of Peace, venting their own confusion and frustration. The third quotation, from William Lyon Mackenzie, is very perceptive. A dissenting Presbyterian, Mackenzie recognized that "the outward form of their worship," rather than doctrine, was the single most distinguishing feature of the Children of Peace. Essential to that outward form were their buildings, which were three-dimensional embodiments of the beliefs of the Children of Peace. These buildings were, in a sense, their distinctive creed.

Defining belief in words was particularly difficult for someone of Quaker background. Quakers emphasized the importance of the Inner Light, the guiding spirit of God that was accessible within the heart and mind of every person. Nonetheless, Quaker consensus on belief and action was expressed through the publication of a *Discipline* by each yearly meeting. Some Quakers emphasized mysticism and individual autonomy more than others, leading to the Orthodox/ Hicksite schism of 1828. Some, like David Willson, downplayed the importance of scriptural authority and the sacrifice of Christ. Beyond stating what they did not believe, it was difficult for Willson or others like him to describe their faith to the satisfaction of others. At first it was enough to say that Scripture and Christ's atonement were not sufficient to bring people to salvation, and that good works were needed as outward signs of true godliness. Willson wrote that his opponents' actions proved that the spirit of God was not in them.[5] Virtually all dissenters in the history of Christianity started with the same premise: others must be wrong because their actions were not governed by their love of God.

Throughout his ministry, Willson remained consistent in his belief that creeds and written statements of faith were of little value. In a manuscript entitled "A short account of the origins and principles of the people that constitute the worship of God, and alms giving in Sharon East Gwillimbury," Willson wrote, "They accept not of theory, or articles of faith, as a distinguishing mark of religion, but will accept of practice only."[6] In two autobiographical sketches, published in 1852 and 1860,[7] he likewise emphasized acts of love and charity as signs that the spirit of God dwelt within the souls of believers. Drawing on Quaker heritage, Willson stressed the importance of remaining open and receptive to the spirit of God. He believed that by doing so his followers would not only be inspired to do good works, but would also find peace and happiness within themselves. In his longest literary work, *The Impressions of the Mind*, published in 1835, Willson clearly set out his belief in the life-giving role of God's spirit. A collection of sermons, essays, poems, and hymns written between 9 October 1832, just after the completion of the temple, and 29 January 1835, *The Impressions of the Mind* drew deeply on Quaker mysticism. Even the title was a phrase familiar to Quaker readers. For example, in a memoir on the life of John Pemberton, published in the Philadelphia-based periodical, *Friends' Miscellany*, from January 1836, Pemberton is described as being "so attentive to the impressions made upon his mind, that he was ready to follow the pointings of Truth, even in what might be termed small appearances."[8] In Quaker usage, the word *impressions* described effects of the Inner Light that prompted the believer to action.

In a compelling passage from *The Impressions of the Mind*, David Willson wrote:

The mind is an atmosphere in itself, containing wonders to us unknown. He that doth not improve his own mind, liveth in ignorance all his days, and dieth short of the intended city, or salvation of the soul. A field improved is productive – a land cultivated is enjoyed, for then we reap the product of our labour; and it is so with the mind. The atmosphere changeth by an over-ruling providence, and there appeareth to be life and motion, in the whole moving system, and this to me is the distant and uncomprehended life of God. He hideth in the cloud, he obscures himself in the clearest sky – he liveth in the deep waters, the living is there, they have their course to run, and I am not afraid to say that nature has a God, and there is not a plant nor tree without him, bud, leaf, or flower. We cannot see anything, but God is there – he is perfect in the storm, he orders the waves of the sea, they rise and fall at his command, there is no space where he is not, and man is as part of these; and God is likewise in the soul, he is the order of life, and the joy of all living, – the stars sparkle with his light, and he commands the rays of the sun to their most extensive bounds. My thoughts, come home into thine own house, and begin to measure thine own habitation, and declare to the world the wonders of thy God; prove that thou art acquainted with him, by leaving an evidence of his light to bear witness of him to the sons and daughters of men. He hideth himself in the mind as in the cloud, and in the waters; and we must seek and find him there.[9]

Another passage that captures the essence of Willson's mystical belief is the following:

A historian can give an account of a nation or country we never saw, why may not religious men reveal the things of God? The contents of the mind to them that never saw them? If a country affords an encouraging history, we will sometimes haste to remove there to better our condition of life, why not speak of the fertility of the mind, and induce some wandering souls that are seeking for a residence of rest, to leave this world and its common source, and inherit the mind, improve it as a new country, and enter into rest, enjoy the fruit of our labour and be at peace; for this is where God hath ordained praise, and where he will satisfy the soul in itself, for a man is a kingdom of his own and he needeth not be as an alien in a far country, and a servant of men.[10]

Literary scholar Thomas Gerry has compared Willson's writings to those of German mystic Jacob Boehme (1575–1624) who, he believes, profoundly influenced the work of George Fox and other early Quaker writers.[11] While Willson did not know of Boehme's work directly, he certainly had access to the writings of George Fox. Before his break with the Society of Friends, Willson was librarian of the small collection of books owned by the Yonge Street Meeting, which included George Fox's *Journal*.[12] Gerry has also linked Willson's thought to the mysticism of William Blake (1757–1827), who he argues, was also influenced by Boehme.[13] Links could be made as well with other English writers of the early Romantic period or with New England transcendentalists, such as Ralph Waldo Emerson

(1803–1882) and Henry David Thoreau (1817–1862). Essential to their beliefs was a sense of the spirituality of all creation. They were convinced that the human mind could transcend tangible boundaries and thus find unity with a spirit that inhabits all things.

The Impressions of the Mind shows Willson to have been intensely concerned with spiritual matters, advocating an inward-turning mysticism that saw the human mind as a new country to be explored, cultivated, and celebrated. One of the central metaphors in the book, his comparison of the mind to a new land was particularly appropriate to the time. Willson, like his neighbors, knew the reality of arriving as a settler in the midst of a dark forest; of cutting trees, clearing land, and growing crops for food; and of watching the clearing spread year by year until farms, roads, and villages came to dominate the landscape. Within one generation, Willson and his contemporaries witnessed a transformation of their environment from wilderness to open, productive farmland. His view of the mind as a new country had special meaning for the Children of Peace, suggesting a boundless potential for change and development. Another common metaphor in *The Impressions of the Mind* linked the mind to a house, residence, or habitation – a place of shelter and rest from the outside world. Again, the frontier environment, where shelter often stood in striking contrast with its surroundings, gave special resonance to such words.

These comparisons with a new country or a house show Willson's tendency to link the workings of the mind to important, tangible things around him. They recall his comments to traveller Patrick Shirreff that the temple itself was "the work of the mind." The mind that designed the temple and wrote books was an active one: developing and extending metaphors, searching for mystical significance in day-to-day occurrences, and seeing the spirit of God present in all creation. For Willson, the temple itself became a metaphor for the mind: outside, rather plain and unadorned; inside, a rich play of space, light, shapes, and materials. This interpretation also fits with Willson's concept of himself: his own "simplicity and plainness of speech"[14] resembling the exterior of the temple and the "wonders" of his mind[15] resembling the interior.

Willson's mysticism, expressed in architecture and writing, was a foundation of his belief. Essentially, he hoped that others would learn to cultivate and explore their own inner selves and find God as he had done. Providing them with a written creed would have gone against his conviction that the spirit of God could be found within the mind of each person. In this belief, Willson was building on his Quaker heritage. What led him away from the Quakers was not his emphasis on the Inner Light *per se*, but the direction that he believed the Inner Light had given him.

Another of Willson's preoccupations was with the Jews, defining who they were and how they related to Christians. There were definite signs of this interest from the start. In his visions and on the two painted banners, children represented Christians and Jews in peace and harmony. His design for the temple was based on Old Testament accounts of Solomon's Temple, on New Testament visions of the new Jerusalem, and on certain aspects of Sephardic synagogue design. In 1828, another vision confirmed Willson's conviction that he was called to play a special role in the restoration of Israel. Willson saw "a beautiful young man clothed in a scarlet robe" that, he was told, stood for the blood of Jesus Christ. The youth then stripped the garment from his own shoulders, put it on Willson's and disappeared, "naked and beautiful." At first Willson felt discouraged: "I will here note that I hitherto had received some hope in having part in the restoration of ancient glory, and therefore was the more grievously disappointed, as expecting by what I had received, I should have part in the Christian Church only." The next morning, however, the young man reappeared wearing a garment inspired by creation itself, "coloured as the skies, ornamented with the lights of heaven wholly, and sparkling with unusual lustre, with a border of gold compassing the mantle round about." The heavenly visitor then carefully and gently lifted up the scarlet robe from Willson's shoulders and placed his own underneath it. Interpreting this, Willson declared: "I saw that Jewish glory was nearest to my heart, and the last visitations of God to His people, and that He would come hereafter, and dwell with them Himself, and receive all glory; I now had received an assurance that I had part both in present and ancient order, but that I must first ornament the Christian Church with all the glory of Israel and afterwards become nothing myself therein, but resign all to God's protection, for He, after me, would take care of His own people."[16]

Willson's earlier visions came in response to the spiritual crisis that he and other Quakers endured during the War of 1812. Their central, female figures were symbols of peace, protection, and nurture. In the 1828 vision, the figure was a young man, but a young man described in androgynous terms: "beautiful," "careful," and "gentle." Why did this figure come to consciousness in 1828? That was the year the North American Quaker community split into two camps: Orthodox and Hicksite.[17] The schism recalled Willson's own earlier dispute with the Quakers and must have awakened memories of 1812. Other members of the Children of Peace saw the Orthodox/Hicksite schism in mystical terms as well. In 1835 Samuel Hughes, for example, published his own pamphlet, *A Vision Concerning the Desolation of Zion*, based on the sorry division of the Quakers.[18]

Willson's conviction that he was called to "ornament the Christian Church with all the glory of Israel" became a fundamental tenet of his belief, a major theme in his writings from the late 1820s and 1830s, and an important influence on the patterns of worship and ritual observed by the Children of Peace. In a poem entitled *A Song of God's appointments or decrees*, written on 26 October 1831, Willson expressed his growing interest in Jewish tradition and tied it implicitly to his visions of 1812 and 1813. Addressing "Wisdom," whom Carl Jung and others have linked with the child-bearing woman of Revelation, Willson wrote:

> Wisdom how clean thy feet appears
> Thy breast like mountains clothed with snow
> Thy mournful cheeks are wash'd in tears
> Thy throne as bright as suns below ...
> Thou wast with Jacob when alone
> With Abram on the mournful plain
> And thou hast come to us unknown
> To seek thy ancient home again
> 'Tis eastern glorys thy delight
> Thou lost thy loving bridegroom there
> To us thou wandered through the night
> Thy bosom and thy feet are bare
> I saw thee e'er the sun arose
> And I embraced thee for my own.
> I leave my kindred and my foes
> To walk with thee by night alone ...[19]

Here Willson, like the author of Proverbs 8, sees Wisdom as a woman whose counsel guided the Jewish prophets and patriarchs of old. In describing Wisdom's return to earth – "And thou hast come to us unknown/To seek thy ancient home again." – he creates a link between his own community and ancient Israel. "'Tis eastern glorys thy delight," he writes, bringing to mind the 1828 vision that so inspired him. For Willson and his followers, the temple symbolized the return of age-old wisdom to the earth and the genesis of a new order that would arise. In this poem, Willson describes not only the return of Wisdom, but also his own embrace of Wisdom as his bride. Since Wisdom lost her loving bridegroom in ancient times – referring to ancient Israel's disobedience of God's commands or their rejection of

Christ – Willson places himself in the role of new bridegroom. By doing so, he implies not only a link with the past, but also a new beginning to start from where the Israelites left off.

In the 1830s visitors to the Children of Peace quickly became aware of the sect's identification with the Jewish people. One of them wrote: "This singular sect, though professing the doctrines of Christianity, appear to consider it as indispensable to unite with it as much as possible the observance of some part of the ordinances contained in the Mosaic law. They profess to take the model of their institution from some parts of the book of Kings."[20] This reference to Kings no doubt refers to descriptions of Solomon's Temple. Captain Thomas Sibbald also remarked on the sect's links with ancient times when he described the temple as "an Eastern-looking building of the most fanciful description."[21]

Willson proclaimed his interest in Israel beyond the bounds of his own community through the publication of a book, *Letters to the Jews*, in 1835. That year was a particularly busy and fruitful one, since it also saw the publication of Willson's *The Impressions of the Mind*. Each book was different, but their publication during the same year suggests that Willson's interest in Judaism arose from the same well of mysticism that had nourished his much longer book. In *Letters to the Jews*, Willson saw the Jewish people as both a physical and a spiritual nation. To the Jews, he wrote, "I am not minded to invite you to change your name, or nation, or mix your blood, till ye see the promises of God to your father fulfilled, and then the Scriptures will be fulfilled, and your chastisements and miseries will honour the living God."[22] Here and elsewhere in his book, Willson saw the Jews as God's chosen people still. His own understanding of Christ as a prophet, which had helped lead to his break with the Quakers, did not permit him to see Jesus as the Jewish Messiah whose coming was foretold in the Old Testament. In *Letters to the Jews*, Willson wrote that the New Testament ought to be read as a book of prophecies for Jews and Gentiles alike. He also believed that the New Testament foretold that "another dispensation shall come upon the world, and this dispensation is, the salvation of the Jews, the chosen of the Lord."[23]

Willson saw the Jewish people not only as they existed in 1835, a dispersed people living under persecution, but also as they were in the Old Testament days of Solomon and David. "The world is unstable as water; but Israel is an immovable pillar in it,"[24] Willson declared, contrasting his belief in the historic strength and stability of Israel with the current state of affairs, as he saw it, in the Christian world. No doubt recalling his own disputes with Quakers and Methodists, Willson described Christians as "far from peace," "divided in their faith," and having a thousand different temples, whereas the Jews had only one.[25] As a metaphor for unity and stability, the Jews had a strong appeal for Willson and his followers, in contrast with continuing disputes between various Christian groups.

The Jews were also appealing as a metaphor for people who received revelation directly from God, in contrast to Christians who emphasized the intermediary role of Jesus Christ. In *Letters to the Jews*, Willson wrote that the word of God was given directly to the ancient Israelites and said, "I believe, *in spirit*, I must become the Jew."[26] Thus, he established a link between his long-standing emphasis on the personal experience of God's presence and his concern for the Jewish people. Willson saw them as a symbol for what Christians should be, guided directly by the spirit of God, the Inner Light, "impressions," or whatever term was used to describe divine power. His autobiographical *Collection of Items of the Life of David Willson* states his belief in the future restoration of Israel and in the prophets of ancient Israel, who might appear in the mind and speak to the soul.[27] Similarly, in a postscript published with *The Impressions of the Mind*, several of Willson's followers stated: "His [Willson's] mind (as he has often intimated to us) has travelled backward from the last dissenters, until his mind dwelleth much with Abraham, Moses, David and the prophets, and latterly he has been engaged in writing some manuscript in favor of the restoration of the Jews, and the downfall of Christian sectarianism."[28]

The temple and the process of building it were striking, tangible expressions of Willson's identification with the Jewish people. If a visitor, or even a member of the Children of Peace, could not understand the fine points of David Willson's theology, they could still see the temple and its construction as embodying Willson's beliefs. Patterns of worship and ritual also became compelling metaphors for theology and ideas. These patterns were essential parts of the cultural framework that inspired the building of both meeting houses and the temple itself. An understanding of these buildings depends not only on analyzing the beliefs of their builders, but also on discovering how each building was used.

In their earliest meetings, held in the Yonge Street carpentry shop of Amos Armitage or in David Willson's Queen Street house, the Children of Peace gathered "to wait on the name and power of God in silence."[29] Meetings were held on First Day (Sunday) and Fifth Day (Thursday),[30] since Quakers used numbers to signify the days of the week. As the *Discipline* of the Queen Street Preparative Meeting recorded, Quakers were "bound to differ from the world in several respects; such as ... our callings the months and days of the week by their numerical names, instead of those which are derived from the Heathen deities, &c."[31] Willson followed Quaker practice initially; however, in writings that were intended for a wider audience, he used the more common terminology – Sunday, Monday, Tuesday; January, February, March; and so on. He also adopted the Quaker practice of holding mid-week meetings as well as First Day meetings.

These early meetings probably included preaching by David Willson and other members of the Children of Peace, such as Rachel Lundy, whom Willson chose as a close confidante and adviser, as well as Israel Lundy, Murdoch McLeod, William Reid, and Samuel Hughes. In the late 1820s, William Lyon Mackenzie referred to David Willson as "their principal minister,"[32] indicating that Willson did not hold exclusive rights to ministry, despite his role as founder and leader of the Children of Peace. The presence of several recognized ministers continued the Quaker practice of calling those with special talents in preaching *minister*. These ministers were not paid, since Quakers distrusted the "hireling ministers" of other denominations and believed that all those blessed with gifts of preaching should share their gifts with others free of charge. Ministers of the Children of Peace also received no remuneration for their services, and Willson's followers were careful to point out that their leader was not a *pay preacher*.[33]

Just as their doctrine was loosely defined, the organizational framework of the Children of Peace gave evidence of great latitude and variation. In general, it followed models established by the Society of Friends, but was open to amendment as the need arose. In 1815, David Willson's report "To the Celect Meeting of the Children of Peace"[34] referred to a body within the sect comparable to the "select meetings" of ministers and elders, who oversaw the spiritual life and conduct of members of the Society of Friends.[35] Among the Children of Peace, this body oversaw a monthly Youths Meeting, designed for "admonishing and encouraging" young members.[36] Monthly meetings "for the strengthening and admonishing of each other, and for the reception and disowning of members"[37] came to be held in the meeting house prior to the almsgiving service at the temple on the last Saturday of every month.[38] These corresponded to the Quakers' monthly meetings, their principal local disciplinary and executive body.[39] Additional meetings were called as required. Twelve elders, including women as well as men, were appointed by the membership to represent them in certain matters;[40] however, a majority vote of the members present at a meeting was required for decisions on important matters.[41] Voting was not part of Quaker practice, which sought instead to arrive at consensus in meetings.[42] Perhaps the increasing involvement of the Children of Peace in the political affairs of the colony led them to adopt this way of making decisions. For business meetings, men and women met together, with young people over twelve taking part occasionally. While early efforts were made to create two distinct charity funds, one controlled by men and the other by women, the attempt was later discontinued.[43]

In the 1830s, the Children of Peace tried to tighten their organizational structure by creating a committee system to look after specific concerns and by defining more precisely who was a member and who was not.[44] At that time, they also began holding yearly meetings of committees, corresponding roughly to the yearly meetings of the Society of Friends.[45] Presiding over these and the monthly meetings was an elected clerk,[46] John D. Willson, David's oldest son. Written motions were presented to him, and no one could speak more than twice on any motion.[48] Generally, David Willson remained in the background at meetings for business, communicating to the members through the elders.[49] By doing so, he may have sought to downplay his own role as leader, so that all who sought the guidance of the Inner Light might have an equal voice.

At times, young members of the sect met separately to deal with their own concerns.[50] In 1845, a meeting of members of all ages decided that younger members should draw up recommendations to be put before the sect as a whole.[51] Like the earliest Friends, the Children of Peace did not generally hold separate business meetings of men and women. The involvement of women, along with teenage girls and boys, must have given these occasions the feeling of a family gathering. Just as women and children were listed along with husbands and fathers as builders of the temple, so was their involvement in meetings integral to the sect's concept of itself as a new church that was open to all people.

Records of the business meetings held by the Children of Peace are fragmentary. When they exist at all, they record decisions made and topics discussed. They do not record the opinions of individual members or give detailed accounts of debates or voting. In these ways, they are much like the records of Quaker business meetings and suggest that the Children of Peace also sought to reach consensus on important issues and were not interested in recording details of arguments that might have arisen along the way. The fact that David Willson did not preside directly over these meetings, despite his position as founder and leader of the sect, also ties their meetings to Quaker practice.

Unlike Quaker ministers, Willson sometimes preached from written sermons or wrote his sermons down for others to preach. This went against Quaker emphasis on the power of the Inner Light to direct and inspire, but was not unlike the practice of Methodist itinerants, who preached both spontaneously and from written texts. Written sermons also recall Willson's Presbyterian roots. As leader and founder of a new religious movement, he may have felt the need to put his thoughts on paper in order to inspire others who might follow him. Certainly, he was a careful record keeper. Throughout his ministry, several women members of the Children of Peace acted as Willson's amanuenses, copying his sermons, poems, letters, and other miscellaneous writings into bound volumes. In one such volume, several lines are crossed out alongside a note in Willson's hand, "not worthy of publication."[52] This suggests that Willson believed the rest *was* publishable and confirms that he saw his ministry in terms of written, as well as spoken, words. Even as early as 1815, Willson penned some verses, "written on the prospect of death,"[53] implying the need to put his thoughts in writing in anticipation of the time when he could no longer teach and preach in person.

One of the most striking deviations from Quaker practice was the use of music in the early gatherings of the Children of Peace. Instrumental music, carefully structured and planned, was avoided in Quaker worship since it contradicted their belief in the spontaneous direction of the Inner Light. It is said that the Children of Peace organized their first choir in 1818 or 1819 and their first musical ensemble or band shortly thereafter.[54] About that time, they acquired the services of Richard Coates, musician, organ builder, and painter of the banners. He had served as a bandmaster in the British army and, like many others Englishmen, found himself out of work after Britain defeated the armies of Napoleon at Waterloo.[55] Arriving in York in 1817, Coates busied himself with a wide variety of pursuits, including the sale of barrel and keyboard organs, both imported and of his own manufacture.[56] In 1820, Coates installed a barrel organ in the square meeting house the Children of Peace had built on David Willson's farm the preceding year.

This organ had two barrels, each pinned for ten tunes. It has been estimated that the process of pinning these tunes, a highly complex, mathematically challenging operation, may have taken up to a year or more to complete. All but one of these tunes were British in origin and would have been known to Coates before he emigrated to Upper Canada. The one exception was the tune "China," written by an American, Timothy Swan, and published in Boston in 1793. Its presence may suggest that the Children of Peace – being of American, rather than British, background – participated in the selection of tunes that the organ was programmed to play. Only one of the chosen tunes was not written to accompany hymns: this was a secular tune known as "In the Cottage" in Britain and *"La Bonne Aventure "* in France. The presence of secular melodies mixed with popular hymn tunes was relatively common among barrel organs meant for church use.[57] The travelling Quaker, Jacob Albertson, noted the presence of this organ in the meeting house in October 1820 and remarked that the dissenting Children of Peace were going "farther and farther from friends."[58] The New York traveller, F. Hall, described the instrument as "a good organ" on his visit in 1825.[59] It survives today in playing condition in the Sharon Temple Museum.

Besides building organs, Richard Coates taught members of the Children of Peace to play a wide variety of musical instruments for use in their services and processions. At a service held in 1829, Coates played a concert horn, while others played violoncelloes, clarinets, German flutes, octave flutes, a bassoon, a violin, and a flageolet. A choir of six or eight young women sang in three-part harmony. Describing this event, which may have attracted as many as three hundred people, newspaper editor William Lyon Mackenzie declared that the Children of Peace had presented "a band of vocal and instrumental performers such as are seldom to be met with, unless in choirs, or perhaps at the grand festivals for sacred music, which now and then occur in England."[60] At first members of the band paid for their instruments out of their own pockets. In 1844, however, it was decided to subsidize these costs out of the Charity Fund. This came about as a result of a plea by the musicians: "persons in ordinary circumstances, having no income except that derived from the labour of their own hands ... They have Houses and families to provide for, and all the cares of life resting upon them common to the labouring class of People ... Musick requires much devotion of time and preparatory exercise to perform it respectably on publick occasions."[61]

In mixing vocal and instrumental music in worship, the Children of Peace followed an old English custom typical of many rural parish churches up until the early-nineteenth century. In his novel, *Under the Greenwood Tree*, Thomas Hardy painted a vivid picture of this practice about the time it was dying out in England. He told of amateur musicians gathered in a gallery and enthusiastically, if not always skilfully, accompanying the singing of a church congregation. Richard Coates no doubt brought knowledge of this tradition with him to Upper Canada. There must, however, have been more direct sources of inspiration for the considerable musical interests of the Children of Peace. It did not come from their Quaker heritage. Quakers used no rehearsed instrumental music in their meetings for worship, although spontaneous singing might sometimes be heard as a manifestation of the Inner Light. The Methodists are a more likely source of inspiration. Methodist itinerants visited the Yonge Street community during its earliest years and Quakers returned the favour by visiting Methodist meetings. Though advocates of simple and uncomplicated forms of worship, Methodists sang hymns. Preachers were likely to carry two books with them: the Bible and a hymnal by Charles Wesley (1708–1788), brother of John Wesley (1703–1791), founder of the Methodist movement. Charles Wesley published over four thousand hymns during his lifetime, making him the most prolific hymnodist in the English language and making the Methodists famous for their congregational singing.[62] Willson and his early followers likely heard music used to advantage in worship at meetings held by Methodist itinerants on the Yonge Street circuit. Coming from a tradition of silent worship, broken only by the words of those who felt moved by the Inner Light, they must have been impressed by the power of singing to inspire and unite a congregation.

On one of his visits to York, David Willson must have met Richard Coates and engaged his services as teacher, so that the Children of Peace, unused to playing instruments and singing, could learn the rudiments of music. Supplying a barrel organ would have been a necessary part of Coates's method of instruction. Before his arrival, there was probably no one in East Gwillimbury able to play a keyboard organ to accompany hymns. A barrel organ, which was operated simply by turning a handle and pumping air into its bellows, would have been an essential piece of equipment. With it, the Children of Peace could learn to sing hymns and play tunes for use in their worship. Willson's interest in hymns grew as time went on. While never as prolific as Charles Wesley, the founder of the Children of Peace did publish three books of hymns[63] and left many others in manuscript. Other members of the sect wrote hymns as well. In 1828, William Lyon Mackenzie noted that, "They compose all their own hymns and psalms to suit the occasions on which they are sung,"[64] thus preserving something of the Quaker tradition of spontaneity.

Music was not the only aspect of worship influenced by the Methodists. The Methodist love feast or *Agape* meal, which John Wesley borrowed from the Moravians and linked with the earliest practices of the Christian church,[65] likely inspired the feasts held by the Children of Peace. Another source could have been the love feasts held by the Tunkers, or River Brethren, who settled in nearby Markham Township in 1804.[66] The first feast held by the Children of Peace took place in 1818 on the site of their first meeting house.[67] They continued to be held in the open air until about 1835, when enough of the second meeting house was finished to accommodate them.[68] Feasts were then moved into its spacious interior, and food was supplied from a separate cook house built next door. Among the Methodists, love feasts were often held at the time of a camp meeting or in conjunction with their quarterly observance of Holy Communion. Although the Children of Peace, like the Quakers, did not observe the Lord's Supper, they may have seen their feasts in that context. Their June feast, at first in honour of David Willson's birthday, was later held to commemorate the Jewish Passover, just as the original Lord's Supper had. In fact, the Children of Peace sometimes referred to their second meeting house, where their feasts were held, as the Communion House.[69] Feasting is a very old form of celebratory activity. For a frontier community that depended directly on the food it produced, a feast was a symbol of prosperity, plenty, and unity. Since the first feast of 1818 followed several lean years of wartime shortages and poor crops, it was an appropriate celebratory act for a group newly formed and hopeful for the future.

Another custom that set the Children of Peace apart from the Quakers was their use of processions. In 1825 the New York traveller, F. Hall, said that the Children of Peace "go in procession to their place of worship the females taking the lead, being preceded by banners and two of their number playing on the flute." Women and men walked separately in these processions, just as they sat on separate sides of their meeting house. The banners, whose symbolism recalled David Willson's early visions, reminded the marchers of the divinely inspired mission of their founder. The music of the flutes added to the sense of solidarity among the marchers by masking distracting noise, while the tempo of the music helped them maintain a consistent pace. Thus, a procession became a strong statement of unity. Marching to worship in procession provided an experience considerably different from arriving one by one. The custom strengthened group identity within the sect, which was so important during the early years when adherents were being individually admonished, disciplined, and disowned by the Quakers. Processions provided a sense of peer comfort and support during difficult times. Willson could have based these processions on the marches of early trade and craft associations, which he may have witnessed in New York City from 1798 to 1801. That was a time of growing labour unrest and early union activity in New York. Such activity led to an increasing number of processions involving workers carrying tools, finished goods, and symbolic insignia, often to the accompaniment of music. These secular processions also provided a sense of group unity and strength, remaining an important civic ritual in North American cities through most of the nineteenth century.[70] They could well have inspired Willson as he sought to develop distinctive forms of worship for his followers.

The 1819 meeting house, which had doors on its north, south, east, and west sides, was designed with symbolism and ceremony in mind. It is not known whether processions broke into four parts to enter the meeting house. Perhaps the doors were meant only to symbolize that people were welcome to enter from all four cardinal directions. Once inside, worshippers found themselves within a building ideally suited to congregational singing. In the days before widespread literacy and plentiful copies of printed hymn books, a precentor would sing or read out hymn verses line by line for the congregation to follow. The precentor may also have conducted the music and established the proper tempo through gestures. Such instruction was particularly important for former Quakers who were unused to public singing. The square meeting house was ideal for singing, since all its occupants were at a short, relatively equal distance from the musicians at the middle.

Processions to the meeting house were forerunners of the more elaborate ritual planned for the temple. Believing that he was called to "ornament the Christian Church with all the glory of Israel," Willson declared, "We have built a house for the purpose of off'ring to God, *Israelite fashion*."[71] In fact, temple services did not follow any specific patterns described in the Old Testament. As links with "Israelite fashion," they were held on the Jewish sabbath, involved ritual movement and action, and included both vocal and instrumental music – all features having Old Testament precedents. Even before the temple was finished, a ceremony was held. When the first storey was completed, "twenty-four females ascended and sung an evening anthem just as the sun was sinking in the west."[72] The building itself had a setting sun painted on it, along with the word *Armageddon*, to signify the end of the world. The event was yet another allusion to the Apocalypse, which like ancient Israel, inspired much of Willson's early theology.

When the temple was ready for its first service, a more elaborate ceremony was held on the last Saturday of October 1831. That ceremony established the pattern for temple worship, thereafter held on the last Saturday of every month. At eleven o'clock in the morning, trumpets sounded to summon the Children of Peace to their meeting house. At noon the band and choir performed a musical selection, which was repeated three times. Silence followed as the congregation continued to gather. Then David Willson preached a sermon. Following that, the congregation rose and left the meeting house by the east doors, facing Queen Street. There they grouped themselves into a procession with twelve elders taking the lead, followed by musicians and then the rest of the congregation ordered according to age. At the temple gate, farther north on Queen Street, the procession divided into four parts, each part entering through one of the four doors of the temple. The musicians entered by the east door, climbed the steep staircase to the gallery, and repeated a piece of music three times. They then descended to the main level of the temple and deposited their instruments on a green-covered table on the east side of the altar. Then the eldest male and female present arose and approached the altar. Others followed and placed offerings of money on four small, covered tables. The money was counted by both a man and a woman, and the total was announced by the treasurer. A precentor dressed in black then rose and stood west of the altar, facing east. He read out the lines of a hymn composed specifically for that service, which was then sung by the congregation with the support of a choir of men and women gathered around the altar, accompanied by musicians playing in the gallery above.[73]

In a poem dated 16 December 1828, Willson described the clothes worn by members of the band and choir. In summer, both men and women wore "spotless white." In winter, the women continued to wear white, along with a scarlet apron and "shoulders clothed with green" – presumably, green shawls. The men dressed in blue during the winter, and each wore a red and gold band around his waist. Willson began his poem:

> Come little lads save all your pence
> And maidens do the same
> To clothe yourselves for providence
> Jehovah is his name.

In subsequent verses, Willson linked white with purity, red with the blood of martyrs, and gold with the ancient patriarchs of the church. This corresponds roughly to the symbolic use of colours on Richard Coates's banners. Willson did not specify his symbolic interpretation of the colours blue or green.[74] Perhaps more important than their meanings was the fact that he prescribed colours at all. Colourful clothing for worshippers was a major departure from Quaker practice, which set the Children of Peace apart from others and added to the splendour of their worship. All the colours mentioned, with the possible exception of green, were produced using commercial dyes. They would have contrasted with the "homespun blueish mixture" that characterized the clothing of the sect as a whole, according to an observer from the early 1830s. Thus, colourful garments for musicians and singers became another element of Willson's grand plan to recall the glory of ancient Israel.

Visitors to temple services were welcomed and asked to sit on benches fixed to the walls around the perimeter of the interior. Each member of the Children of Peace sat on a painted, wooden chair that had the name of its occupant written underneath the seat. Once a service began, two female door-keepers bolted the doors to prevent anyone from entering while the service was in progress. These doorkeepers were chosen by a council of women and were given control over the temple keys. They were not to open the temple except at the direction of "seven patriarchs" of the Children of Peace.[75] At first David Willson did not enter the temple during services. He preached in the meeting house beforehand, but made a special point of not participating in temple worship. In his writings, Willson stressed that the guiding spirit of God was available to all people. His absence from the temple emphasized that idea, leaving his followers to worship by themselves. A "statement signed on behalf of the Brethren" by Murdoch McLeod, John Doan, and Ebenezer Doan declared, "We think ourselves done with the sectarian plan of worship ... We think that no priest can preach us to a better end than the purpose of our present house ..."[76] One purpose that was central to temple worship, and which did not require Willson's presence, was the collection of alms for the poor and needy. In his "Short Account of the origins and principles of the people that constitute the worship of God, and alms giving in Sharon East Gwillimbury," Willson made no mention of temple ritual itself, but simply stated, "They contribute to the relief of the poor, once a month, and give alms according to necessity."[77]

In the temple and in temple worship, all aspects of Willson's thought and theology came together. His Quaker heritage was exemplified by his refusal to act as the sole leader of worship and by the equal role women were given in temple services. His desire to glorify ancient Israel was expressed in his use of music, ritual, ceremonial clothing, and processions. His practical concern for the poor and oppressed was reflected in the central role that almsgiving had in temple services. All these features must have been seen as fulfillment of Willson's divinely appointed mission to rescue and care for the church.

Worship in the temple may be seen in a broader context as well. There were similarities between the origins of the Children of Peace and the Shakers and between their forms of worship also. The Shakers developed a community structure in which members experienced earthly millennial life and anticipated the experience of heavenly life. They stressed the virtues of cooperation, love, mutual assistance, and peace. These they saw as characteristic of the thousand-year reign of peace and prosperity that would follow the second appearing of Christ on earth. In Shaker belief, founder Mother Ann Lee was that second incarnation of Christ. They simulated the experience of the heavenly life by developing intricate spatial regulations involving movement, posture, and personal distance that were facilitated by their architecture. As Dolores Hayden has demonstrated, the Shakers deliberately restricted and carefully controlled all movements that were related to day-to-day earthly living. The buildings in which the Shakers lived in communal "families" were designed to reinforce concepts of uniformity, regularity, repetition, and simplicity, which were associated with earthly movement. Even the paths between Shaker buildings were laid out in strict geometric form, allowing little possibility for deviation in going from one building to another. In contrast with restricted earthly space and movement was the freedom Shakers associated with heavenly life, which they experienced in worship. There, flowing movement, represented by ritual dance, was seen as a foretaste of heavenly freedom. Its impact was all the greater because of the contrast it offered to the regulated, restricted movements of day-to-day living.[78]

The Children of Peace did not live together communally like the Shakers; however, they did stress the importance of mutual assistance through their services in the temple and experimented with systems of cooperative marketing and controlled land ownership and sales. They also adopted a code of plainness and simplicity in their everyday clothing and houses. While not going to the same extreme as the Shakers, the Children of Peace did follow certain codes of behavior that restricted individualism and self-expression in the best interests of their community and in obedience to what they felt was the will of God. Like the Shakers, their contrast to worldly restriction and self-denial was their experience of worship. Even Sunday morning worship at the meeting house involved movement, music, colour, and pageantry, as members of the sect walked in procession and played or listened to music. During temple services, other rituals focused on the time when members rose one after another to place their charitable contributions by the altar. Participation in rituals stood in contrast with patterns of worship members of the Children of Peace had known while they were Quakers. Their worship must have also contrasted with their daily lives as frontier farmers. Census records for East Gwillimbury in 1834 indicate that most settlers lived in simple houses amid large tracts of land yet to be cleared.[79] Their experience of worship in spacious, finely crafted frame buildings, complete with the music of an organ, band, and trained choir, may have inspired the same sense of heavenly life that ritual dance brought to the Shakers.

Shaker influence could have been direct, since David Willson spent his childhood and adolescence in Dutchess County, New York, not far from Mount Lebanon, the centre of North American Shaker activity. It is more likely, however, that similar background, beliefs, and conditions led to similarities in worship. For both sects, ritual acts brought a sense of unity and solidarity, factors important to any minority group. Through ritual, they linked their actions to something bigger than themselves. The Shakers linked theirs to the freedom they would experience in heaven, whereas the Children of Peace linked theirs to an identification with Israel, God's chosen people. For both sects, ritual offered a sense of release from worldly concerns, just as the "jerks" experienced by early Methodists in their camp meetings provided release from the constraints and proprieties of everyday life.

While the temple was used primarily for monthly services of almsgiving, it was opened on three other occasions as well: on the first Friday night in September for the Illumination, on the following day for the Feast of the First Fruits, and on the first Saturday in June. On the evening of the illumination, candles were placed in each of the forty windows of the temple and in the twelve corner lanterns as well. In later years, small lamps were used instead of candles.[80] In the poem, *For the Illumination evening,* written on 26 August 1837, David Willson spoke of the light of the Children of Peace shining out across the land:

> Deep is the grief a saviour bears
> And righteous is his throne
> And deep affliction from his prayers
> In woods and fields alone
> Tis for his name these walls arose
> Thats 'luminated round
> A light more righteous than his foe's
> Amidst our land is found ...
> This night for him the harp doth sound
> King David's royal name
> Amidst our court in peace is found
> His offrings rise again
> Let every lamp of light appear
> To father and to son

And each attentive listening ear
Think on his holy one ...[81]

Light had special meaning for people of Quaker background, recalling the Inner Light that was so important to their belief. The light of the temple became a metaphor for the light of God. Illuminating buildings was an old custom practised in many communities to mark a special event, anniversary, victory, or celebration. The Moravians are particularly associated with this tradition; however, it was a widespread practice and by no means confined to religious observances. Willson and the Children of Peace gave this custom new meaning within the context of their own beliefs. Worship was held in the temple on the illumination evening and on the following day, before the Feast of the First Fruits was served in the meeting house.

On Christmas morning, a special service was held in the meeting house, following breakfast and a 5:00 A.M. illumination. That hour was believed to be the time of the birth of Jesus in Bethlehem. After their service, the Children of Peace celebrated with a noonday dinner.[82] Their celebrations differed from the Quakers, who allowed Christmas Day to pass without any festivities or observance, preferring to consider all days equal in the sight of God. Ironically, Willson left the Quakers partly because of their accusation that he had denied the divine nature of Christ. Like his 1837 poem about the illumination service, the elaborate Christmas celebrations of the Children of Peace reaffirmed their belief in themselves as Christians, despite the criticism of their opponents. However, while they joined certain Christian denominations in celebrating Christmas, the Children of Peace did not hold special services at Easter. Instead, their major spring festival was observed with a feast on the first Saturday in June. Originally held in honour of David Willson's birthday, it was later instituted as "the passover."[83] In this observance, they asserted once again their identification with ancient Israel.

When the second meeting house was completed in 1842, the older structure came to be called the Music Hall and was used primarily for band practices.[84] Sunday services were moved to the larger building, which offered a very different experience of worship. The first meeting house was only 1,600 square feet in size; the second was 5,000. The second meeting house was a less intimate space, not only because of its larger size, but also because of its rectangular form. Except for the presence of band music, its order of worship was similar to that of most Protestant churches of the mid-nineteenth century: organ voluntary, sacred piece by the band, scripture reading, hymn by the choir, prayer, anthem, sermon, hymn, and closing voluntary by the organ. Music continued to play an important part in services and probably reached higher levels of accomplishment in the 1840s than ever before. In January 1846, Daniel Cory was brought from Boston and, according to Emily McArthur's 1898 pamphlet on the history of the Children of Peace, "a systematic training in all the rudiments of singing was engaged in with black-board and all conveniences required." This training lasted for over two years. In 1848, Richard Coates, still active after nearly thirty years with the Children of Peace, supplied the meeting house with a keyboard organ.[85] This in itself signified a higher level of musical accomplishment and indicates the presence within the sect of keyboard musicians.

To all outward appearances, the Children of Peace were thriving by the late 1840s as never before. However, their newly completed meeting house would be the last building project of this sect, which had come to be known for unique architecture and design. By the time it was completed in 1842, David Willson had reached his sixty-fourth birthday. Old age was approaching, and Willson had no obvious successor. Two years before, master builder Ebenezer Doan had resigned his membership in the Children of Peace.[86] Shortly before that, Samuel Hughes, another prominent member, had left to join the Hicksite Quakers. These were ominous signs, suggesting that the Children of Peace had lost some of their original vigour.

The eventual decline of the Children of Peace was spelled out in the very fabric of their 1842 meeting house. It could accommodate more people than either of their earlier buildings, and its design incorporated many details used previously in the first meeting house, the study, and the temple. However, its floor plan and its order of worship suggested a closer association with mainstream Protestantism than ever before. They suggested that the Children of Peace were losing sight of some of those qualities that had marked their earlier years: their Quaker heritage, their introspective searching for the Inner Light, their emphasis on equality, their love of ritual, and their conception of themselves as a unique people chosen by God to reform and rebuild His church. In their adoption of a new type of building that lacked the square plan of the first meeting house and the temple, they approached the spatial norms of other churches whose members focused their attention on one leader and minister. From the beginning, David Willson had provided leadership and inspiration, yet his message had always been that the Children of Peace should look within their own minds for divine guidance. The square meeting house and temple reinforced those doctrinal emphases by causing their congregations to look inward upon themselves. They required their congregation to face each other rather than facing one focal point. This gave little opportunity for one person to dominate in the way that a minister standing in a pulpit or a priest presiding at an altar could.

The second meeting house did not abandon all the earlier practices of the Children of Peace, but its "affecting presence" was significantly different from that of the first meeting house and the temple, reflecting major changes in the organization, practices, and beliefs of the sect as a whole. Even services inside the temple gradually became more like those of other denominations. David Willson, who at first refused to take part in temple services on principle, eventually began to preach there.[87] Increasingly, he assumed the role of a parish minister, probably in response to challenges to his own leadership. As those challenges intensified, fueled by controversies over the Rebellion of 1837, Willson found it necessary to assert his own authority in a stronger manner. This marked the beginning of a new era in the history of the Children of Peace.

Throughout their history, the Children of Peace centred their activities around their meeting houses and temple in East Gwillimbury Township, but always saw their mission to the Christian church in broader terms. Willson published his earliest writings in New York and Pennsylvania and travelled to Quaker meetings far afield. He had followers in Uxbridge, twenty-five miles east of Yonge Street, and held worship services in nearby Markham and at various locations in and around York. Announcements in the *Colonial Advocate* in 1831 indicate that the Children of Peace held worship meetings in Markham on the third sabbath in August, September, and October as well as on the last Sunday of December; they planned to continue regular services there in 1832. The sect also announced regular services "at Thomas Sheppard's, Yonge Street," just north of the provincial capital. In York itself, they held Sunday services at the York East School House, the York Hotel, and the Old Court House. Often services were announced for both eleven o'clock in the morning and three o'clock in the afternoon.[88] Evidently, the Children of Peace were well enough supplied with ministers during the 1830s that David Willson's frequent absences to lead services elsewhere were not a problem.

As they did at home, the Children of Peace walked in procession before their services in York. On 19 September 1833, the *Colonial Advocate* announced a procession consisting of "a few musicians and singers, male and female, bearing representations," which were, of course, the banners. The announcement invited the people of York to march with the Children of Peace, four abreast, the males taking the two right-hand lines and the females taking the left. Newcomers were given detailed instructions as to how and where to walk, conforming to a pattern established by the sect. Such patterns reinforced the confidence of the Children of Peace as they walked through the streets of a town far bigger than their own, where they were outsiders, rather than the majority. By teaching their marching to others, the Children of Peace gained a tangible sense of control and mastery, so their religious procession promoted a sense of unity, confidence, and common purpose.

Processions were used as a prelude to secular events as well. In February 1834, David Willson and some members of the Children of Peace attended a convention of political reformers in the capital. A newspaper announced, "They will be accompanied by music and banners, as on the occasion of the late County Election, and they request the friends of freedom, truth, justice and Constitutional right to take part in the procession."[89] The newspaper writer who recorded this event, presumably political reformer William Lyon Mackenzie, wrote of "the splendid band," of music "well sung," of oratory "with great force and effect," and of "the greatest order and good humour." In contrast with this picture, British traveller D. Wilkie, who visited one of Willson's Sunday morning services in York, recorded that it was attended largely by "servant-girls, working lads, and apprentice-boys about town." Evidently, Willson's reputation as a reform-minded preacher had gained ground and attracted an eager audience.

Wilkie summarized Willson's sermon as follows: "The burden of his discourse seemed to be the injustice practised towards the world by all those who possess an abundant share of the good things of life. That they are all usurpers and tyrants; that there ought neither to be masters nor servants; that all mankind are equal; and that it is the duty of the poor to pull down the rich." Wilkie belittled Willson's "crude ideas and shortsighted dogmas." He ridiculed Willson's rhetorical powers, and thereby betrayed his own conservative stance. His descriptions of both the instrumental and choral music at the service also showed intense dislike. He reported the presence of a choir of several young women, accompanied by four or five men with musical instruments grouped around a table in front of them. David Willson acted as precentor, reading aloud the lines of a hymn he had composed, with the singers and musicians responding. According to Wilkie, "the tune, however, did not tally with my ideas of appropriate church music; it had more the character of a careless rant." After a pause intended as an opportunity for the congregation to meditate on what they had heard, Willson again read out the lines of a hymn "while the girls and musicians joined in full band, and created what was little better than a varied noise, and well calculated to dissipate any religious musings ..."

The period of silence between the two hymns was one of several Wilkie noted in his description of the service. One took place at the beginning, before Willson entered the room; another occurred after the second hymn, before he began his sermon. These pauses reflected the Quaker tradition that placed high value on periods of silent meditation and quiet reflection as worshippers sought the Inner Light. Willson's posture during the service and his manner of preaching also reflected his Quaker past:

> The general expression of his countenance was dry solemnity ... His posture was erect and he remained for several minutes with his right hand clasping his left arm behind; his eyes fixed on vacancy, and some solemn thoughts seemed to be revolving in his mind ... Without recourse to the Bible or other text-book, he abruptly entered on his discourse with the words, "The apostle Paul says." But I do not recollect the passage; but I well remember this much, that the rambling rhapsody which followed could not have drawn its perverted spirit from any part of the apostle's inspired writings. Our preacher soon lost sight of affairs of a spiritual nature, and expiated upon those of a worldly sort. He employed neither genuine argument nor deduction ...[90]

Wilkie's description of Willson's preaching is similar to that written by Francis Higginson, a critical observer of a Quaker preacher in the seventeenth century:

> His countenance severe, his face downward, his eyes fixed mostly towards the earth, his hands and fingers expanded, continually striking gently on his breast; his beginning is without a text, abrupt and sudden to his hearers, his voice for the most part low, his sentences incoherent, hanging together like ropes of sand ... sometimes full of sudden pauses; his whole speech is a mixed bundle of words and heaps of nonsense, his continuance in speaking is sometimes exceeding short, sometimes very tedious, according to the paucity or plenty of his revelations. His admiring auditors that are of his way, stand the while like men astonished, listening to every word, as though every word was oraculous; and so they believe them to be the very words and dictates of Christ speaking in him.[91]

Wilkie was less complimentary about his subject's ability to arouse his audience, declaring that Willson did not "in any material degree appear to be capable of appealing to the passions of his hearers." Nonetheless, despite his own low opinion of Willson's service, Wilkie noted that the meeting place was nearly filled to capacity, and this was certainly not the first time the Children of Peace had held services in the capital. Had the music and preaching been as unappealing as Wilkie claimed, Willson would not have attracted the following he had.

A comparison of Wilkie's account of David Willson's preaching style with that of Francis Higginson is revealing. Both preachers began with a period of silent meditation and started their sermons very abruptly. Both proceeded in a seemingly random manner, without a clear beginning or end to their arguments. Neither based his remarks closely on a biblical text. The observers of these two preachers clearly preferred their own "religion of order" over the "religion of experience" exemplified in the preaching style of Willson and the Quakers. Anglican sermons of the time followed a much more orderly pattern. Following a brief introduction, their progress was divided into three parts: primary principles were set out, these principles were applied to the topic at hand, and then all was drawn together in a systematic way. Each point was made to stand on the conclusions of the previous one.[92] An Anglican sermon was like a Georgian building in its logic, balance, and tripartite organization.

In their search for order and logic, observors like Wilkie and Higginson were blind to the emotional impact that other kinds of preaching could have. The Reverend Henry Caswall, for example, wrote of visiting a Methodist chapel in New York City in the 1830s: "Here I found an immense congregation, the females seated on the left, and the males on the right. They appeared to be an entirely different class of persons from those whom I had seen at Grace Church and St. George's [Episcopal], and were listening with the most profound attention to a sermon in which I could discover neither point nor connection; but a bare repetition of the same phrases, with violent emphasis and gesticulation."[93]

None of these three observers understood the power of repetitive and rhythmic preaching to awaken the response of a congregation. In a perceptive commentary, Richard Bauman has written: "To the extent that the auditor of such preaching could begin to anticipate the repetitive words and cadences of the minister and to be caught up in expressive collaboration with him, there might well arise a sense of immediate co-participation in the utterance that would make the listener feel that the minister's words were echoed within himself."[94] That sense of co-participation was strengthened, not only because of the familiar repetitions of the preacher's own words and rhythms of speech, but because those words and rhythms often echoed the familiar King James Bible. Thus, the words of the minister and the thoughts and feelings of his listeners could be one – a key to understanding the impact of the preaching of David Willson and of the Quakers and Methodists of the past.

Another key may lie in these preachers' identification with the economic and social concerns of their listeners. Both Wilkie and Caswall described a congregation composed largely of working class people or servants. Higginson did not describe the Quaker preacher's audience in detail, but we may assume it was similar because of the Quakers' early identification with the plight of the poor and oppressed. By mixing theology with social, economic, and political concerns – which David Willson undoubtedly did – another potent ingredient was added to the elixir of preaching.

The Children of Peace, like the Quakers, abhorred formulaic creeds; but through books such as *The Impressions of the Mind* and *Letters to the Jews*, David Willson attempted to provide his followers with the basic tenets of a religion. He emphasized what Quakers called the Inner Light and incorporated both Christian and Jewish tradition. In planning worship and other gatherings, Willson drew on Quaker and Methodist traditions; incorporated feasts, illuminations, and processions, which had come to be associated with secular as well as religious observances; linked theology with social concern in the elaborate ritual associated with almsgiving services in the temple; and created his own imaginative links with the practice of the ancient Israelites.

At his meetings in York, Willson sometimes linked religion with politics and often spoke out against the economic injustices of his day. In the village of Hope, particularly, David Willson's religious beliefs were mixed with concern for the social and economic well-being of his followers. There, in addition to designing unique buildings for worship, Willson attempted to lay the foundation for a model community whose meeting houses and temple would be surrounded by prospering farms, well-ordered households, and efficient educational institutions. If outsiders and even some Children of Peace could not always understand the fine points of Willson's religious beliefs, they could still be inspired by his words and find evidence of his divine appointment in the sect's forms of worship, their buildings, and their prospering community.

6 Life and Work in the Community

In 1803, scarcely two years after his arrival in Upper Canada, David Willson had a dream that would later provide a pattern for community life among the Children of Peace. Willson dreamed about a poor man who had no money to find lodging in the city where he had moved. The man decided to move out onto the lake that lay in front of the city. There he built a church that was shaped like a house, but surmounted by a tall spire and flooded with light. Beside the church, he built a house that was also very bright, although not as bright as the church. Beside that, he built a stable a little less bright than the buildings he had built before. Amidst these buildings, the man lived contentedly for the rest of his days. Willson placed a record of this dream, along with other documents recording the early history of the Children of Peace, in the altar at the centre of the temple. The dream symbolized Willson's view of an ideal earthly home by combining church and farm in close proximity, all brightened by the Inner Light. Its setting symbolized separation from the rest of the world in both spiritual and material terms. Water, where the outcast's home was located, was in Willson's visions a place where the church would be rescued and where wisdom would be received from God. In remembering and recording his dream, Willson envisioned the kind of community he hoped to build in East Gwillimbury: separate and distinct, a home for outcasts, and shining with the light of God.[1]

In their descriptions of the community established by the Children of Peace, early-nineteenth-century travellers told of a place that fulfilled many of Willson's hopes and plans. They wrote primarily about the temple, the two meeting houses, and David Willson's study, but seldom failed to remark on the orderly and prosperous village around them. At first that village was officially known as Hope, although some referred to it as "Davidtown" and to the Children of Peace as "Davidites," because of the prominence of their leader, David Willson.[2] After the establishment of a post office on 6 February 1841, the name Sharon was used.[3] Since Hope could have been confused with Hope township in the Newcastle District on the shores of Lake Ontario, the colonial government may have insisted that a distinctive name be chosen for postal purposes. The name, Sharon, came from the biblical Song of Solomon 2:1 – "I am the rose of Sharon, and the lily of the valleys" – and referred to the church, the prefigured bride of Christ. For David Willson, who had long been fascinated by female figures representing the church, the name Sharon would have suggested a fulfillment of the mission the Children of Peace. By 1841 there were reasons for such satisfaction: the community had established a temple, a pair of meeting houses, a study for their leader, and a prospering village.

Whether writing about Hope or Sharon, nineteenth-century observers commented on the village's appearance in flattering terms. Thomas Duncumb, author of *The British Emigrant's Guide*, published in London in 1837, declared: "[It] is most decidedly the neatest village I almost ever witnessed in the inhabited wilds of North America; the surrounding lands were so prettily cleared, the fields being conveniently divided by snake fences; substantial, and erected with the utmost ingenuity and regularity; with spacious green swarth roads; completely cleared of loose logs and old tree stumps; a scene very unusual on this continent."[4] In 1861, a newspaper correspondent provided the following description: "The village is built upon one street, a concession line, running north and south, and is about a mile and a half in length. Both sides of the street are bordered with maples, elms, evergreens and willows. The houses, which are all of wood and either 'rough cast' or painted white, are by no means crowded together, and peep out modestly from the deep green maples and oaks by which each and every one is surrounded. In the foreground stand two large white buildings, the places of worship of the villagers; while to the south and east rise majestic forests of maple and beech, furnishing a pleasing background to our picture."[5]

David Willson and the Children of Peace were inspired by at least two sources in establishing and governing their community: first and foremost, by Quaker tradition; secondarily, by the writings of Scottish reformer and philosopher, Robert Owen (1771–1858). Sharon was a long, narrow settlement, like the one that grew up around the Yonge

Street Friends meeting house earlier in the nineteenth century. It resembled the "street villages" of the mid-Atlantic states and reflected the geographic origins of many of the people who settled there. Many of the people of Sharon remembered the cooperative Quaker households and communities of the Delaware valley, from which they had come; however, the cooperative tradition went back even farther to late-seventeenth century England. From the earliest days of the Society of Friends, English Quakers had been interested in community projects. Quaker reformers introduced higher standards of living and better working conditions without threatening existing patterns of private ownership. Their achievements included the industrial ventures of the iron masters of Coalbrookdale and the chocolate-makers of Bournville.

Robert Owen, whose writings were familiar to David Willson, acknowledged that Quaker experiments had influenced his own "villages of cooperation."[6] Owen began his experiments in social reform in the textile-milling town of New Lanark, Scotland. In 1824, he went to the United States, addressed Congress concerning his plans, and purchased 2,000 acres of land at New Harmony, Indiana.[7] When visited by the Scottish traveller and writer, Patrick Shirreff, members of the Children of Peace asked anxiously about Owen's work in Scotland and the condition of the working classes there, but seemed pleased when they were told that the New Harmony experiment had failed.[8] Owen lost many of his supporters by speaking out against organized religion and by establishing cooperative communities on purely secular grounds. David Willson was among those alienated from Owen's work because of its secular nature, for he never separated his theology from his concern for the physical well-being of his followers. Among his earliest writings, prose and poetry condemning those who oppressed the poor existed side by side with accounts of visions and theological debate. Both men envisioned ideal communities inspired by Quaker tradition; however, when Owen abandoned the religious grounds for his work, Willson lost interest in him.

David Willson could have learned of Owen's work through the newspapers of his day, particularly the *Colonial Advocate* published by William Lyon Mackenzie, an admirer of both Owen and the Children of Peace. Willson's knowledge of Owenite principles could also have come from news of the reformer's work in Scotland or from the one Owenite community in Upper Canada. Maxwell was located on Lake Huron in the southwestern part of the colony, in what later became Sarnia and Plympton Townships. Henry Jones, a retired British naval officer, secured a grant there of 800 acres, with a promise of several thousand more, and brought about fifty people to the site in 1829.

These settlers moved into a large community house with separate apartments for families and a common kitchen and dining room. By 1831, most members left the community, however, when they discovered they could individually lay claim to land in Upper Canada for themselves.[9] Unlike the community of the Children of Peace, Maxwell did not allow for private enterprise. It represented a more radical departure from the norm. In the early 1830s, George Henry Hume contrasted the Children of Peace with the followers of Robert Owen when he wrote: "They are not absolutely embodied in one and the same society, as is the case with Mr. Owen's establishments: but though living in one community, and having their laws and regulations within themselves, yet, as to personal property, each individual is distinct."[10]

Other early travellers, commenting on the social and economic organization of the village, compared it to models they had seen elsewhere and sensed that it was different from most frontier communities of the time. The New York traveller, F. Hall, wrote in 1825 that the Children of Peace "reside in families and close to each other, forming a community something like the Shakers."[11] Mary O'Brien of Thornhill, just north of York, wrote in her diary in 1829 that David Willson had "collected about him persons enough to form a tolerably large village and persuaded them to consider him as a prophet and resign their substance into his hands and their conduct to his direction."[12] In 1836, Dr Thomas Rolph of Dundas, some fifty miles west of York, claimed that "the founder of this new sect has managed to induce many farmers to dispose of their farms to take an acre lot in this new village."[13] All these writers exaggerated or were mistaken to some degree, yet all knew that the village of the Children of Peace represented a departure from the norm of community organization in North America.

Records from the early 1830s show that David Willson and the Children of Peace set out to create a village that, if not communal in the manner of an Owenite or Shaker community where all property was held in common, still attempted to promote a spirit of cooperation and mutual assistance among its members. The sect attempted to maintain the distinctive identity of its community by regulating the sale of land and by controlling who should be allowed to settle there. In a document entitled "My will and desires for the house of the Lord, and the land of our predestination," David Willson wrote that a member of the Children of Peace should "dispose not of his ground to strangers, that after this date may come among us, but keep it for his children that shall succeed their fathers in the house of the Lord, nor marry with strangers, least we shall bring in a wicked generation of

Canaanites that know not the will of the Lord ..."[14] This reflects the Quaker heritage of the Children of Peace. Quaker families placed great emphasis on buying, exchanging, and preserving land for their children.[15] They also strongly discouraged marriage outside their own religious community, disowning sons and daughters who married non-members of the Society of Friends.[16]

David Willson exceeded the Quakers in his attempts to maintain the identity of his community by controlling the way newcomers would be allowed to settle there. He declared that strangers should be settled at a distance and tried for seven years before they could be considered part of the community.[17] On 2 April 1831, the Children of Peace adopted a more specific regulation that required a newcomer accepted as a settler to be overseen by a group of nine people – four chosen by the settler and five by the congregation. At the same meeting, members agreed that no individual could sell his lands without the consent of the entire congregation or its chosen council. Their resolution declared: "Be it known to all from this date, who wish so to do, that we hereby assign our property, as well as person, for the general cause of salvation, and the glory of God on earth; and well knowing the present age of the world to abound with speculation and craft, and sectarian divisions, we only will part with our property with the following restrictions. That is to say, that no individual shall dispose of lands to kindred or friends, without the consent of the whole assembly, or our chosen council to act in behalf thereof, as the case may require ..."[18]

Why did the Children of Peace wait until the early 1830s, some twenty years after their founding, to enact regulations such as these? Perhaps they were not needed prior to that time. Land records for the parts of East Gwillimbury Township where the Children of Peace settled show relatively little buying, selling, or dividing of property prior to the late 1820s. Initial grants of Crown land ordinarily amounted to 200 acres, more than enough for the first generation to clear and plant. Newer arrivals in Upper Canada could easily obtain land of their own elsewhere. Thus, few families needed to acquire more land at that time, and few opportunities arose to sell land at a profit. Samuel Hughes, who took up a farm immediately south of David Willson's on Queen Street, did not bother to take out a patent on his land until 1833.[19] There were many others like him. However, the picture started to change as sons of the original settlers began to need land of their own. Shortly after Samuel Hughes secured a patent for his 200-acre farm, he sold off thirty-six acres to Hugh D. Willson, David Willson's youngest son. David Willson himself maintained his original 200-acre grant intact until 1828, when he sold off a small lot to Elias Doan, a son of master builder Ebenezer Doan.[20] Land sales and divisions had increased by the late 1820s and early 1830s. It was not until then that guidelines and regulations were necessary to ensure that future generations of the Children of Peace would be able to obtain land nearby. Surviving records do not indicate, however, whether the sect ever did try to prevent the sale of land by a member or stop a newcomer from settling near them. In practice, they preserved the spirit of their laws by following customs that were familiar to their Quaker forebears.

The land transactions of Ebenezer Doan and his family illustrate this phenomenon. In Bucks County, Pennsylvania, Doan had farmed near land owned by his father, Ebenezer, Sr, and his brothers, John, Joseph, and Mahlon.[21] When the Doans moved to Upper Canada, they acquired land close to each other on or near Yonge Street. When they left the Yonge Street Quaker settlement to follow Willson, the Doan brothers took up land in East Gwillimbury Township. In 1818, Ebenezer purchased 200 acres, the west halves of lots thirteen and fourteen in the third concession, for $4,000. In 1831, he acquired a Crown grant of one hundred acres, part of lot fifteen, immediately to the north. The following year, he purchased for $1,000 another hundred-acre plot, part of lot eighteen in the second concession, northwest of his earlier holdings. In 1842, Doan sold eighty acres from lot eighteen to his son, Ira (b. 1810), for the sum of $800, equal to what he had paid ten years earlier. In 1851, he sold forty-five acres from lot thirteen to his son, Oliver (b. 1807), for $1,000, roughly equivalent to what he had paid in 1818.[22]

These transactions indicate that Ebenezer Doan acquired land close to his original farm for his own use and for his two sons, Ira and Oliver. He did not give them this land, however. He sold it to them for the same price per acre that he had paid originally. This practice of selling land to his sons, rather than giving it to them, was perhaps meant to avoid jealousy or charges of favoritism within the family. A question remains, however, as to how Ira and Oliver could have acquired money to purchase land from their father, no matter how fair the price was. A letter to relatives in Bucks County, written in 1830 by Oliver Doan, provides a clue. In that letter, Oliver described work on his father's farm and remarked, "Ira had all the fallow ploughed and wheat sowed and harrowed when I got home, there is twenty five acres of it, five belongs to him and I."[23] This passage suggests that, long before any recorded land transactions took place, Ebenezer Doan assigned portions of his land to his sons. Those sons, in effect, became his tenants. By saving the profits on their part of the crop, his sons could eventually buy land from their father.

In his will, Doan eventually bequeathed to his sons land close to their purchased properties: Abraham received nearly seventy acres; Oliver, sixty-five acres; and Ira, fifty acres. David was given title to the "home farm" of approximately sixty-five acres, and Elias got a house and lot on Queen Street along, £25 from the sale of his father's stock or movable property, and the cancellation of a seventy-five dollar debt. Doan's will affirmed actions he had taken earlier, since after each reference to the legacies of Abraham, Elias, Oliver, and Ira, it stated "which I have give him a Deed for it." Doan looked after the interests of his wife by granting her the use of his home farm until the time of her death. To each of his daughters, Hannah and Sarah, he bequeathed £43.15s to be paid by their brothers – Abraham, Oliver, Ira, and David – in proportion to their legacies' value. Doan's will was scrupulously fair in dividing his estate among his family.[24]

Ebenezer Doan's eldest sons, Abraham (b. 1802) and Elias (b. 1805), were both able to acquire land on their own initiative, close by their family's holdings. Abraham purchased fifty acres immediately south of his father's farm in 1828 and a further forty-eight acres just to the west in 1845. Elias also acquired land in the neighbourhood.[25] Doan's two daughters, Hannah (b. 1812) and Sarah (b. 1815), did not acquire land of their own, but both married farmers. Hannah married Jacob Lundy in 1833, while Sarah married Israel Haines in 1836.[26] Both Lundy and Haines were active members of the Children of Peace and owned farmland close to Ebenezer Doan. Ebenezer's wife, Elizabeth Paxson Doan, shared her family's concern for acquiring farmland. In 1840 she purchased twenty-five acres of lot twelve, concession three, from Elias and a further twenty-five acres adjoining it from John Rogers. Rogers's land had previously belonged to Elias as well.[27] This instance of a parent buying land from a son, though unusual was consistent with earlier practice within the Doan family. In 1789, for example, Jonathan Doan had sold thirty-nine acres in Solebury Township, Bucks County, to his father, Ebenezer Sr, for the sum of £180.[28] Whether the sale was from parent to child or from child to parent, the aim was the same: to maintain adjacent parcels of land under family ownership.

Meanwhile, in 1834, Ebenezer Doan had sold fifty acres of his holdings on lot fourteen to Hiram Harrison. The Harrisons were members of the Children of Peace, so this sale was consistent with the objectives of the community, even if it did diminish Doan family holdings. More serious breaks with custom occurred when the Doans sold land to purchasers who were neither family members nor, as far as can be determined, members of the Children of Peace. In 1836, Ebenezer and Elizabeth Doan jointly sold fifty acres of their land on lot fifteen to

Colin (or Orlin?) Williams for $350. In 1838, they sold their remaining fifty acres there to Thomas G. Bond for $500.[29] In both instances, the Doans made money on land that they sold. Their holdings on lot fifteen had been acquired in 1831 by means of a Crown grant. Had they sold them to their sons at any price, they would have gone against their practice of transferring land ownership within the family at the original cost. Nonetheless, these sales to Williams and Bond went against the sect's 1831 decision not to sell land to outsiders. They may have contributed to the dispute that caused Ebenezer Doan to resign from membership in the Children of Peace in 1840.

The family's general practice of acquiring and maintaining or nearby plots of land for their own use was a logical response to conditions of life on the frontier. It made sense at a time when most farm work was done by hand with the assistance of family and neighbours, and when communication over an area even as small as a township could be difficult. Yet Quakers and Children of Peace stressed the concept of familial cooperation more than most of their contemporaries. Albert Schrauwers has shown that in the 1830s sixty-four per cent of the Children of Peace were land renters, and thirty-six per cent were owner/operators.[30] Among residents of East Gwillimbury who were not sect members, the opposite was true: thirty-seven per cent were renters, and sixty-three per cent owner/operators. The low percentage of owner/operators among the Children of Peace was an indicator of the "moral economy" of the sect, whereby parents held land in trust for their children and children were less likely to own land at an early age. The Children of Peace followed the Quaker custom of familial land ownership to fulfil their objective of building a distinctive community. The sect itself did not own land. In fact, during David Willson's lifetime, the Children of Peace did not even own the land where their places of worship were located. In 1829, Willson declared his intention to give the sect that portion of his farm where the meeting house and temple had been built,[31] but this gift was not formally registered until after his death. Nor was the schoolhouse located on land belonging to the sect as a whole: census records from 1851 list it on property owned by William H. Willson.[32]

The Children of Peace also followed Quaker custom in discouraging marriages with partners who were not from their religious community. One traveller, George Henry Hume, maintained that Willson acted as an intermediary when unmarried men of the sect proposed marriage: "Any of the unmarried men of the sect, who takes a fancy to either [sic] of the virgins, makes known his ideas to David, who communicates to her the proposal made; and if she should wish to enter into the holy state of matrimony, an appointment is made for a meeting of two hours' duration; (which is all that is allowed;) and when a final decision, either favorable or otherwise is made."[33] Willson himself stated that many of Hume's comments about the Children of Peace were inaccurate,[34] making it difficult to assess the truthfulness of this particular report. However, young members of the Children of Peace were encouraged to hold him in high regard as an adviser; they referred to him as "grandfather Willson" during his later years.[35]

In addition to receiving advice from David Willson personally, young members could also expect to be guided and admonished by the sect as a whole. Early in December 1831, for instance, a meeting was called to discuss "the expediency of our young males and females meeting together on such subjects as is common on earth." The assembled men and women considered this practice "as being injurious to the female character, and unprofitable to the male, as the evil most generally outreaches the good, and upon the whole is injurious to society."[36] In an important sense, *community* and *family* became almost interchangeable, as adult members sometimes fulfilled disciplinary roles similar to those of parents. Based on religious convictions and Quaker heritage, this practice reflected the fact that, by the 1830s, many of the original families who had formed the Children of Peace were becoming closely related by marriage. They were becoming literally, as well as metaphorically, an extended family. By 1851, fully a third of the sect's members belonged to either the extended Willson or Doan family.[37]

Also in keeping with their community-oriented values, the Children of Peace took the same approach to buying and selling merchandise as they did to transfering land. The rights of free enterprise and private ownership were tempered by family ties and concern for the well-being of their community. If a merchant disregarded the welfare of others by charging exorbitant prices, members of the sect were expected to take their business elsewhere in protest. An 1832 statement signed "on behalf of the Elders" by John Doan and Rachel Lundy advised: "If merchants are found to be extravagant, in their sales and popular in wealth, far beyond the bounds of their laborious brethren; Chastize their trade, by with drawing your custom and promote these that are moderate, that extravagance and popular wealth, may be shut out from amongst you."[38]

At that time, there appear to have been two stores operating in or near the village. Just north of Hope, on lot sixteen of the third concession, was a store run by John Reid, who had married David Willson's daughter, Sarah, in 1821. Closer to the centre of the village, on lot seven of the third concession, was another shop run by Charles Doan, who had married Willson's daughter, Mary, in 1831.[39] One of their few competitors was likely Eli Beman, who owned a store in the northern part of the township.[40] Beman was well-connected to the governing elite of the colony, being a stepbrother of the future chief justice, John Beverley Robinson.[41] An 1825 tax assessment roll for the northern half of East Gwillimbury Township shows that Beman's taxes that year were the highest on the list, signifying a man of wealth and property. To the Children of Peace, Eli Beman was an outsider; Reid and Doan, however, were part of their community. Had the sect been a communal organization in the strictest sense, it would have opened its own store, directly under the supervision of the sect's membership. As it was, the business of shopkeeping was left to two of its members, John Reid and Charles Doan. In theory, Reid and Doan represented free enterprise. In practice, however, their close family connections to David Willson likely tempered their roles as capitalists and entrepreneurs, ensuring that their stores would operate with the well-being of their community in mind.

One account book from the Doan store, containing entries from 10 July 1837 to 4 February 1839, has survived.[42] Among the store's customers were many of those recorded as "builders" of the temple, including the Willsons, Doans, Dunhams, Morrises, Harrisons, Haineses, Rowans, Mainprises, Lepards, McLeods, Brammers, Kings, Kavanaughs, Kesters, Hills, Reids, and Terrys. Among them in equal numbers, however, were other township families who were not members of the Children of Peace: the Atkinsons, Purdys, Drapers, Metcalfs, Fentons, Parks, Glovers, Goodells, Wilders, and Munroes, for example. If Doan had relied only on members of the Children of Peace to purchase goods at his store, he probably could not have stayed in business very long. At least half of the purchases recorded in his account book were made by outsiders. In this respect, the Doan store was probably little different from others in the colony at the time: it relied on the neighbourhood for customers, and the religious affiliation of its owner did not dictate who would choose to do business there.

Sales of commodities specifically intended for joint use by the Children of Peace were not handled differently from any other transaction at the store. For example, "Dishes for feast," sold on 4 September 1837 for 19s 8d, were charged to the personal account of member Peter Lepard, rather than to the sect as a whole. Similarly, "3 Cobbs Spelling Books," worth three shillings, were charged directly to John Reid, rather than to the school, on 15 November 1837. On 31 August 1837, candles for the September illumination and ingredients for a large cake to be served at the autumn feast were charged to an account called "Feast." It is surprising that some of the ingredients listed would have been purchased at a store at all. The quarter pound of "spice" and one-and-a-quarter pounds of "Loaf Sugar" could not have been obtained otherwise, but ingredients such as "5 lb Sugar" (presumably brown or maple sugar since it was not specified as "Loaf Sugar"), four pounds of butter, and two dozen eggs could easily have been supplied from members' farms. These purchases, like those by Peter Lepard and John Reid, were further indications of the loose organizational framework of the Children of Peace. A truly communal organization would have obtained common commodities such as maple sugar, butter, and eggs from its own members, rather than buying them at a store. It would have also set up its own accounts for supplying the feasts and the school.

The shelves of the Doan store were stocked with a wide range of hardware, household goods, spirits, medicines, clothing, cloth, sewing supplies, and foodstuffs. The 1837–39 account book contains many references to the sale of glass, nails, and household goods such as candles, candlewick, bed cord, ticking, brooms, combs, handkerchiefs, soap, starch, cooking utensils, tablewares, and chamber pots. It reveals that many members of the Children of Peace drank substantial quantities of liquor, including whisky, brandy, gin, and sometimes, wine. They also purchased shot and tobacco at Doan's store, along with sulphur, camphor, castor oil, "British oil," and "Harlem oil" to cure their ills. They bought a few items of clothing there, including suspenders, hats, bootlaces, and occasionally, shoes. Doan's customers, like others of the time, made most of their own clothes, buying large quantities of cloth, including cotton, linen, flannel, and fustian (a mixture of cotton and linen), as well as decorative calico, "stripe," "check," and "vesting," and "linings." For ornament, they bought ribbon, tape, "trimmings," and "bobbinet," an early kind of machine-made lace. For sewing, they purchased thread of various sorts, skeins of silk, pins, buttons, and hooks and eyes. Foodstuffs recorded in the account book included local goods like butter and eggs, but mostly consisted of items imported from farther afield. Among these were pepper, salt, peppermint, ginger, cinnamon, saleratus (baking soda), loaf sugar, rice, coffee, and both black and green tea (the latter denoted in the account book as "hison"). Payment was made in cash or by bartering farm products such as meat, butter, and wheat.

The account book indicates that, by the late 1830s, the people of Hope were not a producer culture in the strictest sense of that term, nor were they a modern consumer culture either. A broad range of consumer goods was available for them to purchase, including items such as candles, soap, and flannel, which they could have produced themselves. The goods that they purchased supplemented, rather than replaced, those they could produce in the community. The candles Doan sold, for example, may have been hard candles made of spermaceti, styrene, or beeswax, commercially produced and both longer-lasting and more fragrant than candles made from beef tallow. Similarly, the soap in Doan's store likely supplemented what was produced on the farms using lye and fat. The flannel he offered may have been purchased only by those who did not own their own sheep. Census information from 1851 indicates that substantial quantities of both flannel and fulled cloth were still being produced on farms in the neighbourhood. (Flannel was coarse, loosely woven, woollen fabric, whereas fulled cloth had been shrunk and thickened through moistening, beating, and pressing.) Of the thirty-two farms worked by members of the Children of Peace, and for which data are available, twenty-five produced flannel, with yields ranging from a high of forty-nine yards to a low of ten yards and averaging 26.5 yards for each producing farm. Twenty-one farms produced fulled cloth, yielding from seven to twenty-five yards and averaging 16.6 yards for each producing farm.[43] Most of the cloth sold in the Doan store was made of cotton, linen, or a mixture of the two, and was likely more decorative than fabric produced at home. It would have supplemented, rather than replaced, homespon woollen cloth, just as the store's array of spices and seasonings added variety to homegrown foodstuffs.

The account book only occasionally lists sales of staples such as meat and vegetables. Evidently, these commodities were produced at home or exchanged directly between producers and consumers, avoiding a middleman. Opportunities for such sales must have been limited since most area residents lived on farms and supplied themselves. Therefore, sending goods to market in York provided an important supplement to family incomes. This activity, like so many others of the Children of Peace, illustrated the sect's combination of individual enterprise and communal activity. A traveller's account from the early 1830s noted that "The general produce of the community is deposited with him [David Willson] and conveyed to York, for sale, regularly twice a-week; and he accounts to the different members for the amount of the produce sent to market."[44] Another observer wrote, "The produce is sent to York Market weekly in common, yet individuals are left to guide themselves."[45] The communal aspect of this activity was shared transportation for goods; members attended and received the proceeds from sales individually.

Having defined their approach to land transactions, family life, and commerce, the Children of Peace considered other aspects of community life as well. In the early 1830s, this process was spurred by growing membership and the need to regulate and guide sons and daughters who were reaching maturity. On 9 August 1832, a "solemn assembly" called members together to deal with a number of problems that they saw arising. In response, they created eight committees (later pared down to six): first, "To support a House of Public Entertainment with reputation and honor in the world"; second, "To correct our female Institution"; third, to see that the business of the sect was conducted with truth, sobriety, and justice, and to deal with all "hurtful accusations"; fourth, "To remove such from our lands and houses as corrupt the order of the house of the Lord by inattention to worship of any kind, disrespecting the sabbath or sacrifices fit to be offered unto the Lord"; fifth, to supervise dealings with hired servants, making sure that they were properly paid; sixth, to advise against "idle diversions"; seventh, "To see that all things are in order for our public feasts," and to distribute the leftovers to the needy; and eighth, to care for the sick and the needy, help look after funeral arrangements, and tend the cemetery.

These committees were to report at a meeting of the Children of Peace scheduled for three o'clock on the Saturday two weeks prior to the September feast each year. If necessary, though, a special meeting could be called by a committee with the consent of twelve elders. Brief records of a few of these annual meetings survive. They contain few specifics about the committees' work, but include brief statements declaring, in a rather formulaic way, that some progress had been made during the previous year and more work remained to be done in the next. At these meetings, elections were held for committee membership. However, the committees seem to have ceased operation by the 1840s, leaving their work to the elders and other interested members.[46]

Charity and mutual assistance long remained major concerns, and many observers commented on these distinctive aspects of the community life of the Children of Peace. George Henry Hume noted that their most striking principle was "a mutual assistance to each other."[47] Even the traveller, D. Wilkie, who wrote so scornfully of David Willson's preaching, claimed that "their lives are represented as being simple, and their actions charitable. Their stores are ever open to the needy ..."[48] The residents of York first learned of the charitable actions of the Children of Peace through the pages of William Lyon Mackenzie's *Colonial Advocate*. On 19 July 1830, the following account appeared, written by a traveller who had passed through the village of Hope on his way to Lake Simcoe:

In the house of Samuel Hughes, a member of this new society, I found an undoubted evidence of practical Christianity. Three years ago, an old decrepit negro who had up to that time begged for a subsistence, was struck with the palsy in his body and one of his sides; and lost the use of his limbs and one arm. Mr. Hughes took him in – had a chair with wheels made for him – and continues to wait upon and assist the helpless object, who can do nothing for himself. Whether he and his family do this altogether at their own expense or whether they get some help from the society I know not, but their conduct might put to the blush many who make extraordinary professions of that meek faith, of the effects of which their proud lives afford but a faint specimen.[49]

This account shows the individual generosity of Samuel Hughes. In addition, the Children of Peace jointly operated an institution known as the Poor House or Orphan House. Located on the farm of Amos Hughes, it is mentioned only briefly in surviving records. During the cholera epidemic of 1832, the people of York witnessed the charitable work of the Children of Peace at first hand, when David Willson and Murdoch McLeod distributed among widows, orphans, and the afflicted the sum of seventy dollars. This had been gathered from 113 followers in Hope and a further thirty-one in Markham.[50]

Contributions at the time of the cholera epidemic were part of a special relief effort, and not drawn from the monthly collections held in the temple. Part of those monthly contributions was intended for the relief of the poor. Twelve elders had jurisdiction over how this money should be used, up to the sum of five pounds per year. Beyond that, a majority vote by the congregation was necessary. Two men and two women formed a committee to visit the needy, report on their condition, and provide them with assistance as discreetly as possible.[51] The Charity Fund, as it came to be called, was also a source of loans for members. At first it was intended that these loans be granted without interest; however, late in 1832 a majority of members voted that interest should be charged.[52] Members of the Children of Peace had the right to borrow from this fund as the need arose and could transfer their rights to their children and grandchildren.[53] A report from 1844 shows that contributions for the preceding year amounted to £26.7s.6d. Interest paid on loans brought that year's total income to £36.3s.8d. The total worth of the fund stood at £226.4s.5d., with £132.12s.11d. on loan and £93.11.6 d. on hand.[54]

Records of the Charity Fund are incomplete, but they point to an important aspect of life within the community of the Children of Peace. Like other features of village life, the existence of the Charity Fund suggests a strong sense of mutual concern and community identity. Initially, their almsgivings may have been inspired by the "meetings for sufferings" that Quakers had held since 1676 to gather and distribute alms for the poor.[55] The Quaker *Discipline* followed by the Queen Street meeting stated, "Each monthly meeting should have regular quarterly collections made, and the money placed in the hands of the treasurer of said meeting, for the exclusive purpose of assisting [the poor] ..."[56] Some monthly meetings also provided loans for members.[57] The Charity Fund was based on these Quaker precedents and provided both relief for the poor and a source of loan money for members. They could borrow to make improvements to their farm, add to their house, make repairs to their shop, or otherwise add to their family's material well-being.

Other tangible evidence of cooperation and mutual concern lay in the support the Children of Peace gave to schooling. Unfortunately, records of their schools are scarce. As noted earlier, the sect established a boarding school at least as early as 1817 on Yonge Street, before they had begun to congregate around the village of Hope. The curriculum the school followed is not known, nor is there a record of its facilities. The very existence of a boarding school at that time and place is evidence of the importance the Children of Peace placed on educating their young. A partial list of regulations shows that the school operated *in loco parentis*, teaching manners and regulating behaviour as well as imparting practical lessons. During the school term, which ran from early November to early April, the part of the year when children would not be required for work on their families' farms, the young scholars were required to attend worship once a week. Their conduct and cleanliness were scrutinized to the last detail through regulations such as: "All bedding belonging to the boarding room be changed or washed once in the month by those to whome they belong" and "If any hath an ocation to clean the nostrils as is frequent amongst children in the case of taking sudden colds let them step to the door or use a handkerchief which will prevent blowing the nose on others or on the floor." The school's teacher was William Reid, one of David Willson's earliest followers, who continued his teaching duties after the school moved to Hope. There Reid is known to have taught practical skills such as blacksmithing and carpentry to boys who came as boarders.[58]

Emily McArthur's 1898 pamphlet on the history of the Children of Peace records that a girls' school was opened in Hope in the winter of 1818. This school may have been conducted at first in David Willson's house. In 1820, the Quaker traveller, Jacob Albertson, recorded that Willson had "taken in 12 or more young women in his house for what purpose I don't know; their parents say they have sent them because he can bring them up better than they can."[59] Willson's operation of the girls' school in his own home gave rise to charges that he maintained "an extensive harem."[60] Willson's critics outside the village used these charges to try to discredit him and his followers in the eyes of both the people and the government of Upper Canada. One unidentified prankster went so far as to draft a petition to the Upper Canadian House of Assembly, purporting to come from David Willson and requesting a £500 grant to finish building the temple. Its author declared that Willson felt commanded by God to "Take unto [himself] married and unmarried women and people the world ..."[61]

When the first school opened in Hope, David Willson was living on his farm on lot ten of the third concession, for which he had obtained a Crown grant in 1805. Willson's house was demolished early in this century; however, two late-nineteenth-century photographs show it to have been a Georgian style frame structure with one or two added wings. Perhaps this was the site of the first school. McArthur states, however, that the Girls' House was first located in a small log building, then in a frame structure, and finally, in a two-storey building, thirty-feet square, called the Square House. This last school building stood opposite the 1842 meeting house and must have recalled the design of the first meeting house, which was square.[62] In one of these early structures in 1828, William Lyon Mackenzie observed young women receiving instruction in "knitting, sewing, spinning, making chip and straw hats and bonnets, spinning wool, and other useful accomplishments of a like description." Mackenzie went on to say: "There is a male and female superintendent resident in this ... school; the pupils cook, make their own clothes, keep the garden in order, receive lessons in reading &c., and work at their various avocations. I counted nearly a dozen wool-wheels in one of the rooms; among the pupils I saw either one or two young girls from York; and they all seemed happy and contented."[63] By emphasizing the mastery of household skills that ordinarily were taught at home and passed from mother to daughter, the school's curriculum gives evidence of the value the Children of Peace placed on community life. In their school, girls were taught traditional skills, but outside their traditional context.[64]

Willson's plan for his followers' well-being included a concern for plainness and simplicity in clothing and other material possessions. In his early writings of 1815, Willson stated: "I have had some months serious reflection on the nature of fine dress, with its consequences in the world, with other things of like nature and affect, in which mankind are proud of earthly things and circumstances, or states of life, with different characters therein, Viz; fine and large buildings, with unnecessary furniture therein ..." Willson objected to these luxuries not only on theological grounds, but also because to him they symbolized the oppression of the poor: "All your grandeur, fine buildings, and needless apparel, with all other such possessions, is robing the Poor, and the needy of their proper rights ... Therefore arise divide and separate that which ye have, that there may be a comeing together in this world, give on earth that ye may receive in heaven, give to the poor that ye may receive of them." Willson knew that some might be tempted to pursue simplicity only in terms of style and ornament and might still demand only the most expensive materials. (The black silk Quaker bonnet shown in figure 3 could symbolize this tendency.) He recognized that "these that profess plainness and moderation, are verry particular in colour, price, and quality" and chastised such people for their actions.[65]

In 1815, Willson condemned extravagance during a year of scarcity, just after wartime shortages and poor harvests had brought hunger and want. In that context, overspending on elaborate clothing, furniture, or other possessions would have seemed particularly ill-advised. Even in more prosperous times, however, Willson continued to advise against luxury. "Be moderate in your buildings and your apparel," he warned in 1832, citing practical reasons for moderation: "Abstain from large quantities of salt and sweet diet and you will abstain from doctor's fees – abstain from strong drinks of all kinds such as are used in common and God will increase your health; keep the body warm, summer and winter – and in particular the feet, for a constant persperation is bodily health – be moderate in labour, and keep out of storms; when sweating in a particular manner sudden colds obstruct persperation and fevers ensue ..."[66] Willson's advice was coupled with concern for his followers' health at a time when cholera raged in York and the surrounding countryside.

In 1845, Willson penned a long manuscript entitled "Advice in the Economy of life in a temporal Interest, and the glory of Religion." Using an often light and humourous style, he combined his concerns for plainness and simplicity with practical advice on good farming practices, the care of farm animals, the treatment of servants, sobriety and frugality. He advised his followers:

Do not clothe thyself with the cloth of another, when thou can get of thy own, lest another should say, that man is wearing my cloth, and others laugh at thy folly and the just remark ... Teach thy wife and daughters to wear out their old clothes before they get new ones, not to wear muffs and tippets, veils and gold rings and Jewelry, till they have cups, plates, pots and pans for house keeping; lest they should want the price to furnish the Table and bed-room with needful supplies ... Not to wear umbrellas without necessity, lest they hinder others wondering at the cause ... Not to get many dresses at a time, lest they become out of fashion and the old ones have to be altered at cost or laid up for food for moths ... Not to let a hole in a garment that is no larger than the eye, go without mending till it is as big as the head.[67]

The repetition of these and similar directives over many years suggests that his advice was not always followed. The sale of large quantities of cloth in the Doan store as well as decorative ribbon, calico, silk thread, and machine-made lace confirms this suspicion. Nevertheless, the Children of Peace on the whole, like the Quakers and early Methodists, attempted to adhere to a regimen of plainness in dress. George Henry Hume, recorded in the early 1830s that David Willson "in common with the whole sect, wears a homespun blueish mixture."[68] Patrick Shirreff described him as "dressed in a short brown cloth jacket, white linen trousers, with a straw hat, all perhaps home-made."[69] A portrait of Willson (Fig. 2) and a photograph taken when he was an old man also suggest that he dressed plainly.

The 1862 probate inventory of John Doan indicates that he too dressed plainly. Doan's inventory is unusual in its completeness and provides a rare glimpse at the clothing owned by a member of the Children of Peace. His clothes included: "1 fulled cloth Coate, 1 vest, 1 pair pants, 7 pair wool Socks, 2 pair wool Mitts, 1 pair fulled cloth pants new, 2 pair flannel pants, 2 leather caps, 1 pair leather Mitts, 1 over coat drab cloth, 1 pair blue grey pants & suspenders, 6 woollen shirts, 4 pair drawers," and "1 pair woolen Gloves." All of these could easily have been produced in the community, using homemade cloth and homespun wool. Doan also possessed, however, "1 Satnett Coate, 1 blue vest, 1 figured vest," and "4 fancy Silk hats." "Satnett" was probably satinet, which used a cotton warp and woollen weft and was noticeably smoother and more satin-like than homemade flannel or fulled cloth. His "Satnett Coate," along with the blue and figured vests, could have been made in the village. Its value, four dollars, exceeded any other item in his wardrobe and was among the highest in his inventory as a whole. The four silk hats definitely would have been imported luxuries. Thus, despite simplicity, there was variety among Doan's clothing: sturdy, functional, everyday clothing contrasted with more elaborate garments worn to services and meetings. It is important to note, however, that Doan could have afforded much more: at the time of his death, he left an estate valued ultimately at well over eight thousand dollars.

Clothing had important symbolic meaning for David Willson and the Children of Peace. In describing his visions, Willson was careful to record the meaning of the clothes worn or discarded by his heavenly visitors. The woman in red, for instance, wore a robe that symbolized the blood of Christian martyrs. The beautiful young man wore a mantle that stood for the glory of ancient Israel. In planning ceremonies, processions, and services of worship, Willson paid close attention to the clothing that he deemed appropriate: colourful uniforms for the band, white dresses for the young women, and a black robe for the precentor. Clothing worn by those who led services of worship was intended to contrast with what the Children of Peace wore as they went about their daily lives. That contrast could be achieved through bright color, as in the uniforms of band members, or through simpler garments entirely of white or black. Just as the complex symbolism and design of their buildings suggested a spiritual world in contrast with the earthly sphere around them, ceremonial clothing was designed to contrast with the plain clothes worn every day. Elaborate clothes, like elaborate buildings, were reserved for the worship of God: they would have lost their meaning within the material culture of the sect if adopted for everyday use.

David Willson also used clothing as a metaphor for his own leadership. Addressing his followers early in 1832, Willson wrote: "My garments are beyond my choice, and I often would put them away, but I dare not; I know from whence they came, and I am afraid to offend the Lord ... I am not proud of my garments, but mortified where I go that I am not like my elder brethren, for I am not proud of the clothes I wear ..."[70] In these words, Willson recalled one of his visions and expressed his faith that his role as leader was given to him, like a garment, from God. He maintained that he did not choose that role, or garment, himself and was not proud that it was different from those of others.

As former Quakers, Willson and his followers were accustomed to thinking of the metaphorical and symbolic overtones of plainness and elaboration. Quaker attitudes regarding clothing were well-summarized in an oft-repeated anecdote concerning Quaker leader William Penn and King Charles II of England. King Charles supposedly asked Penn how the religious beliefs of the two men differed. Penn apparently replied, "The difference is the same as between thy hat and mine; mine has no ornaments."[71] In the *Discipline* followed by members of the Queen Street meeting, Quakers were exhorted "to consider seriously the plainness and simplicity which the gospel enjoins; and to manifest it in their dress, speech, furniture of their houses, manner of living, and general deportment." Plainness in material possessions was linked by the *Discipline* to plainness in the non-material aspects of life. It was not intended to exist apart from spiritual concerns; otherwise, plainness in itself could become a vain ritual. Instead, Quakers were encouraged to view simplicity as something "which truth leads into" – a sign that a believer was following the Inner Light. Quakers also viewed plainness as a hedge, protecting what it enclosed and keeping away evil influences from the outside world. According to the *Discipline*, "In ages of pride and extravagance in dress, the adoption of it [plainness] may make us appear singular, yet, in relation to us, this singularity is not without its use. It is in some respects like a hedge about us, which, though it make the ground it encloses rich and fruitful, yet it frequently prevents those intrusions, by which, the labour of the husbandman is injured or destroyed."[72]

By practising plainness, Quakers not only manifested their allegiance to unadorned spiritual truth as they defined it, but they also gave themselves a sense of group identity. This must have been a particularly important means of control to people who emphasized that the Inner Light was available to all. Such a belief could lead ultimately to antinomianism – lack of law, authority, and direction – and thence to disruptive individualism. Their creed of plainness set the Quakers apart from the rest of the world. It also enforced a sense of community identity that otherwise would not have existed for a group so intent on emphasizing personal religious experience. Conformity to plainness defined the Quakers as a group and allowed them to maintain their belief in the spontaneous promptings of the Inner Light, while still adhering to the discipline imposed by their hierarchical structure.[73]

The use of clothing to set believers apart from the rest of the world had other practical advantages as well. As the *Discipline* stated, it was an effective means of preventing young men and women from straying from the teachings of their elders. Conformity to the ways of the world and abandonment of plain clothing were seen by the *Discipline* as "opening the way for some of our youth more easily and unobservedly to attend places of public resort, for the exercise of sports, plays, and other pernicious diversions, from which truth taught our ancients, and still teaches us to refrain."[74] A distinctive style of clothing made a young Quaker stand out from the crowd, so he could be watched and controlled more easily by vigilant Quakers. Attending "places of public resort" and participating in sports and "plays" brought Quaker youth into contact with dangerous influences from the world outside and, Quakers feared, could weaken their spiritual resolve. Excessive drinking associated with taverns and public houses and the display of physical prowess linked with sports could lead ultimately to sexual misconduct.

Quakers linked clothing to many aspects of human behaviour. Playing on the similarity of the words *dress* and *address*, their

Discipline often juxtaposed these terms and combined admonitions regarding the use of plain clothing with instructions regarding "plain speech." The Queen Street *Discipline* stated: "In our address, also, we are bound to differ from the world in several respects; such as using the singular number [i.e., "thee" and "thou" instead of the more formal "you"] in speaking to a single person; our disuse of the appellation of master, mistress, &c., in a complimentary manner to such as do not stand in these relations to us; and our callings the months and days of the week by their numerical names, instead of those which are derived from the Heathen deities, etc."[75] Dress and address – clothing and speech – both were metaphors for aspects of Quaker belief. Both were part of a Quaker's *conversation*, a word used by Quaker writers to define a believer's whole style of living and his relationship to others. This usage came from the seventeenth-century definition of *conversation* as it appeared in the King James Bible. It was maintained by Quakers, for whom distinctive habits of speech became symbols of belief and metaphors for their way of life.

Richard Bauman has used the term, *rhetoric of impoliteness*, to describe Quaker refusal to use empty phrases of greeting or departure and their disdain for customary habits of deference. Although founded on a desire for sincerity and simplicity and on a belief that people should offer deference only to God, such customs were misinterpreted by outsiders who characterized Quakers as proud and impolite in their speech and general conduct.[76] David Willson may have earned a similar reputation for similar reasons. One resident of Sharon, David Graham, who understood Quaker tradition, wrote that Willson was "of a sedate and reserved nature yet possessing that peculiar disposition that rather repelled than drew persons to him who were unacquainted with him. Yet he was endowed with that rare magnetism that made him a ruler of others and his power over his members was almost absolute, which he used for the good of his Society."[77]

Graham saw in Willson a man who could both repel and attract. Others described Willson's appearance and manner favourably if they admired his achievements, but were repelled by his appearance and manner if they did not approve of what he had done. For example, Thomas Duncumb, who found the community of the Children of Peace to be "the neatest village I almost ever witnessed in the inhabited wilds of North America," described Willson as having "the appearance and gait of a naval officer," although "very homely in manners and habits."[78] Duncumb's description recalls the fact that Willson had once been a seafarer, during the days when he and his brother sailed on *The Farmer* between New York and the West Indies.

George Henry Hume, a more critical observer of the sect, wrote that Willson "squints much, and has a flat heavy appearance ... He appears to move as if he were pulling his legs after him; his speech has a strong nasal twang."[79] Another critic, Patrick Shirreff, claimed that Willson met him with "a cold suspicious reserve."[80] Graham, Duncumb, Hume, and Shirreff all described the same man. The disparities between the positive impressions of Graham and Duncumb and the negative reactions of Hume and Shirreff related to their differing opinions regarding the Children of Peace as a whole. Hume and Shirreff, like those who disparaged the early Quakers, may not have understood the role which plainness took in the lives of Willson and his followers any more than critic D. Wilkie had understood the power of Willson's preaching style.

Significantly, the Children of Peace did not always follow the plain speech of the Quakers. In his early writings, David Willson referred to the months and days of the week by numbers and used the familiar *thee*.[81] By the 1830s, however, when he published *The Impressions of the Mind* and *Letters to the Jews*, he largely abandoned Quaker practice. Willson was not born a Quaker, so some Quaker speech patterns may not have come naturally to him. Other members of the sect, such as Oliver Doan, would have learned these patterns from their Quaker parents, as surviving documents attest.[82] Willson did not stress adherence to plain speech to the extent that he stressed simplicity in clothing and other material possessions. This served to distance him and his followers from the Society of Friends, revealing a more fundamental difference between the two groups. The doctrine of plainness espoused by the Children of Peace was clearly based on Quaker precedent. However, the very existence of their temple and other elaborate buildings and artifacts connected with their worship shows that plainness had a different place in the theology of the Children of Peace. For them, plainness of clothing and possessions provided a way of visibly identifying with the poor and oppressed. It also allowed them to separate earthly from spiritual concerns in a way that the Quakers would not have condoned. Willson's advocacy of plain clothing and personal possessions contrasted with his plans for elaborate forms of public worship and ritual. Thus, it served to heighten the impact of worship and ritual. Quakers, on the other hand, strove to reflect in their meeting houses and worship the same spirit of plainness that they sought to maintain in their daily lives.

A desk made by John Doan (Fig. 12) illustrates how the Children of Peace applied their doctrine of plainness to items of household furniture. In describing this piece, the word *plain* is of little use. The desk is made of figured bird's eye and striped tiger maple. This was a locally available material, but carefully selected for its warm, golden color and the rich pattern of its grain. The desk is made to look lighter at its front corners by the use of decorative quarter columns. It is supported by carved ogee bracket feet, while the transition from foot to case is accomplished through the use of a concave moulding. Standing behind the writing surface of the desk is a bank of small drawers and compartments. Two document drawers with convex, reeded fronts flank a hinged door with additional compartments behind. The desk owes more to the background of its maker than to any specific doctrine of plainness: its quarter columns and ogee bracket feet reflect cabinet-making traditions of the Delaware valley, the birthplace of John Doan. Probably constructed in the 1830s, the desk follows a style that first came into popularity seventy years earlier. Thus, while it does not reflect plainness in an objective sense, it does reflect a conservatism that was either the conscious choice of its designer or an expression of a community with little interest in the current fashions of the world outside its boundaries.

According to his 1862 inventory, cabinet-maker John Doan's living quarters seem to have been furnished simply and rather sparsely; however, it should be remembered that he was then a ninety-four-year-old widower living with his sixty-year-old unmarried son, John, Jr. By that time, he may already have given away many of his belongings to his children and grandchildren. Beds and bedding, as in many other inventories of the period, constituted the most highly valued items then in his possession. Sometimes beds (which at that time described mattresses rather than frames) were considered so important that they were specified in bequests. In his 1850 will, for example, Sharon resident Thomas Dunham bequeathed to his youngest daughter, Mary, "one good feather bed with bedding Suitable and Sufficient for the Same" on the day she married or the day she turned eighteen, whichever came first.[83] Doan's inventory reflected this tradition by listing beds and bedding first. His "1 Feather bead & 2 Pillows" were valued at twelve dollars, a sum equalled only by the value of his bureau. The inventory also included "2 pair bead Steads" ($5.00), "1 Feather bead 1 Bolster & 2 pillows" ($6.00), "7 Cheque woolen blanketts" ($10.25), "1 coverled" ($1.25), "3 woolen bead quilts" ($1.50), "8 woolen blanketts" ($5.00), "4 linen sheets" ($4.50), "2 linen straw ticks" ($3.00), "1 linen straw tick" ($1.00), "1 cotton sheet" ($.50), and "5 pillow cases" ($.50). The cotton sheet certainly was an import. Linen probably was as well, since detailed census data from 1851 recorded no raising of flax or production of linen in East Gwillimbury Township. The amount of bedding listed in Doan's inventory was more than enough to equip his two bedsteads: such quantity suggests that much of it had already been retired from use.

Along with his two bedsteads, Doan's furniture consisted of "1 Looking Glass," "1 Beauro" ($12.00), "1 Chest" ($2.00), "1 Table & dough Trough" ($.75), "6 Winser Chairs" ($3.00), "4 splint bottomed chairs" ($.50), and "1 Green Chair" ($.25). This list was appropriate to the needs of a father and son, living alone in perhaps two or three rooms of their house. Suggesting Doan's long career as a builder and cabinet-maker were "1 compass Saw" ($.25) and "1 pair Compasses" ($.25). An interest in the world outside Sharon was shown by his copy of Macaulay's *History of England* ($.50), "1 coppy New World" ($.10), "1 coppy Bonapart" ($.50), and "1 Map of the world" ($.50). An entry listing "1 Fiddle & Bow" ($1.00) confirmed that music was a part of Doan's life as well.

Few ceramics or tablewares were listed. Perhaps most of these had already been divided among his children. In the inventory are "1 Chamber Sett," "1 Brit[annia] tea pot," "1 Glass decanter," "1 ground Tumbler," and "1 white water pisher," the values of which are indecipherable. Exploratory archaeological investigations on lot ten of the second concession, where David Willson and his family lived, suggest that the ceramics and glassware of the Children of Peace were typical of most other Upper Canadian households during the first half of the nineteenth century. The fragments excavated came from earthenware and stoneware vessels as well as from mass-produced pearlware and ironstone, decorated by both hand-painting and transfer-printing techniques.[84]

The individualistic orientation of the theology of the Children of Peace meant that many variations existed among the members' personal possessions. Their theology of plainness influenced their perceptions of material objects without dictating the appearance of those objects.[85] More important than any detail of line or ornament was the way material possessions fit into the everyday lives of their owners. If material possessions became stumbling blocks to faith by absorbing too much of their owners' attention, resources, and energy, or if they served to promote divisions and jealousy within the community, there is every reason to suspect that they would have been condemned. That condemnation resulted from how objects were used and perceived, and not from their design *per se*. Fine pieces of furniture, such as the desk made by John Doan, were not condemned for their lack of plainness, but they might have been, had their owners used them to flaunt their wealth or position in the community. John Doan's inventory indicates that he did not use his cabinet-making skills or his possessions in that way. It shows that his home was furnished according to his own particular needs and that he had already taken steps to distribute possessions among his children and their families. His simply furnished rooms were as much an outward sign of his old age and infirmity as they were the manifestation of religious belief. As in so many other aspects of the everyday life and work of the Children of Peace, practical concerns intersected with religion.

The community of the Children of Peace, with its doctrine of plainness and blend of private enterprise and cooperation, was described in the words of David Graham, who was born in the village of Hope in 1827: "The Sharonites were an economical people in the true sense of the word, they believed in doing for themselves and by themselves, whatever could be done at home, they were largely a co-operative people, in turn helping each other and not depending on an outside market for their supply; consequently almost every trade had its representative, so that the general public, as well as themselves, could get their wants supplied at Sharon ..."[86] *Smith's Canadian Gazetteer* for 1846 noted "one tannery, two stores, one saddler, two blacksmiths, one tavern, one wheelwright, one tailor, one tinsmith, and one weaver" under the heading, "Professions and Trades in the village of Sharon", but this list may have been incomplete.

The gazetteer estimated the population of Sharon at "about 150" and stated, "The congregation, including children, number about 200."[87] The list of temple builders begun in 1831 recorded 250 names,[88] William Lyon Mackenzie's 1834 *New Almanac for Canadian True Blues* estimated about 280 members,[89] and the 1851 East Gwillimbury census listed 298 people as Children of Peace. Since Jesse and Abraham Doan, both prominent members of the sect, were census-takers, the latter number is probably fairly accurate for that date. Examination of the 1851 census provides a more complete picture of the households and activities of the Children of Peace than any other source. Table 1 shows the sect at the height of its numbers, when many of its original members were still active.

The fifty-six households listed here ranged in size from eleven members to one, the average number of people per household being 5.7. This compares with an average of 6.1 in the nearby township of King, to the southwest.[90] At that time, King Township was predominantly rural, wheras that part of East Gwillimbury where the Children of Peace lived included the village of Sharon as well as the surrounding farmlands. The average number of people living in farm households was 6.6, somewhat larger than in King Township. This relates to the fact that sons of members of the sect tended to remain as tenants of their parents longer than young men outside the community and were slower to establish independent households. In non-farming households including those in the village, the average size was 5.2. The larger size of farming households was due to working conditions of the time: many hands were needed, whether family members or

133   Life and Work in the Community

Table 1
Members of the Children of Peace

Head of Household	No. of Others in Household	House Description	Occupation
Brammer, George (w. Ellen)	9	1-storey frame	yeoman
Briggs, Caleb (w. Mary)	3	1½-storey plank	farmer
Brodie, Rbt. [Presb.] (w. Phebe Ann)	2	2-storey frame	carpenter
Crone, Nelson (w. Mary)	0	1-storey frame	innkeeper
Dennis, Enos (w. Sarah)	0	1-storey brick	yeoman
Doan, Abraham (w. Eliza)	5	1-storey frame	yeoman
Doan, Ebenezer [Quaker] (w. Eliz.)	2	1-storey frame	yeoman
Doan, Eli (w. Josephine)	2	1-storey frame	yeoman
Doan, Elias (w. Wait)	9	2-storey frame	yeoman
Doan, Ira (w. Elizabeth)	3	1½-storey plank	farmer
Doan, Jesse (w. Wait Ann)	6	2-storey brick	yeoman
Doan, John, Sr	2	1-storey frame	carpenter
Doan, Judah (w. Anna)	9	1-storey frame	yeoman
Doan, Oliver (w. Ann)	8	1-storey frame	[not listed]
Dunham, Benjamin (w. Anna)	2	1-storey frame	yeoman
Elmer, William (w. Mary)	1	1-storey log	farmer
Gillvrie, Andrew (w. Hester)	8	2-storey frame	carpenter
Graham, William (w. Elizabeth)	6	1-storey frame	yeoman
Haines, Charles (w. Anna)	2	2-storey frame	shoemaker
Haines, Israel (w. Sarah)	6	1-storey frame	yeoman
Harrison, Joshua (w. Sarah)	8	1½-storey plank	carpenter
Hughes, Job (w. Elizabeth)	6	1-storey frame	yeoman
Kester, George (w. Martha)	6	1-storey frame	shoemaker
Lepard, Mary	2	1-storey frame	widow
Leppard, Benjamin (w. Moriah)	4	1-storey log	yeoman
Leppard, Peter (w. Elizabeth)	3	1-storey frame	cooper
Leppard, Savina	0	1-storey frame	[not listed]
Linsted, William (w. Martha)	8	1-storey log	farmer
Lundy, Jacob (w. Hannah)	5	1-storey frame	yeoman
Lundy, Judah (w. Elizabeth)	6	1-storey frame	yeoman
Lundy, Rachel	1	1-storey frame	widow
Lundy, Reuben (w. Mary)	6	1-storey frame	miller
Maguire, John [C. of E.] (w. Grace)	5	1-storey frame	bailiff
Mallow, William (w. Rebecca)	1	1-storey frame	yeoman
McLeod, Wm. D. (w. Martha)	6	[not listed]	yeoman
Morris, John (w. Eliza)	4	1-storey frame	tinsmith
Reid, John [Quaker] (w. Sarah)	6	2-storey frame	innkeeper
Reid, Willson (w. Hannah)	4	2-storey frame	tanner
Reid, Wm. Jr (w. Mary)	2	1-storey brick	bailiff
Rowan, Peter (w. Deborah)	5	2-storey brick	blacksmith
Stokes, John (w. Martha, C. of E.)	1	2-storey frame	carpenter
Terry, Elizabeth	0	1-storey frame	single woman
Terry, John (w. Sarah)	5	1-storey frame	tanner
Ward, Wm. [no relig.] (w. Abigail)	1	1-storey frame	[not listed]
Willson, Charles (w. Elizabeth)	1	1-storey frame	carpenter
Willson, David (w. Phebe)	0	1-storey frame	[not listed]

Table 1 (cont'd)

Head of Household	No. of Others in Household	House Description	Occupation
Willson, Hannah [?]	0	1-storey frame	single woman
Willson, Israel (w. Mary)	4	1-storey frame	yeoman
Willson, James (w. Pricilla?)	2	1-storey frame	tailor
Willson, John D. (w. Moriah)	1	1-storey frame	yeoman
Willson, John D. (w. Rebecca)	4	1-storey frame	tinsmith
Willson, Phebe	6	1-storey frame	[not listed]
Willson, Wm. H. (w. Sarah)	4	[not listed]	yeoman
[entry unclear]	4	1-storey log	yeoman

Source: East Gwillimbury Township Census, 1851

hired labourers, for planting, cultivating, harvesting, and other chores around the farm. Village households also included hired help, but in the village more people were retired or widowed, bringing the average size of households down.

While nuclear family households, consisting of only parents and children, were the norm within the Children of Peace, census data show considerable variation. For example, the household of Phebe Willson, David Willson's daughter-in-law (not to be confused with David Willson's wife, also named Phebe), included her children: Sally, aged seventeen; William, eleven; and Mary, nine; along with her son, Clinger; his wife, Angeline; and their daughter, Salira [or Salina?], aged four. With Eli and Josephine Doan lived James Kavanaugh and Daniel Moore, a medical doctor. John Doan shared his home with his son John, aged fifty, and sixty-year-old Miriam Webster, who may have been their housekeeper. The household of Job and Elizabeth Hughes included widow Ellen Henderson, aged thirty-seven. Judah and Anna Doan's home included their six children as well as Judah's parents, Mahlon (aged eighty-two) and Rebecca (aged seventy-nine), along with Rebecca Philips (aged thirty-five). Oliver and Ann Doan lived with their seven children and an Irish girl named Eliza Birmingham, aged eighteen, who was likely employed as a servant. Andrew and Hester Gillvrie shared their home with their own three children plus Seba and Abigail Wiggins and *their* three. Mary Lepard, a widow, lived with her son Jacob, thirty-three, and her daughter Emarilla, twenty-three. William and Mary Reid's household included William's father, aged eighty-nine. Caleb and Mary Briggs lived with their two children and "hired servant" Eliza Pegg, aged eighteen. The household of Willson Reid, a tanner, included four men who likely worked for him: tanner Lemuel Doan and Benjamin [?] Corbett, Alexander McArthur, and Benjamin [?] Baskerville, all shoemakers. Households including servants, employees, the aged, and the widowed were common at the time; in this respect, the homes of the Children of Peace were little different from those elsewhere in Upper Canada.[91]

The 1851 census provides a "snapshot" view of the households of the Children of Peace at one moment in time. What was true at that moment differed from conditions a few years before or after. David Willson's own household provides an example. In the 1851 census, he and his wife Phebe were recorded as living in a one-storey frame dwelling by themselves. Sixteen years earlier, however, the Willsons were part of a thirteen-member extended family living in one of the few two-storey houses in the village, south of the temple grounds. That house was shared with son Hugh, his wife Phebe, and their four children, who ranged in age from a few months to ten years old. The household also included son Israel, his wife Mary, and their five-year-old daughter Rebecca. A recently widowed son, John, lived there as well, with his young son Job. They lived on part of lot nine, concession two, immediately south of David Willson's original 200-acre Crown grant.[92] The Willsons lived on lot ten originally, but had consolidated their household on lot nine by 1834. Then, as the third generation grew up, the Willson household divided. By 1851, sons Hugh, Israel, and John all had separate family households, while David and Phebe lived alone. Assessment records from 1860 indicate that David and Phebe lived in a house opposite the temple and meeting house, while John had moved back to the original farm on lot ten.[93] The next year, David and Phebe, both in their eighties, moved into John's two-storey frame house, bringing with them a servant girl, sixteen-year-old Anna Morris. They joined John and his third wife, Irish-born Maria Thorpe (who was twenty-two years his junior), along with John's four children.[94] In that household, they ended their days in the midst, once again, of an extended family.

Occupations listed for heads of households in 1851 follow patterns that were common in rural communities of the mid-nineteenth century. Of the fifty members of the Children of Peace whose occupations were listed, twenty-two were shown as yeomen and four as farmers. The term *yeoman* was used by enumerators Jesse and Abraham Doan, who compiled the census roll for the southern half of the township where most Children of Peace lived. *Farmer* was the term used by enumerators William Cane and George Foster, who surveyed the northern half of the township. Neither Cane nor Foster was a member of the Children of Peace. Perhaps the Doans' preference for the more archaic term *yeoman* reflected the conservative language patterns of their Quaker heritage. Both terms signified the same occupation, although *yeoman* more precisely designated a farmer who owned his own land.

In the census records of 1851, Ebenezer Doan was listed as a yeoman, even though he was also a skilled carpenter who, twenty years earlier, had overseen the erection of the temple. This example shows that census listings do not always describe all the skills present in a community. At best, they indicate the current and chief, but not only, means of earning a livelihood. By 1851, Ebenezer Doan was in his eightieth year and lived with his wife Elizabeth, their son David, and granddaughter Hester Ann, who may have acted as their housekeeper. David Doan was described as a "laborer" and must have done much of the outside work on his father's farm. That farm was sixty-eight acres in size, about a third of the original 200-acre tract that Doan had purchased in 1818. Like other members of the Children of Peace, Doan had taken steps earlier to provide his children with acreage of their own. At the age of eighty, he shared his remaining land with his son, David. They, like their neighbours, practised mixed farming on a modest commercial scale. In 1851, the Doans used twenty-seven of their sixty-eight acres for raising crops, producing 150 bushels of wheat, eighty of peas, 110 of oats, forty of potatoes, sixty of turnips, and eight tons of hay. They also maintained a garden and orchard of one acre, from which they made seventy-five gallons of cider. On their seventeen acres of pasture, they kept twelve sheep, from which they obtained thirty pounds of wool that produced nine yards of fulled cloth and fourteen yards of flannel. The Doans had three milch cows and used the cream from their milk to churn sixty pounds of butter. They also kept one calf or heifer, three horses, and six pigs, butchering four hundred pounds of beef and one thousand two hundred pounds of pork. That same year, they produced sixty bushels of potash and 196 pounds of maple sugar, which provided an important source of cash for Upper Canadian farmers like themselves.

Among the commodities the Doans sent to market were wheat, pork, and beef. This is evident from a comparison of what the four-member Doan household likely consumed with the amount they produced on their farm that year. A study of two families in Georgina township, just north of East Gwillimbury, has shown that one adult could be expected to consume two hundred pounds of flour, 120 to 160 pounds of pork, and sixty pounds of beef per year at that time.[95] Based on these estimates, the Doans required eight hundred pounds of flour for their own use. Their six acres, however, yielded enough

Table 2
Inventory of Jacob Lepard, 1850

Description	Value (£. s. d.)
1 Plough	1.0.0
1 Double Waggon	5.0.0
1 pr. Seed Harrows	2.0.0
1 Fanning Mill	3.0.0
1 Wood Sleigh	1.10.0
1 Lumber Sleigh	1.10.0
Cradle & Scythes	10.0
1 Sett of Double Harness Whipple Trees & Neck Yokes	3.0.0
Dung Fork, Hay Forks & Rakes	7.6
2 Sugar Kettles	1.5.0

wheat to produce roughly double that amount. Similarly, the Doans processed nearly twice as much pork and beef as they could consume themselves. Peas and oats may have been raised for market as well; although large quantities of both would have been reserved for the horses and livestock as well as for household consumption.

By 1851, Ebenezer Doan's farm was smaller than many in the neighbourhood. He had sixty-eight acres, with forty-five of them under cultivation, whereas the average farm among the Children of Peace was just over 103 acres, with nearly fifty-four acres under cultivation. Yet, Doan possessed enough land and livestock to produce roughly double the foodstuffs needed to supply his own small household. Like his neighbours, he produced commodities on a modest commercial scale, much as his ancestors had in Pennsylvania.[96] The Doans and their neighbours farmed their land with tools and equipment little changed since the eighteenth century. Among the few labour-saving devices on the Doan farm was a fanning mill,[97] a device used to separate grain from chaff, which had been available to Pennsylvania farmers since the 1730s.[98] The inventory of Jacob Lepard,[99] a member of the Children of Peace who died in 1850, provides a more complete list of equipment used on a farm of average size (Table 2). Next to a "double waggon," a fanning mill was the most expensive piece of equipment on the Lepard farm.

Four hives of bees were also among Lepard's goods. In the inventory of John Doan, who died in 1862, one hive and ten pounds of honey were listed. Beekeeping was common in most settled areas of Upper Canada,[100] even though it did not appear as a distinct category on the 1851 census. Honey provided a common alternative to maple sugar as an inexpensive sweetener.

Agricultural data appended to the 1851 census show that those not listed as farmers or yeomen often pursued farming to supplement their income. For example, shoemaker Charles Haines lived on a farm of fifty-three acres, thirty-six of which were under cultivation. George Kester, also a shoemaker, occupied twelve acres and kept a few sheep, pigs, and cattle, thereby producing butter, cheese, maple sugar, and woven cloth. Miller Reuben Lundy kept a 160-acre farm, innkeeper John Reid and tanner John Terry each had one hundred acres, and a tinsmith John D. Willson had a 305-acre farm. Others, such as carpenter Andrew Gillvrie, blacksmith Peter Rowan, and carpenter Charles Willson occupied lots ranging in size from half-an-acre to three acres, on which they maintained a garden and kept a cow or two. Clearly the Children of Peace were a farming community, where even craftsmen owned farmland and made a significant portion of their incomes through agriculture. Next to farming, the most common occupation for heads of households was carpentry – not surprising, given the skill displayed in the public buildings of the community. Six followed this trade. The 1851 census listed two persons each as tanners, innkeepers, tinsmiths, shoemakers, and bailiffs. It also listed one miller, one tailor, one blacksmith, and one cooper. Surprisingly, no members of the Children of Peace were listed in 1851 as storekeepers. By that time, Charles Doan had left the village, but assessment records from a decade later show that he continued to own a store in Sharon, then operated by William Doan.

Analysis of religious affiliations listed in the 1851 census show that households occasionally were divided along religious lines. Ebenezer Doan, for example, had by then left the Children of Peace and was listed as a Quaker; however, his wife, son, and granddaughter were all noted as members of the sect. Within the Stokes household, only John Stokes was listed as a member of the Children of Peace, his wife and son being adherents of the Church of England. In the household of William and Elizabeth Graham, their son David was noted as a "Christian," a member of the Disciples of Christ. In the Linsted household, William belonged to the Church of England, his wife Martha to the Church of Scotland, and their eight children, aged three to seventeen, were members of the Children of Peace. Resident employees and boarders also added variety: within the household of tanner Willson Reid lived three shoemakers, one Scottish and two Irish; all three were Roman Catholics.

The Children of Peace were part of the broader culture of their day, their lives comparable to those of countless others across northeastern North America. Yet early visitors noticed a difference. During the first half of the nineteenth century, the Children of Peace created a village that was unique, not only because of its elaborate buildings for worship, but also because it was exceptionally neat and prosperous, presenting an unusually high regard for mutual assistance and community good. By mid-century, the Children of Peace formed a prospering community whose economic mainstay was farming, but whose many trades and occupations made the sect largely self-sufficient. The kinship ties of its citizens also played a major role in confirming their community's independence from the outside world.

The Children of Peace used several strategies to maintain the distinctive identity of their community and establish boundaries against outside interference. They linked land ownership with kinship, as members sought to maintain family ownership of adjacent plots of ground. They further strengthened family life by encouraging members to marry within their own community and by showing active concern for the conduct, discipline, and education of the young. They allowed free enterprise to operate in the buying and selling of merchandise and foodstuffs, but tempered commerce with concern for community well-being by encouraging members to do business in their own village, warning against over-charging, and jointly transporting their crops to market. To look after the sick and needy, they established a charity fund to which all members contributed and from which all members could borrow. In addition, they gave tangible form to their distinctive community life, not only through religious ceremonies and architecture, but also by using plain clothing and speech in their daily lives.

7 House and Home: The Ebenezer Doan House

Written documents of many sorts can be put together to provide a picture of life and work in Sharon at various times during its history. Imperfect and incomplete as it may be, that picture offers us glimpses at the way the Children of Peace lived day by day: how they worshipped, farmed, practised trades, fed and clothed themselves, purchased goods, cared for each other, educated and controlled their young, furnished their houses, and practised a rule of plainness. Alongside written documents, houses can offer insights as well. Unlike most documents, however, houses usually change over time. Paper that has been saved from the scrap basket may suffer a slow or rapid decline, depending on its degree of acidity and conditions of storage, but even then, the essential information it contains may be successfully copied and stored. Houses that are saved, however, usually undergo tremendous change, as each generation leaves its mark in the form of major or minor alterations to the original fabric.

In Sharon, only one early house survives today in virtually its original condition – an accident of history really, since it served for many years as a farm storage building without the added plumbing and electrical wiring almost all other houses possess. In 1958, it was moved from its original location on the Doan farm to the grounds of Sharon Temple Museum. Like the temple, it deserves a close look on its own terms. The Ebenezer Doan house (Fig. 16) provides an important example of a largely unaltered dwelling built and occupied by a family closely associated with the Children of Peace. It is one of those described by a visitor to Sharon in 1861: "The houses, which are all

The Ebenezer Doan House

Figure 16 Ebenezer Doan house, built 1819, East Gwillimbury Township, Ontario. Now at Sharon Temple Museum.

of wood and either 'rough cast' or painted white, are by no means crowded together, and peep out modestly from the deep green maples and oaks by which each and every one is surrounded."[1] For other houses in Sharon today, alterations themselves can provide important information regarding historical and cultural change. Here, however, is a house that gives insight into the life, work, and thought of one of the most prominent members of the Children of Peace, standing much as it did in 1866 when Ebenezer Doan died.

When the Children of Peace concentrated their activities around David Willson's farm in East Gwillimbury, Doan sold his land on Yonge Street and purchased one hundred acres, the west half of lot thirteen, on the third concession. This was roughly one half mile north of Willson's property, on the other side of Queen Street. Doan purchased this land, along with the hundred-acre west half of lot fourteen, for $4,000 from Joseph Sutherland in 1818.[2] At first, the Doans may have lived in a log house once occupied by the Sutherlands. Soon after his purchase, however, Doan began work on a larger house for himself; his wife Elizabeth Paxson Doan

(1783–1874); and their children: Abraham (b. 1802), Elias (b. 1805), Oliver (b. 1807), Ira (b. 1810), Hannah (b. 1812), and Sarah (b. 1815). Their seventh child, David, was born in the house on 30 September 1820.[3]

The two-storey Doan house has timber frame construction, a gable roof, and a nearly symmetrical three-bay façade. Downstairs are three principal rooms plus a rear vestibule, scullery, and pantry; on the second floor are four additional rooms. In 1820, this house was larger than most in York County, since Doan's household was larger than most. There were nine family members, when the district average was less than four,[4] and hired help may have lived there also. When Doan acquired the property, his oldest son was only sixteen; thus, additional help likely was necessary for farming and clearing his land. With a large family and live-in help for at least part of the year, Doan needed a large house with numerous rooms.

Brian Coffey has determined that, prior to the mid-nineteenth century, the majority of people in York County lived in one or two-room log houses.[5] Assessment and census records from 1825, 1834, and 1851 indicate, however, that most of the Children of Peace lived in frame houses that were larger and more substantial.[6] If the records are accurate, the majority of members lived in one-storey frame buildings; however, these records list even the Doan house as a one-storey frame structure. As there is no structural evidence to suggest that the Doan house was originally a one-storey building, the accuracy of these documents may be questioned. Property taxes were based, in part, on the number of storeys a house had. Thus, local record-keepers may have been purposely inaccurate in their descriptions in order to reduce payments to an unpopular government. Perhaps many more members of the sect lived in two-storey houses than the official records suggest, setting them apart even further from the county norm.

In a survey of surviving Ontario buildings, Darrell A. Norris has described the two-storey, gable-roofed house as a vernacular type concentrated particularly in the area from York County westward to the Niagara Peninsula. About twenty-one per cent of surviving York County houses built before the mid-nineteenth century fit into this category. The most common surviving house type, the one-and-a-half-storey house, comprises nearly twenty-three per cent of the total.[7] Research by Coffey and Norris, along with the East Gwillimbury assessment and census records, suggests that the Ebenezer Doan house was indeed larger and more substantial than most in York County during the first half of the nineteenth century. However, it may not have been greatly different from those occupied by the majority of the Children of Peace. Members of this sect formed households that were generally larger than the norm in neighbouring areas, so their houses would have been larger as well.

Since Doan was a skilled craftsman, he was well-equipped to erect a two-storey house with a hewn timber frame. The house he built may be interpreted in two ways: as a document relating to the life and work of Doan and his family and, more generally, as a document that illustrates the diffusion of vernacular architectural forms across North America. It is worthwhile to examine the Doan house within the general concept of diffusion and then return to analyze what insights it may give into the lives of the Doans themselves. The concept of diffusion has often been used in studies of North American vernacular architecture to account for the spread of building types and plans, methods of construction, and forms of decoration from one place to another.[8] These studies suggest several things. Firstly, there is a need to search out the sources used by Ebenezer Doan, consciously or unconsciously, as he built his house. This involves identifying his models, which were houses he had known in the past. Secondly, it is important to study how Doan modified or combined these models to build something suitable for his own needs. Throughout this process, it should be remembered that buildings meet not only the physical needs of their occupants, but their psychic needs as well. Doan chose from his store of architectural knowledge, not only to provide shelter for his family against the weather, but also to give three-dimensional form to his concept of what family life should be.

Many small houses exhibiting similar front and rear elevations were built at that time in Bucks County, Pennsylvania, birthplace of the Doans. Examples include the Abdon Hibbs house, not far from the farm where Doan's father once lived,[9] and several small houses in Solebury Township, close to where Ebenezer himself had a farm. Many were built after the Doans had left the area and attest to the continuing popularity of the three-bay form. The symmetrical façades of these houses may have derived as much from vernacular tradition as from any "trickling down" of the Georgian style of more elaborate dwellings. Small houses with symmetrical, three-bay façades appeared in the British Isles in the seventeenth century and may have inspired some of the early houses built in Bucks County by English, Welsh, and Scots-Irish immigrants.[10] Furthermore, as Henry Glassie has pointed out, "Bilateral symmetry was, in fact, an essential feature of western European folk design."[11]

Several features set the Doan house apart from most of its Bucks County contemporaries. For example, its first-storey windows are wider and more in keeping with earlier fashion. Also, it is of frame construction, whereas most Bucks County houses were built of stone. In Doan's time, frame houses may have been slightly more common in Bucks County than they are today. Surviving tax and assessment records for Solebury Township, where Doan lived, do not provide detailed information regarding house construction and size; however those for Plumstead, immediately to the north, do. Of the 187 Plumstead buildings listed in preparation for the Direct Tax of 1798, only one was of frame construction. Sixty-five were of log, while 121 were of stone.[12] To the south, in Upper Makefield Township, a similar pattern appears in a tax list compiled in 1795 or 1796. There, one of the few frame houses in the township was owned by Ebenezer's great-uncle, Benjamin Doan.[13]

When building a house in Bucks County, Ebenezer Doan would have worked with stonemasons and supervised their work. The masons built the walls, chimneys, and fireplaces, while Doan added the interior partitions and trim, floors, windows, doors, and roof. As a carpenter, he would have drawn the plans and subcontracted any additional work in joinery, glazing, plastering, and painting. The dominant role of the carpenter is evident in Joseph Moxon's widely read manual, *Mechanick Exercises or the Doctrine of Handy-Works, Applyed to the Art of House Carpentry*. That role persisted even in parts of America where houses built entirely of wood were rare.[14] Doan's working life as a carpenter in Upper Canada must have been very different from what it had been in Pennsylvania. In East Gwillimbury, frame houses were much more common, so he could have been responsible for building a house from start to finish.

The dimensions of the Doan house, twenty-five-and-a-half feet long by twenty-one-and-a-half feet deep, set it apart from most Bucks County examples. British settlers there tended to build longer houses, at first only one room deep, with end chimneys and fireplaces. The ground floor of these houses generally contained up to two rooms, a hall/kitchen and a parlour, with one opening into the other.[15] By the latter third of the eighteenth century, they built increasing numbers of two-storey houses that were two rooms deep.[16] The 1798 Direct Tax records for Plumstead, which list forty-six two-storey houses, give average overall dimensions of approximately twenty-nine by twenty-one feet, indicating that rectangular houses remained the norm. The Doan house, however, resembles the square houses built by Pennsylvania Germans,[17] rather than the rectangular houses built by most settlers of British background.

It also adopted the German three-room plan, which included a large hall/kitchen with two smaller rooms off to one side. In the Doan house, one of these two rooms is rectangular, while the smaller one behind it is nearly square, again in keeping with German tradition. One variation is the hall/kitchen, which has two adjoining anterooms. The smaller of these has built-in shelves on three sides, like a large cupboard, and could have served as a pantry for storing tableware, utensils, and foodstuffs. The larger anteroom is approximately five by seven feet and lit by its own window. Wider shelves are found at one end and a dry sink stands by the window, suggesting the room's use as a scullery. In another variation, the boxed-in stairs are placed near the middle of the back wall of the Doan house, rather than in a corner location, as favoured by most German three-room-plan houses. Another major difference lies in the Doan's use of end chimneys rather than a central chimney. Even this, however, does not remove the Doan house from Pennsylvania-German precedent in Upper Canada. The Daniel Stong log house, built northwest of York by a Pennsylvania-German family in 1816, has an end chimney with a three-room plan, while the Stongs's three-room-plan frame house of 1832 has a central chimney.[20] The example of the Stong houses upsets any attempt at a neat chronology of assimilation: the Stongs's second house in Upper Canada was more typically Pennsylvania-German than their first. Many variations were made in the traditional German plan, even by settlers of Pennsylvania-German ancestry.

If the Doan house does indeed reflect Germanic influence, Bucks County precedents may still be found, despite the British background of most local people. Among Bucks County's eighteenth-century German settlers was Anna Savilla Sloy, Ebenezer's mother.[18] Also, the county's Hilltown, Bedminster, Tinicum, and Plumstead townships were home to German Mennonites, including at least sixteen families who, between 1786 and 1802, made their way to Upper Canada.[19] On Ebenezer's father's side, the Doans were originally Quakers whose ancestors had come from Wales.[21] Their Quaker origins and Welsh background suggest two other possible origins for the Doan house plan. One is the so-called *Quaker plan* house, said to have been inspired by a promotional pamphlet printed in 1684, once attributed to William Penn. That pamphlet gave instructions for building a house with one large room and two smaller rooms off to one side.[22] A more compelling argument could be made that the three-room plan came to Bucks County as a long-standing British precedent, particularly from the north and west of England and from Wales, where the majority of Pennsylvania's Quaker settlers originated.[23] While less common than one or two-room houses in those areas, three-room plans and their variants may be found.[24]

Since Ebenezer Doan's Bucks County house no longer survives, a direct comparison with it cannot be made. However, surrounded on three sides by land once owned by the Doans stands an eighteenth-century stone house that is similar to the Doan's Upper Canada house in several important ways. Measuring approximately thirty-two by thirty-four feet, this house is also nearly square and contains three rooms on its main floor. Like the Doan house in East Gwillimbury, the Solebury Township house has a front door set in the middle of its three-bay façade. In both cases, this door leads directly into a hall/kitchen with a large cooking fireplace set against the gable wall. In the Solebury house, two smaller rooms of roughly equal proportions are located to the right. A boxed-in stairway ascends to the second floor from beside a back door that, as in the Doan house, is located directly opposite the front door. Ebenezer Doan must have been familiar with this house, since his farm was located immediately next to it.[25] With its similar shape and floor plan, this house provides a tangible link with Solebury Township precedent. The plan and construction of both it and the Ebenezer Doan house suggest a mixture of traditions, both British and German, which came together on the Pennsylvania frontier and then were taken far and wide, wherever Pennsylvanians settled, only to be changed again to meet the needs of new situations. Like the Friends meeting house on Yonge Street or the temple itself, the Doan house has a complicated pedigree, but one that clearly reflects the background and origins of its builder.

But does it reflect anything more than this? To answer this question, it is important to look at the way Doan finished his house inside. A striking contrast exists between the façade of the Doan house and its hall/kitchen. The façade is largely in keeping with early-nineteenth-century vernacular design, while the hall/kitchen is designed in the manner of a century before (Fig. 17). This contrast of an up-to-date exterior and traditional interior is reflected in the construction of the front door. Aside from the glazing of its upper panels, from the outside the door appears to be a standard six-panel Georgian door. Inside, however, it is faced with beaded boards, trapezoidal in shape, giving it the appearance of a much earlier style. Also on the inner face, large hand-forged nailheads serve as decoration, conforming to the location of the stiles, rails, and muntins of the Georgian door visible outside. The front door itself embodies the transition from the symmetrical, Georgian façade to the more traditional hall/kitchen within.

Beaded pine boards were used for partition walls and sheathing throughout the hall/kitchen, its anterooms, the rear entryway, and the stairwell. Beams running from the front to the back of the house are exposed throughout the hall/kitchen area and are beaded at their lower edges. The ceiling boards they support are also beaded. This beading is part of a reductive aesthetic dating from the mid-

Figure 17 Hall/kitchen of the Ebenezer Doan house, built 1819, East Gwillimbury Township, Ontario. Now at Sharon Temple Museum.

eighteenth century and used widely in vernacular houses. Beaded beams and ceiling boards were, however, less common than beaded wall boards. The care given to finishing them where they are exposed in the hall/kitchen suggests the importance Doan must have attached to this part of his house. Unusual too are the pair of raised panels over the fireplace and the four panels above them, two of which are hinged cupboard doors. The fireplace in the hall/kitchen never had a mantel; instead, a band of dark stain was applied around its opening. A similar band that simulates a baseboard runs around the rest of the room. While the walls were never painted or stained, the four-panelled interior doors were coloured a dark reddish brown, imitating a more exotic and expensive wood than the pine used throughout the house. The ceiling too appears to have been stained a dark colour originally, although it is now covered with darkened varnish, probably from the late-nineteenth century.

There was no oven built into the fireplace of the Doan house, indicating that an outdoor bake oven may have been located in a separate outbuilding, as in many Pennsylvania precedents. As in other Upper Canadian households, an iron bake kettle or reflector oven would have been used to bake indoors on the hearth.[26] Other tools and equipment may have been similar to those used in the home of

Ebenezer's brother, John, whose probate inventory for 1862 included "1 Table & dough Trough, 1 Brass kittle, 1 Copper kittle, 1 meal Sive, 1 Grid Iron, 1 Shovel & tongs, 1 Frying pan, 1 Sugar box, 1 cream crock, 1 weigh ballance, 1 bake Iron," and "1 bake oven."[27]

The size of the hall/kitchen, its large open hearth, and the exposed beams of its ceiling recall rooms from earlier houses. Like them, this room served as a place where many daily activities of work and recreation took place. This would have been true particularly in winter, when the hearth offered warmth and comfort not available elsewhere. Ebenezer Doan demonstrated the importance he placed on family ties when he moved with his father, brothers, sister, and other family members to Upper Canada as part of an extended family. He continued to show a high regard for family unity by providing land for his sons close to his home farm. It was appropriate, then, that the hall/kitchen, which served as a focal point of domestic life, should have been the most traditionally arranged and decorated room in the house. Much that Doan sought to do during his lifetime was inspired by Quaker tradition. Tradition was a major factor in determining how this symbolic centre of the home should look.

Less important rooms in the Doan house were more subject to changing modes of design and finish. For example, the adjoining parlour and downstairs bedroom both had plaster ceilings and walls. Their doors and windows were trimmed with simple surrounds, which were painted dark green. Beaded baseboards and chair rails, also painted dark green, provided the only other ornament in these rooms. The smooth plaster walls and beaded woodwork of these rooms followed neoclassical ideals and were more in keeping with fashion than the traditional hall/kitchen beside them. Upstairs, baseboards, chair rails, and door and window surrounds are virtually identical to those below. Their simplicity was in keeping with the aesthetic of plainness espoused by the Quakers and Children of Peace. At the same time, however, they were similar to those found in many other small houses throughout eastern North America during the first third of the nineteenth century – a time when plainness and simplicity were part of the prevailing neoclassical taste. Relating more specifically to southeastern Pennsylvania tradition is the *hook strip* with nails for hanging things, found in the small room at the top of the stairs.

More unusual are the small fireplace and fully panelled end wall in one of the two front bedrooms. This wall contains three hinged closet doors and is similar to a panelled end wall in the Isaiah Paxson house in Bucks County. The Paxson house displays a date stone inscribed "1785." Through tax records, it is known that Ebenezer Doan lived near the Paxson house from 1783 to 1786, probably in the household of his father or brother. Ebenezer himself did not become a landowner until 1801, the year of his marriage to Elizabeth Paxson, a distant cousin of Isaiah. Ebenezer must have known the Paxson house and could even have had a hand in building it. Similarities may also be found in the front doors of the Paxson and Doan houses: both have glazed openings in the upper panels.

Strong similarities exist between the house Ebenezer Doan built for his family in East Gwillimbury and the houses he had known in Bucks County. His house illustrates the diffusion of architectural forms across hundreds of miles. This provides three-dimensional evidence of cultural diffusion in its broadest sense. When Doan replicated in Upper Canada many features of houses he had known in Pennsylvania, he did so in the midst of a community that included numerous members of his family who had lived near him before his emigration. He followed a religious faith that also preserved much of what he had known in the past, first as a Quaker and then as a member of the Children of Peace. His farming practices and his successful efforts to obtain land nearby for his children also preserved traditions and patterns that had been familiar to him for many years. In this context, it was to be expected that Doan would build a house that also embodied much of his Pennsylvania heritage.

The size of his house and its relatively large number of rooms were determined by the large size of the Doan household. Since the hall/kitchen of the Doan house was the centre of the household's activities, its design must have been particularly important in a symbolic sense. Its old-fashioned appearance may be a more important sign of Doan's outlook than any other feature of his house: it may be key to understanding why, after following David Willson for nearly thirty years, he eventually returned to the Society of Friends. The architecture of his own house shows Doan to have been a conservative man at heart – a man who eventually returned to the religious faith of his ancestors. The temple that Doan helped to design and construct shows him to have been, at times, an innovator, yet those qualities existed hand-in-hand with a strong respect for tradition and continuity with the past.

The mixture of tradition and innovation found in the buildings built by Ebenezer Doan was typical of the mixture of old and new in the beliefs, worship, community life, and material culture of the Children of Peace as a whole. The Children of Peace, in setting about to establish a new church, retained much of their devotion to the old Quaker doctrine of the Inner Light. They erected a meeting house and temple influenced by Quaker heritage. They attempted to build a cooperative community, which had its roots in the Quaker-dominated Delaware valley of Pennsylvania. They rooted their new church in traditions that were familiar to them, while creating something that still could claim uniqueness and originality. Ebenezer Doan, for a time, joined their quest, while living in a house whose very plan, construction, and finish reminded him of the past. He supervised the building of an innovative three-tiered temple in the wilderness, but returned each night to a house that must have been comforting in its familiarity. In the end, it seems a truer representation of his own beliefs and convictions since he eventually left the Children of Peace and went back to the Quakers.

8 Religion and Politics

From the beginning, the Children of Peace looked beyond their own affairs to the world at large. While seeking to build a new church and a model community, they were influenced by events in the world around them and, in turn, often sought to influence the course of those events. When David Willson and members of the Children of Peace attended a political convention in Toronto in February 1834, they walked in procession and carried two banners: "a black one with white border, and 'the constitution' inscribed in silver, and a sky blue one, with an amber border, motto 'Peace and Justice,' in gold, shaded." By doing so, they linked religion and politics in a tangible way. They followed a pattern established as part of their religious services, which were also preceded by banners and processions. Both occasions also included band music, although the convention featured secular tunes – "Jubilee Waltz," "Huntsman's Chorus," "Number 1 Quadrille," and *"Le Petit Tambour"* – rather than hymns.[1] Similarities between the religious and secular ceremonies of the Children of Peace demonstrated their conviction that religious belief and secular affairs could not be separated. Their community in East Gwillimbury, with its distinctive approach to land ownership, schooling, and mutual assistance, was the principal illustration of how the sect tried to put its beliefs into practice. Involvement in political events, however, shows that Willson and his followers did not intend to close themselves off from the rest of the world, but hoped to influence affairs outside their community for the broader good of the colony.

The banner bearing the words, "the constitution," in silver on a black background with white border, must have suggested mourning through its sombre combination of funereal tones. In early 1834, many Upper Canadian reformers had reason to believe that the British Constitution was indeed to be mourned. Their most colourful spokesman, William Lyon Mackenzie, had been ejected several times from the Legislative Assembly for his outspoken views. To many moderate reformers, Mackenzie was an embarrassment, but to his constituents, who included the people of East Gwillimbury, Mackenzie was something of a folk hero, standing up for the rights of the people against the Family Compact, which included the lieutenant-governor and his associates. Mackenzie and his followers often despaired of ever achieving reform under the existing political system.[2] The funereal banner carried by the Children of Peace showed that they too mourned this sad state of affairs, through which constitutional government in the colony of Upper Canada appeared to be endangered. However, their other banner, proclaiming "Peace and Justice" surrounded by the blue and amber colours of daybreak, offered a more optimistic view.

When the procession ended and the banners were suspended over the speakers' platform, members of the Children of Peace sang a song that conveyed their disappointment at the state of political affairs in the colony. Like the blue and amber banner, however, their song also offered hope that things might still improve by reason of the innate goodness of the British Constitution and the presence on the throne of King William IV, who was widely believed to be a reform sympathizer. Their song said, in part:

> When Parliament becomes our foe,
> We find our glass has run so low
> We let our king and country know
> We cannot be contented so
>   With King or Constitution.
>
> We would not have the pillars move
> But that the workmen would improve,
> And Parliament their subjects love
> Inspiring praise to these above
>   To King and Constitution.
>
> We truly wish King William knew
> One half the mischief that ye do
> He'd send Lord Goderich o'er to you

And he would make their numbers few
That break our Constitution.

And for a Parliament we'll try
That's just and true, not prone to lie,
Then with their prayers we will comply
And stand for "William" till we die
And for our Constitution.[3]

These verses, probably written for the occasion by David Willson, contained ideas that were similar to those of reform-minded Americans during the years leading up to the American Revolution. Both claimed loyalty to King and constitution and spoke out against Parliament and corrupt local officials. They demanded the rights of British subjects to constitutional government and did not advocate abolishing ties with the motherland.

Willson and his American predecessors obtained much of their knowledge of the British Constitution – a loosely defined body of statutes, common law, and precedent – from William Blackstone's *Commentaries on the Laws of England*. Blackstone's book, first published in 1765, was an immensely popular treatise. Willson would have known of the *Commentaries* since he had a knowledge of law and had "liberated hands from lawyers' fees and the judges' sentence at court" by acting as arbiter of his followers' disputes. Willson was an acquaintance of Henry Blackstone, who was a lawyer in nearby St Alban's (Holland Landing) and a grandson of the great jurist himself.[4]

In his song, Willson not only expressed faith in King William IV and the British Constitution, but echoed a theme familiar to his followers by employing metaphors of architecture and building. In the buildings he designed for the Children of Peace, Willson tried to capture the essence of his religious faith. In referring to his desire that Upper Canada remain under the authority of the British Constitution, while still achieving reform, Willson wrote, "We would not have the pillars move/But that the workmen would improve." In these lines, Willson linked King and constitution to the supporting pillars of a building and compared political reformers to builders and renovators. A second song carried similar themes:

O that our sun may set in peace
And that offences all may cease
That Truth and Justice may increase
  Our liberty!

O may our great design be blest,
May William set our hearts at rest
And move the load that hath oppressed
   Our liberty!

May William for our grief atone
That we may bless him on the throne
When all our griefs to him are known
   For liberty!

We trust we'll state our cause so clear
That all his Parliaments may hear,
For we're resolved to plead sincere
   For liberty!⁵

Again, Willson saw King William IV as a champion of liberty in opposition to an oppressive Parliament. The opening line of this song, "O that our sun may set in peace," recalled the apocalyptic image of the setting sun painted on the outside walls of the temple and created a link between Willson's political views and his theology. This metaphor set his plea for political reform in the context of his belief in the coming millennium, when peace and justice would reign on earth.

Willson's mixture of theology with social and political reform went back to the earliest days of his ministry. In preaching, both in the capital and in the townships, Willson strove to extend to the world the ideals that inspired his community in East Gwillimbury. Traveller D. Wilkie exaggerated only slightly when he wrote of one of Willson's sermons from the 1830s: "The burden of his discourse seemed to be the injustice practised towards the world by all those who possess an abundant share of the good things of life. That they are all usurpers and tyrants; that there ought neither to be masters nor servants; that all mankind are equal; and that it is the duty of the poor to pull down the rich."⁶ Another contemporary, the Reverend H.H. O'Neill, claimed, "His public services consist of political harrangues against the Church, Tories, Clergy Reserves &tc."⁷ Each observer recognized the strong links among Willson's religious, social, and political beliefs.

Willson made his political opinions known to the world beyond his little band of followers as early as 1815, when he included an "Address to the Crown of England" in his pamphlet, *The Rights of Christ*, published in Philadelphia. In it, Willson declared his loyalty to the King, but bridled against the opposition he suffered at the hands of Quakers and civil authorities. Boldly, he said to the King, "Now choose whether I should, or might be your servant ... I am a man under the visitation of God's power in your land ..."[8] About that time, Quakers and Methodists had brought charges against David Willson before the civil magistrates. The nature of those charges is unknown; however, Willson's account of the incident stated: "The uproar increased mightily and the magistrates was stirred up by evil reports, chiefly of the Quakers; after which I was visited by two of them, to inquire into the truth of the business, but finding no cause for imprisonment, or execution of laws, I was suffered to return home in peace, leaving the magistrates to look after my accusers for further satisfaction, as none of them was willing to come forward to prove the things to my face, of which I was rongfully accused."[9] Through this incident, Willson may have felt that civil government was on his side and that his real enemies were the religious leaders of his day. Certainly he was anxious to proclaim his loyalty to Britain at a time when the War of 1812 had brought considerable suspicion against American-born residents of Upper Canada. The Alien Question led, for a time, to exclusion of new American immigrants and curtailment of the rights of those already in the colony. Only in 1828 did controversy end, when Americans already in Upper Canada were permitted, after meeting certain residence requirements, to take an oath of allegiance and secure full civil rights and privileges.[10]

Willson's longest political tract, *A Friend to Britain*, printed and bound together with *The Impressions of the Mind* in 1835, shows that he remained a strong supporter of the monarchy and the British system of government. The decision to bind this tract with Willson's longest theological work again suggests how closely religion and politics were linked in Willson's mind. The following passage from *A Friend to Britain* provides a key to understanding why Willson supported British institutions: "Reform began in Abram, and succeeded through his generations till a Messiah was born, an evidence of the Prince of Peace, and the one universal Father of the whole inhabited earth. Reform has begun in Britain as in Abraham, and will spread through the whole earth. It is without a priest, but not without the Spirit of God, or his Son Jesus Christ. Truth, justice and mercy is in it; these are principles of peace and will descend to the whole world. Britain is restoring the poor to their right, and pleading for a free circulation of just principles, and the preaching of the Gospel on the principles it began in Israel and Judah."[11] Here, Britain is pictured as a new Israel, leading the way to social reform. Willson would have valued this image since he and his followers saw themselves as a new Israel, leading the way to spiritual reform. His optimism may have been based on events that had only recently taken place in England: the 1828 repeal of the Corporation Acts, which had once bolstered the power of the Church of England at the expense of dissenting sects, and the passage of the Reform Bill of 1832, which expanded the British electorate and abolished many of the most blatant abuses of power in the British parliamentary system.

The 1830s were also the era of Jacksonian democracy in the United States, but Willson was no admirer of the American system. He wrote in *A Friend to Britain*, "England has not to flee to republicanism to make herself happy, she has wisdom on her own shores, and it will shine to the western world when republicanism will tremble like a leaf."[12] Willson's aversion to republicanism may have owed something to the experiences of his father many years before. The American settlers who came to the Yonge Street Quaker community at the beginning of the nineteenth century could not be called Loyalists, but David Willson's father, an Irish-born Presbyterian, *was* a Loyalist. During David Willson's infancy, John Willson actively opposed the Revolution and was fined and imprisoned several times for his beliefs.[13] Stories of those times may have inspired a dislike of republican ways among his children. In *A Friend to Britain*, Willson wrote: "It is in vain to flee from the British constitution for a better, or from king to congress. The storm has arisen *there* that is not yet seen to abate. Self-interest is of one effect every where, destroys the name of religion and the peace of the nation."[14] Speaking out against the "self-interest" of the Americans, Willson contrasted the American tradition of individualism and private enterprise with the kind of cooperative community he was trying to build in Upper Canada.

David Willson's views were influenced by his belief that the monarchical system of British government was established by God himself as a modern-day equivalent of the governing structure of ancient Israel. Willson declared: "I love the order of a monarchical government, it is designed to the Son of God, and the throne of David for him to sit upon; he is a prince of mercy, and I trust he will arise from small things and ascend to the heart of our king, and that his judgment and justice will be seen to all, descending from our king and Britain's throne to all the world."[15] Willson's admiration for ancient Israel and his desire to follow Old Testament models and practices were well-established in the design of the temple and in his *Letters to the Jews*. His preference for a monarchical system of government, believed to be based on divine decree and symbolized by the throne of David, fit well with his overall identification with ancient Israel.

Many irritants arose to challenge Willson's faith in Upper Canada's British ways, not only during the time leading up to the convention of 1834, but earlier as well. Among the most serious was the lack of "responsible government" in the colony. In 1791, the British Parliament had passed the Constitutional Act, which established the form of government that would prevail in Upper and Lower Canada. This form of government, which Upper Canada's first lieutenant-governor, John Graves Simcoe, claimed was "the very image and transcript" of the British Constitution,[16] consisted of a three-tiered system like that of King, Lords, and Commons in England. At the top was a lieutenant-governor, who was advised by an appointed Legislative Council. Below the Legislative Council was a Legislative Assembly elected by the people. This three-tiered system was not autonomous, however. The lieutenant-governor was responsible to the Colonial Office in England. Moreover, neither he nor his council was responsible to the elected Assembly for their actions. When the Constitutional Act was proclaimed in 1791, many precedents had been set in England to establish the authority of the House of Commons, particularly in matters of finance. The Upper Canadian Assembly, however, had little power. Its wishes could be ignored by the upper house and by the lieutenant-governor and his council. When Upper Canadian reformers called for responsible government, they demanded a system wherein the upper levels would be responsible to the elected representatives of the people – a form of government that had been evolving in Britain for well over a century. Only the most radical reformers based their demands on American models, which did away with appointed positions and declared that all those in power were directly responsible to the electors.[17]

The Constitutional Act also brought controversy by establishing clergy reserves, which comprised one-seventh of all the land in the colony, scattered evenly throughout all the townships. These were meant "for the Support and Maintenance of a Protestant clergy," but the Constitutional Act did not specify which denomination. Church of England clergy assumed that Parliament had meant *them*. Representatives of the Church of Scotland argued that *they* should be included since theirs was also an established church in Great Britain. The majority of settlers, however, belonged to neither church and objected to any special favours granted to support these religious minorities. Few settlers were interested in renting clergy reserve lands when they could obtain grants of land or buy land of their own nearby. This left many clergy reserves unoccupied for years. With no settlers living on them, there was no one to clear or maintain the roads in front of them. This added considerably to the difficulties of travel and communication within the colony. When Yonge Street was surveyed in 1794, no clergy reserves were established on either side in order to avoid the problems they would cause. Less important roads, such as Queen Street in the heart of East Gwillimbury, had clergy reserves scattered along them at regular intervals.[18] Compounding the problem were Crown reserves, constituting another seventh of the colony's land, which were set aside for the support of government to free it from the financial control of the Legislative Assembly. Whenever David Willson and his followers travelled to Markham or York to hold services and took their wagon loads of produce to market, they were reminded of the presence of clergy and Crown reserves by the unoccupied lands and poorly maintained roads.

Entanglements of religion and politics also affected the marriages of the Children of Peace. In early Upper Canada, only Anglican, Roman Catholic, and, after 1798, Lutheran and Calvinist clergy could legally perform marriages. If there was no licensed clergyman within an eighteen-mile radius, civil marriages were permitted under the authority of a justice of the peace. Quakers were a privileged minority: their marriages had been recognized as valid under English law since 1753.[19] The Children of Peace, however, were left in a difficult position. Marriages performed by David Willson were illegal. Unless they were solemnized a second time by an approved clergyman or by a justice of the peace, they did not exist under law. Children of such marriages were illegitimate, and their rights of inheritance could be challenged in court. Such marriage laws also proved irksome to Methodists and other dissenting groups within the colony.

Reform finally came in 1831, greatly expanding the list of clergy who could legally perform marriages, but still leaving those of the Children of Peace open to question. In the debate over the Marriage Bill of 1831, Solicitor General Hagerman said: "He had heard of a sect called the *Children of Peace* in this country – but they were the *Children of Wrath* – not the inheritors of God's word, and not entitled to the privileges of Christians. 'What! are we going to give the right (of marrying) to every ignorant person, who having addressed a number of people ... may please to call himself a preacher?' He hoped not."[20] The reforms of 1831 gave the right to perform marriages to clergy "regularly ordained according to the rites and form of the church of which he professes to be a Clergyman or Minister." This left David Willson, along with other ministers of the Children of Peace, in a questionable position.

Nonetheless, Willson continued to perform marriages: twenty-two, dating from 1821 to 1841, are recorded in one surviving register. Weddings were held during Sunday services. However, a congregational meeting on 17 April 1833 decided that they should become part of "Seventh day monthly Meetings" instead.[21] Willson added his own personal touch by recording many of the marriages in verse. One poem, dated 21 November 1825, commemorated the marriage of his eldest son, John David Willson, to Sarah Lundy:

> In hand we stand most firm agreed
>   As witness present see
> That from this time we do proceed
>   Bride and bridegroom to be
> United in the marriage tie
>   And bind our promise strong
> We're man and wife until we die
>   Let life be short or long.[22]

The certificate containing this poem was signed by the bride and groom and by five witnesses – not by the entire congregation, as in Quaker practice. To be recognized under Upper Canadian law, however, this marriage must have been performed again by a clergyman from one of the established churches or by a justice of the peace. Not until 1859 were all restrictions on marriages performed by nonconformist sects withdrawn.[23]

David Willson had little reason to love the Anglican church or its ministers. Their privilege was represented by the hated clergy reserves and by their special powers to perform marriages. In *A Friend to Britain*, Willson appealed to King William to ignore the advice of Anglican clergy: "Make a royal decree from thy throne, by and through the advice of thy humble-minded subjects, that the priests' hand shall be bound as with a cord, that he shall withold his iron hand from his neighbour's bread. For, the bishops of England, by their decrees, are advising thy crown down into the dust.[24] However, just as Willson refused to abandon his faith in the essential goodness of the British system of government, he remained in a somewhat ambiguous position regarding the Anglican church.

Despite his criticisms, he described the Church of England as "my mother."[25] His widowed mother, Catherine, had married an Anglican after following David Willson and his family to Upper Canada. Her second husband's name was John Willson, the same as that of her first husband. (Needless to say, this has caused great confusion for Willson genealogists ever since.) The second John Willson was a Loyalist, who originally had emigrated from New Jersey to the colony of New Brunswick. He was also a justice of the peace and could have legitimized the early marriages performed by his stepson, David. John Willson died at the age of ninety in the village of Hope in 1829, having remained an Anglican in the midst of that most un-Anglican village of the Children of Peace. At John Willson's death, John Strachan, the archdeacon of York who would one day become Upper Canada's first bishop, came to the village and conducted an Anglican funeral service in the meeting house.[26] This may have irritated David Willson, but he was anxious to fulfill the last wishes of his step-father.

David Willson and the Children of Peace were not only concerned about responsible government, the clergy reserves, and the right to perform marriages; they were also involved in specific economic controversies of their day. In 1831, for example, the Children of Peace forwarded a petition signed by fifty of their members to their representative in the Legislative Assembly, William Lyon Mackenzie. Their petition opposed the raising of additional funds to build the Welland Canal, then under construction to link Lake Ontario with Lake Erie by the Welland River. Mackenzie became one of the strongest opponents of that project, charging that members of the Family Compact and others close to power would benefit most from the government's large expenditures. The text of the petition sent by the Children of Peace shows how closely connected religion and politics had become. The petition began, "We address you in our home style, from an impression your voices has left on our minds, respecting the loan of money for the benefit of the Welland Canal system."[27] This recalls David Willson's use of the word *impressions* to describe the communicating powers of the spirit of God, as reflected in the title of his book, *The Impressions of the Mind*. This is another instance of that mixture of spiritual and temporal concerns that characterized the thinking of the Children of Peace. Here, a theological metaphor was used in a political context, linking concern over the economic affairs of the colony with the spiritual outlook of the Children of Peace. Complaints against extravagant expenditures on the Welland Canal were set in the same language that was used to express abstract religious concepts. This was the literary equivalent of the sect's use of banners, processions, and music at the 1834 convention. These gave religious overtones to the convention, just as the phrasing of the petition gave a spiritual context to concerns about government expenditures.

Such unity of thought and purpose did not always prevail among the Children of Peace. During the 1830s, political agitation in the colony increased and began to take its toll on the stability of the sect. During the summer and fall of 1831, William Lyon Mackenzie travelled throughout the colony, but particularly along the back roads of his constituency north of the capital, distributing pamphlets and soliciting signatures for grievance petitions. Mackenzie's actions were prompted when the Legislative Assembly, with its conservative majority, approved the British government's request for the establishment of a civil list, making permanent provision for the payment of salaries to certain colonial officials. In return, the government promised the Assembly increased control over customs revenues; however, Mackenzie and many of his reform colleagues were outraged at the Assembly's willingness to give up its prerogatives. In November 1831, Mackenzie used his newspaper, the *Colonial Advocate*, to characterize the Assembly as "a sycophantic office for registering the decrees of as mean and mercenary an Executive as ever was given as punishment for the sins of any part of North America in the nineteenth century."[28] In response, the Assembly voted to expel Mackenzie and call a by-election.

Mackenzie's abusive language alienated many of his more moderate supporters. Diarist Mary O'Brien of Thornhill, about ten miles north of York, wrote, "His unwarranted attack on the Govr will disgust many of his advocates – David Wilson's society are much disturbed thereat and enduring great storms on the subject of the propriety of supporting him."[29] Mackenzie previously gained the support of his constituents in the village of Hope by means of his work as a political reformer, opposing many of the same abuses that David Willson and the Children of Peace opposed. He published flattering accounts of the sect in his newspaper and, earlier in 1831, had defended it in print against the abusive comments made by Solicitor General Hagerman during the debate over the Marriage Bill.[30] However, David Willson began to have second thoughts about supporting Mackenzie. "A red hot radical is like a porcupine, throwing his quills at everything which is not like himself. A more tyrannical spirit is not in existence," Willson later declared.[31]

Some members of the Children of Peace rebuked their leader, causing Willson to write: "Where I have missed censure from one I have received from another, and in the eyes of my friends I am rightly fitted for nothing. I further add that it is my opinion that no saint from heaven could please you nor no man on earth, but God can do for you what I was never given to do, and as I stand I feel too weak to struggle against the oppositions any more."[32] These lines, in which Willson appeared ready to relinquish his leadership, were written less than three months after the triumphal first service in the temple. They suggest how divided the Children of Peace became over their involvement in political affairs. This alarmed the sect's elders and led them to write a reply to Willson's statement, expressing their frustration with trying to understand what Willson wanted them to do. They recognized Willson as the founder of their religious community, but found it difficult to further the work he began: "He laid the foundation, or was the first stone in our present congregation (which has grown to be considerable) and told us to build thereon, and there seems to be a snare for us in the very expression, for when we try to build and forward the fellowship of society we seem to be like putting the new wine in the old bottle, or new cloth in an old garment, do as we will the rent seems to be made the worse, he is silent when we are in action, but observing of our infirmity to act."

Later, the elders resigned themselves to trusting Willson's judgment and declared themselves willing "to serve him, as he hath served us, that he may advise us and our children with Godly care and the respect that a father should have for sons and daughters who is by them respected."[33] The metaphors the elders used, comparing their organization to a family with Willson as father, were appropriate to a community that placed strong emphasis on familial cooperation in everyday life. Willson seemed satisfied with the elders' reply, but warned on 3 January 1832, the day after the electors of the district triumphantly returned Mackenzie to his seat in the Assembly, "Cease to be active in gathering together the congregation or any part thereof without special necessity; do not oppose opposition, but stand firm on the pillars of the Church."[34] Two days later, Mackenzie came out with another vehement attack on the government and was expelled from the Assembly once more. Again, he was re-elected. When prevented from taking his seat, Mackenzie resumed his political tour of the colony and then set off for England to present his grievances there.[35]

In the midst of this continuing political turmoil, Willson saw another vision – a response, it would seem, to the rising tensions around him. Like his visions of 1812, 1813, and 1828, this came at a time of crisis. On 5 February 1832, Willson recorded seeing stars, representing the light of ancient prophets and kings, descending to the earth. He wrote that he gathered the stars together and placed them on an altar, where they created a small lighted space, a refuge in the darkness.[36] This vision brings to mind Willson's fascination with the beliefs and political organization of ancient Israel. Placing their light upon an altar suggests the practice of illuminating the temple and meeting house with candles on special occasions and, more specifically, recalls the temple altar with its five small lamps. As Willson urged his followers to remain aloof from political controversy, he looked inward to the image of a lighted altar shining in the darkness, a symbol of isolation from worldly affairs.

With Mackenzie out of the country, a period of relative tranquility followed. A cholera epidemic in York that summer may have helped reunite the Children of Peace, as they raised money for the support of destitute families and ministered to the sick. Meanwhile, it appeared as if Mackenzie's trip to England had met with some success: the Colonial Office ordered the dismissal of both Solicitor General Hagerman and Attorney General Boulton. The reformers' elation, however, was short-lived. With a change of administration in England, Hagerman was returned to his former position in Upper Canada, and Boulton was promoted to the office of chief justice of Newfoundland. Mackenzie then became increasingly radical, extending his angry campaign in the Colonial Advocate to include the prominent Upper Canadian Methodist, Egerton Ryerson, who had spoken out against some of his radical statements.[37] In the see-saw battle of the early 1830s, when the Upper Canadian reform movement seemed to gain ground and then was pushed back again, David Willson continued to try to keep his followers aloof from the extremes of political controversy. In a statement "To the Public" on 23 November 1833, he declared, "We will take our part in providing Just men to parliament, and influential men may turn aside from our gates ... we will receive no courting from electioneering parties ..."[38]

The political gathering the Children of Peace held in the capital in February 1834, with its banners, procession, and music, was a dramatic public display of unity, which offered no hint at the divided opinions growing within the sect. Scarcely a month earlier, another crisis had arisen over David Willson's leadership, which was serious enough to bring him to the point of resignation once again.[39] Despite the turmoil, 1834 was also the year that the second meeting house was begun. Perhaps Willson saw it, like the gathering in the capital, as a manifestation of unity – a project in which members of the sect could unite, much as they had in building the temple and the first meeting house. Yet some members saw the new meeting house as too large and unnecessary, so Willson accused them of exhibiting "a want of care about our precious buildings that the lord hath given."[40]

The following year, publication of Letters to the Jews and The Impressions of the Mind – along with two shorter works bound with the latter, The Acting Principles of Life and A Friend to Britain – helped clarify Willson's views on certain religious and political issues in response to his followers' complaints that they often had difficulty understanding his teaching. On 31 October 1835, Willson declared, "I have drawn out the acting principles of life – and placed them in the store house, with the merchandize of the land; the goods are taken and the product of my spirit lies still in slumbering Ease."[41] Evidently, once these major works were published, they were not widely read. Willson lamented, "I am but a stumbling block in the way of wealth and mirth."[42]

The years 1836 and 1837 brought increased political tensions to the colony of Upper Canada, leading ultimately to rebellion and deeper division within the Children of Peace. Early in 1836, the haughty Sir Francis Bond Head arrived in the colony as lieutenant-governor. Almost immediately, Head incurred the anger of all but the most conservative members of the Assembly by his staunch opposition to the principles of responsible government. In the spring of 1836, the news broke that Head's predecessor, Sir John Colborne, had endowed forty-four Anglican rectories with twenty thousand acres of the colony's land.[43] Church historian H.H. Walsh has written that the news about the rectories "may well have been the chief factor in precipitating the rebellion of 1837."[44] Certainly, it helped to galvanize public opinion against the government. The endowment of the rectories confirmed Willson's belief that religious and political corruption went hand in hand. Willson wrote, "We must attach our numerous disappointments to the Church of England, seeing they possess exclusive privileges and power in government that no other Church is possessed of."[45] In July 1837, Willson charged that "the principle magistrate, the king, is subject to a certain sect of religious priests – and bishops – he receives his crown and consequently his Kingdom conditionally and is not possessed of that freedom and liberty of sentiment and expression with which every impartial monarch or magistrate ought to be endued."[46] Willson saw temporal and religious matters as inexorably intertwined. Recent events in the colony seemed to confirm his view.

This debate over political and religious concerns came at a time of general economic depression. In 1836, poor harvests of wheat and potatoes hurt farmers, particularly those newly established. At the same time, merchants and tradesmen were demanding payment from their creditors as credit tightened internationally following a long period of economic growth in North America and Britain.[47] The Children of Peace were insulated from many vagaries of the Upper Canadian economy by their charity fund and their cooperative approach to farming; nonetheless, younger and recently established members must have felt apprehensive.

In the election of 1836, Head skilfully silenced all serious opposition within the Assembly by taking part in order to ensure the defeat of most reform candidates. Head appealed to the loyalties of many British-born immigrants, who had flooded into the colony during the early 1830s. Between 1830 and 1833, Upper Canada's population had increased by nearly fifty per cent, continuing to rise substantially thereafter. Most new immigrants were from the British Isles, not the United States, which had been Upper Canada's earlier major source of population. Among those who came to the colony were large numbers of Irish Protestant Orangemen, who responded to Head's plea that a vote for his supporters was a vote for Britain and a vote against republicanism.[48] Recalling the tumultuous elections of that period, Quaker Joseph Gould wrote, "The Orangemen had long been a terror to the peaceably disposed at elections, and, armed with bludgeons, and sometimes with fire-arms, used to take possession of the polls, and they subjected those who differed from them in opinion to all kinds of ill-treatment."[49]

The situation worsened in the summer of 1837, when word arrived of the passage of Lord John Russell's Ten Resolutions by the British parliament. These resolutions were directed at Lower Canada, where agitation for reform by politicians of French-Canadian background was particularly intense; nevertheless, they caused many in Upper Canada to give up any hope that the principles of British constitutional government would ever be extended to the colonies. The resolutions allowed the governor to take funds from the colonial treasury without the Assembly's approval, thus stripping elected representatives of their power and prerogatives. David Willson's frustration with this turn of events shone through every word of his response: "When the Constitution of Britain becomes no more a law for administration – Our thoughts are lost from the means of Improvement – That Constitution that is one thing today and another tomorrow, it is beyond comprehension what will be administered to us next day – and how to enter any mode of meeting the coming Exigencies is beyond the comprehension of our present thought. Therefore as reformers we are Inclined to preserve chast[e] our home Institution, and reserve our independence for the coming day."[50] Willson withdrew from the public arena in the hope that things might improve in the future. A week later, on 7 August 1837, he wrote: "The present administration has brought my mind into a puzzel of what our Constitution is. And when I come to solve the Queree, according to my capacity, It is the variable will of the ministers of the Crown. A Strange Alegiance I have sworn – IE – to be agreeable to the variable dispositions of the human mind. I find I am in fetters by the Cords of my own hands."[51] In this powerful statement of anger and frustration, Willson acknowledged his inability to act and his profound disillusionment with the faith he once had in the British Constitution.

William Lyon Mackenzie, in contrast, offered a radical course of action. On the symbolic fourth of July 1837, Mackenzie started a new newspaper, *The Constitution*, and shortly thereafter began to reprint Tom Paine's *Common Sense*, which had helped spark the move toward American independence in 1776. At the end of July, Mackenzie and his followers in Toronto drew up a declaration closely following the American Declaration of Independence and set up a Committee of Vigilance modelled after those organized by American patriots some sixty years earlier. Mackenzie organized his lieutenants north of the capital: Pennsylvania-born Jesse Lloyd and Samuel Lount, and New Hampshire-born Silas Fletcher.[52]

On 27 November 1837, Samuel Lount rode into Hope and assembled a meeting of twenty-two young men at the Orphan House. Lount has been described as "probably the most popular reformer north of Toronto and a man whose generosity to new settlers and to the Indians of the region was remembered long after he was dead."[53] According to a statement by Charles Doan, Lount told them that there was war in Lower Canada and that martial law would be proclaimed in Upper Canada unless they joined him and others who planned to march down Yonge Street and take over the capital. Lount assured them that they would be joined by hundreds of others from the adjoining townships and, more importantly, by Receiver General Peter Robinson and Solicitor General John Beverley Robinson. He stressed that the city would be taken without firing a gun, but advised them to take guns with them nonetheless. Lount's words echoed those of Mackenzie, speaking at a meeting of reformers in Stoverville (now Stouffville) shortly before.[54] On Sunday 3 December, Lount returned. Knocking on the doors of villagers he thought would support him, Lount instructed them to be ready to leave at nine o'clock the next morning and to put their arms in the wagon of John D. Willson, one of David Willson's sons.

Twelve or thirteen of the original twenty-two young men decided to make the journey and arrived that evening at Montgomery's Tavern, located on a hill north of the capital. There they found a smaller number of people than they expected, and there was no sign of the Robinsons. Instead, they saw mortally wounded Colonel Robert Moodie, a government supporter who had tried to ride past the rebels in order to give warning of their plans. If this was not enough to convince the men of East Gwillimbury that all would not be as easy and bloodless as Samuel Lount had claimed, the actions of William Lyon Mackenzie himself must have confirmed their suspicions. On Tuesday 5 December, they protested in vain as Mackenzie and some of his supporters set fire to the home of Dr Thorne, a government sympathizer. According to Doan, Mackenzie tried to calm their fears, claiming that Sir Francis Bond Head had left the capital and wished Mackenzie and his followers to take over. Doan reported:

Some were willing but mostly all objected, some did come down after dark and the rest went up to Montgomery's. Shortly afterwards those who went down came running back and stated that they had been fired upon by a picket guard and they would not go on at the risk of their lives. Mackenzie called them cowards and asked them to shoot him through the heart. They all went to Montgomery's and stayed that night. During the day on Wednesday, David Willson came down and took his son John David Willson. On Thursday morning we remained until the militia came up. Mackenzie's people went over into the bush to the west of the road and when the cannon began to fire, my brother and myself went off home.[55]

This account was given by a man brought to trial for his involvement in the rebellion, who would have wanted to put his support of the rebellion in the best possible light. It suggests that many of those who took up arms late in 1837 may not have understood the consequences of their actions or the reasons for their march down Yonge Street in the first place.

Some of the people of Hope, perhaps less naïve than Charles Doan, gave their full support to Mackenzie's radical plans. James Henderson and James Kavanaugh both were shot dead on Yonge Street. Richard and Jeremiah Graham were indicted for high treason and fled to the United States. Alexander McLeod, son of prominent sect member Murdoch McLeod, was exiled to Van Dieman's Land (Tasmania) and died shortly after arriving there.[56] Brothers Charles and Jesse Doan and John and Hugh Willson, David's sons, and other Children of Peace who were less seriously involved were imprisoned for nearly five months.[57] Some of those in authority believed that the Children of Peace had been a veritable nest of rebels and, according to one account, it was with difficulty that the militia was prevented from destroying their temple.[58] J.H.S. Drinkwater reported leading the 5th Battalion Company of the 1st Regiment Simcoe militia into Hope on December 10 and taking possession of the village "without the slightest opposition on the part of the Inhabitants."[59] Perhaps their opposition was more subtle. Another contemporary wrote, "When their guns were demanded from the prisoners and their houses searched, about David Willson's village & elsewhere after the first disturbance, they invariably said they had lost them or thrown them away ..."[60]

In their cells, Charles and Jesse Doan and some of the other prison-

Figure 18   Box made in prison by Charles Doan, maple, 2.5" × 3.5" × 2", 1838. (Aurora Museum acc.no. 989.25.1)

ers whiled away the hours by carving little boxes made of wood. Charles and Jesse's father, John Doan, had been the builder of the altar in the temple. He was a highly skilled cabinet-maker who must have passed some of his knowledge to his sons. One box (Fig. 18) constructed by Charles Doan is made of maple and has a sliding top.[61] It resembles a blanket chest supported on four ogee bracket feet, rather tall in proportion to the box's overall dimensions, but not unlike those supporting the desk (Fig. 12) that his father had made. The hollow box and its supporting feet were carved together out of one piece of maple, showing great skill and patience. On the top is an inscription, "Elizabeth Doan/Hope," written within a scrolled border. On one side are the words, "Elizabeth Doan from her son Charles in prison, April 13th 1838." On the other side is a poem:

> Dear mother this I for thee make
> A Token keep it for my sake
> If in yon eastern world I roam
> And parted from my wife and home.

"Yon eastern world" may have meant Van Dieman's Land where some of the rebels were later exiled, or perhaps it evoked the wilderness through which the ancient Israelites had wandered.

Another box,[62] also made from a block of maple, is inscribed, "Charles Doan arrested Dec 10th 1837 committed to prison Toronto where I now remain." On the top is a sketch of a house in a wooded setting, signed "JGP" in the bottom left corner. "JGP" was likely John G. Parker, who was imprisoned for his part in the rebellion and may have shared a cell with the Doan brothers. Parker was later exiled to Van Dieman's Land.[63] In the bottom right corner are the initials "WGE," for William Graham Edmonstone, who was also imprisoned at the same time as the Doans.[64] Perhaps Parker and Edmonstone collaborated on the sketch, while Doan carved the box. Edmonstone, a teacher and printer,[65] may have been responsible for the decorative script above and below the sketch. Framing the sketch on the second Doan box are the words, "Memento of David Willson Doan/who died Aug 18, 1837, aged 16 mo. 10 days." On two sides is the following verse:

In this dear mother lay my toys,
The props that closed my eyes;
These little gifts were e're my joys,
Now in my grave I lie.
My tombstone standing by my grave,
My friends may on it see,
And read the sorrows of my days,
Prepare and come to me.
Dear parents, it's a mournfull day;
In tears your eyes are seen;
Haste not to put your grief away,
May it you blessings bring.
My innocence, dear father, learn,
And press it on thy mind,
From worldly cares and anger turn
That thou may mercy find.

David Willson Doan was Charles Doan's infant son. The verse suggests that this little box was intended to hold some small trinkets, or possibly a lock of hair, associated with the dead child. Its small size, less than three by four inches, means that its use was more symbolic than practical. The box and its verse were a *memento mori*, reminding people of their own mortality and warning them to prepare for their own deaths. The box and verse also perpetuated grief, in the hope that grief might be of benefit to the child's parents by reminding them of the fragility and value of innocence, thereby distracting their minds from worldly care and anger.

This artifact with its few lines of poetry embodies much of the nineteenth century's view of death and dying, sentimental to be sure, but rooted in the belief that grieving over the dead, particularly children, was an important, even uplifting, experience for the living.[66] At a time of high infant mortality rates, this may have filled an essential psychological need and helped make sense out of the seemingly random pattern of disease and infection that claimed so many young lives. As a member of the Children of Peace, Charles Doan was particularly apt to link ideas with objects, worshipping as he did in buildings that were filled with religious meaning and symbolism. The box itself, like the words on it, was a mnemonic device, a reminder of his infant son's death. A tangible reminder was important since Doan's next son, born while Charles was in prison, was given the dead infant's name, David Willson Doan. Mary Willson Doan, Charles's wife, wrote to her husband in prison, "I am well at present and so is the little child. I think its name will be David W D ... I think he will get a box."[67] By his very name, this son was intended to take the dead child's place on earth. Doan may have made the box as a three-dimensional metaphor for his first son's brief life – an object he and others could hold in their hands, keeping alive the memory of their dead child even as they watched over the growth of the new infant who bore his name.

Making this box while in prison linked Doan's personal sorrows with sorrows outside the prison walls. Just as the verse on the box suggested that tears and grief over the death of a child could prove to be beneficial to the living, Doan must have hoped that the sorrow caused by his imprisonment could also serve some good purpose, either for himself or his family. The words he used to describe his own plight, "Charles Doan arrested Dec 10th 1837, committed to prison Toronto where I now remain," were terse in comparison with the florid imagery of the verse about his dead son. Their directness and simplicity gave them power. They also contrasted with the thoughts evoked by the romantic scene sketched on the box's lid: the words telling of grief and confinement, the picture suggesting the sheltered domestic environment that Doan once knew.

Boxes were made in prison by other young men from Hope as well. Elizabeth Graham wrote to her husband, John, saying, "We have all received a box from you but her [John's sister, Jane] and Richard's wife, if you make any more, your mother wishes you to send each of them one."⁶⁹ A box made by Charles Doan's brother, Jesse, was more obviously political in its message.⁶⁸ It is decorated with two inlaid stars, inscribed "U.C." and "L.C." for Upper Canada and Lower Canada, probably alluding to the stars on an American flag and linking the rebels' actions, as Mackenzie did, to those of American revolutionaries. Inlaid lozenges bear the words, "Liberty," "Justice," and "Hope," and the French and Latin mottoes, "*Dieu et la liberté*," "*le bon temps veindre*," "*libertas et natale solum*," and "*Ne cede malis*." These words, recalling the rhetoric of the American and French revolutions, could well have come from newspapers and pamphlets printed by William Lyon Mackenzie, widely circulated during the years before the rebellion broke out.

The rebellious action taken by the Doan brothers, David Willson's two sons, and other young members of the Children of Peace went against Willson's advice to "preserve chast[e] our home Institution" and avoid political controversy. Yet Willson, in a sense, had prepared his followers for that moment for many years. Time and time again he had spoken out against the political and religious establishment in Upper Canada. He had led, or at least approved, his followers' participation in military drill: even the young women of the sect had been trained in the use of firearms. When Willson was questioned about these practices by a member of an American peace society, he had replied that he wished to maintain peace with other religious groups, but did not disapprove of his followers' taking up arms to defend themselves or to take part in just national wars.⁷⁰ Willson's immediate reaction to the events of the rebellion was sorrow, both for the men in prison and for their families back home. In a poem sent to the prisoners in January 1838, Willson wrote:

> Dear Children of our love and care,
> Our evening thoughts, our morning prayer,
> In your deep grief we freely join,
> It is the change and turn of time.
> We see your offspring circling round
> No fathers smiles on them abound.
> Tears flowing from their mothers eyes
> Are mingled with their mournful cries ...⁷¹

Willson's other thoughts can only be imagined: following a "Song for the altar," written on 20 November 1837, pages from the record book were carefully cut out.⁷² The weeks immediately after the rebellion were, evidently, times that members of the Children of Peace wanted to forget. In another manuscript volume, hymns and sermons written during the summer of 1838 conveyed such themes as "Mourn for the altar of the Lord" and "The Lord's chastising hand."[73] In 1838, the Children of Peace were trying not only to recover from the disaster of the rebellion, but also to deal with the resignation of one of their most prominent members, Samuel Hughes, who left to join the Hicksite Quakers. As the year came to a close, David Willson penned a memorial, dated December 27, in which he described his own history: his rejection by the Quakers, his call to lead a new people, and now, it seemed, his rejection by those whom he led. In his "New Years gift to the Church for the year 1839," Willson wrote, "The sons rise above me – And daughters despise."[74] Several years later, still angry over his followers' involvement in the rebellion, Willson complained, "I ... was your Parent until the Rebellion when fools (I boldly say) took you out of my hands from comfortable homes, and cast you into prisons there to pray to your enemies for mercy, and your Parents to weep over you with tears."[75]

In the meantime, change was afoot in the broader political affairs of the colony. Early in 1838, the British government appointed Lord Durham, a strong supporter of the Reform Bill of 1832, to investigate matters in Upper and Lower Canada. Durham's report, first published in Upper Canada in April 1839, angered French-speaking people in Lower Canada by insisting that they must be assimilated through political union with Upper Canada. Within the union, they would eventually find themselves in a minority position, outnumbered by settlers of British and American background. Durham delighted Upper Canadian reformers, however, by advising that self-government and substantial reform should be introduced within this new union.[76] Some organized Durham Meetings to show their support; but far from being orderly political rallies, these meetings sometimes led to brawls scarcely less fierce than the violence brought on by the rebellion itself. The Children of Peace again found themselves caught up in the turmoil: a young member, David Lepard, was killed at a Durham Meeting on Yonge Street in October 1839. In a poem written in Lepard's memory and published as a broadside, Willson assumed the voice of the dead boy and wrote:

This morn I left my peaceful home,
And my dear mother's tender care,
To meet a fate, to me unknown,
Be bruis'd, and bleed and languish there.

My father, and my brothers, kind,
In peace with you I walk'd abroad

On Sabbath days, together join'd,
And went unto the house of God.

But oh! the beating storm arose,
And blood like rain that's in the skies,
Descended from our lawless foes,
They unsuspected did arise.

Vain prospects then betrayed our feet,
We hasten'd to the unknown cause,
Led on that day, my foes to meet,
For liberty, and British laws!

Dear brothers of a tender mind,
Be careful while your years are young;
That you may peace and safety find,
Shun the deception of the tongue!

There were sweet counsels in our way,
Bright cautions from our altar came
But strong delusions led this day
To death, to misery, and to pain.

See, David's with the flock no more,
Nor feeding at our plenteous board;
Remind the dying pains he bore,
He's gone, to never be restor'd.[77]

In this poem, Lepard acknowledges his mistakes in leaving the peace of his community and disobeying Willson's advice. In the final verse, he laments not only his own demise, but that of his leader as well.

Willson continued to lament the sorry state of political affairs in the colony and the division it had brought to the Children of Peace. In 1840, this division was emphasized by the defection of yet another important member, Ebenezer Doan, whose departure must have come as a major blow to David Willson. On a bright day in September, however, an event drew Willson back into the political arena and helped heal some of the wounds his community had suffered. None other than the governor general himself, Charles Poulett Thomson (later Lord Sydenham) made a visit to the village of Hope. Riding slowly into the village on horseback, he was accompanied by the music of the village band. Thomson had been sent to the Canadas to put in place some of the recommendations of Lord Durham's report. Willson addressed him, declaring, "In the fulfillment of the great trust the Queen has reposed in your care, you have our sincere prayers and warmest desires for your success in the accomplishment of every good design, and [we] remain the faithful subjects of our Queen and Country." Skilled diplomat that he was, and knowing that his orders from Britain did not include the granting of responsible government, Thomson replied, "I assure you that my best endeavours will be exerted to introduce and recommend whatever I think of advantage to the country ..." He was then given a tour of the temple. On his departure, "the company gave 3 cheers for the Governor General, then 3 for the Queen; the Tories did not join the salute, but stood still like signposts."[78] Addressing Thomson in a letter printed in a Toronto newspaper in April 1841, Willson declared, "At your word we put our hands to the cause we had silently forsaken."[79]

Politically, the 1840s proved to be a more tranquil time for the Children of Peace than the 1830s had been. During that decade, Robert Baldwin became active in the political affairs of the Fourth Riding of York, which included East Gwillimbury Township. Baldwin was a moderate man, less prone to outbursts of passion and anger than William Lyon Mackenzie had been. He was a man with whom David Willson felt comfortable. Willson's correspondence with Baldwin indicates that the leader of the Children of Peace was willing to rejoin the political fray and was less concerned about keeping his followers isolated from party politics.

In the first election following the union of Upper and Lower Canada in the spring of 1841, Baldwin carried both the Fourth Riding of York and the riding of Hastings. He chose to represent Hastings and decided to make a bold gesture by recommending that Louis-Hippolyte Lafontaine represent the reform party in the subsequent by-election in the Fourth Riding of York. He and other reformers in Upper Canada, by then officially known as Canada West, decided that they could best influence the course of political affairs by supporting their reform colleagues from Lower Canada, newly named Canada East, in the united legislature that had been established that year.[80] Baldwin wrote to Willson to ask what he felt Lafontaine's chances might be of winning an election in the English-speaking Fourth Riding. Willson's reply indicated how active he had become in party politics and political manoeuvres: as a member of a reformers' committee, he suggested the name of a possible returning officer known to be a Baldwin supporter and recommended that the poll be held in the newly named village of Sharon, where it would result in "more honour than at New Market – as the musicians will not attend that place."[81] The musicians appear to have helped on other occasions as well. In March 1844, the Toronto Reform Association offered to donate a new instrument for David Willson's son, Hugh.[82]

In 1844, Baldwin contested the Fourth Riding once again and wrote to his friend to ask his opinion of party strength. Willson's reply suggested the close, comfortable association the two men had come to enjoy: "I would almost say come up as soon as you can and continue in the Riding, doing what may seem best – if a visit to some of the back Townships may be thought proper I will use my endeavours to promote them. You know the humble fare of my dwelling – if agreeable, return and be assured you are welcome."[83] By that time, Willson did not hesitate to combine party politics and religion. During the same campaign, Willson wrote to Baldwin and mentioned that he had announced the politician's upcoming visit to Sharon at the end of a service in the meeting house.[84]

At a political rally held in Sharon in the spring of 1844, Willson served as master of ceremonies, introducing a long list of important speakers, who expounded on the virtues of British government and on their efforts to introduce the principle of executive responsibility to the legislature of the united Canadas. The speakers included Captain Jacob Irving, a member of the Legislative Council; Robert Baldwin Sullivan, who had served as president of the Council during Lord Sydenham's tenure; and James Small, solicitor general for Canada West. Then came a climactic speech by Robert Baldwin himself; its effect is described in a poem Willson wrote for a broadside printed after the event:

Then ROBERT BALDWIN plac'd the seal
  On all that pass'd before,
A grateful heart did Sharon feel,
  Unnumber'd hundreds more.

For voters are the Royal stay,
  The bearers of the Crown,
Now cheerfully we bless this day
  That put dark errors down.[85]

Willson continued to actively support the reform movement throughout the 1840s, following Baldwin's career closely and permitting the reformers to hold meetings in the village school.

However, internal divisions continued to nag the Children of Peace. Records of meetings held in May 1845 indicate that these divisions did not come from differences over politics, but from the "generation gap" that was apparent between the founders of the sect and its younger members. Resentment may have arisen due to Willson's attempts the summer before to promote stricter discipline of younger members. Parents were instructed to enforce stricter sabbath observance and to admonish their sons and daughters to avoid riding for pleasure, visiting taverns, swearing, and visiting unnecessarily from house to house.[86] A meeting on 5 May 1845 challenged Willson's authority. A second meeting, on 31 May 1845, decided that younger members should meet to draw up recommendations to be put before meetings of the older members.[87] That same meeting also decided to make changes in the operation of the Charity Fund, making it more like a modern-day "credit union" from which members could borrow more easily.[88] Perhaps these signs of division between old and young were indications that the cooperative system of village life was breaking down. In 1845, David Willson was sixty-seven years old; his own sons and those of his contemporaries were well into their thirties or early forties. As their participation in the Rebellion of 1837 suggested, they may have become restless under their elders' supervision and anxious to assume more independent roles of their own.

During the next four years, many of Willson's writings were jeremiads – lists of woes – on the decline of his community and challenges to his leadership. In 1848, he wrote to his followers:

You've bruised my heart and burst my mind
But I to you the truth declare
That you shall yet salvation find
If your inclined to hear my prayer.[89]

Two years later, he wrote, "I fear to speak lest I err and write lest it should be without direction."[90] Near the end of that year, he prayed, "Lord thou hast forsaken us, we have sinned before thee, we have gone after strange gods that are in the land. We have bowed down to images that hath done nothing for us ..."[91]

The late 1840s marked an end to a tumultuous chapter in the political history of Canada and, with it, an end to the once intense involvement of the Children of Peace in the reform movement. In 1849, members of the elected assembly of Canada East and West passed the Rebellion Losses Bill, compensating those who lost property during the Rebellion of 1837. Governor General Lord Elgin signed this bill into law despite his own personal opposition. In this way, the principle of responsible government was achieved, not as the direct result of an armed uprising, but with the stroke of a pen, signifying Britain's new relationship with her North American colonies. That relationship came about more as a result of changing economic conditions in the

1840s than because of political agitation. When Britain revoked the age-old Corn Laws in 1846, doing away with many of the advantages that colonial suppliers of grain had once enjoyed in the British market, Parliament decided to give the colonies responsible government instead. Once responsible government was achieved, many old abuses were cut away. The clergy reserves, for example, were finally abolished in 1854.[92] With many of the old issues gone, there were fewer political causes to divide the Children of Peace; conversely, there were fewer causes to unite them as well.

9 The Last Years of the Children of Peace

The 1851 census described the Children of Peace at what was probably the height of their numerical strength, listing 298 members. Over the next ten years, that number decreased alarmingly to 168. In 1871, only thirty-four were listed, nearly all of them members of four closely related families.[1] What happened to reduce the sect's numbers so quickly? The Children of Peace had seen times of crisis before – the 1837 rebellion, for example – but they had managed to weather those difficulties. In the very different world of the third quarter of the nineteenth century, new forces were at work that would bring about the sect's demise and cause its buildings to fall into decay.

In 1851, David Willson was seventy-three, approaching old age, but still fully in charge of the sect's affairs. By all accounts, he continued to lead services of worship much as he had always done. A report in the *Newmarket Era* from 1857 stated that Willson "preaches still with much energy and force" and included an account of the June feast, which attracted more than five hundred people to the village that year.[2] In the 1850s, Willson continued to write sermons, poems, and hymns and published two autobiographical accounts, two books of hymns, at least one devotional tract, and dozens of broadsides printed to commemorate weddings, funerals, and other events.[3] He seems to have gradually withdrawn from political affairs, but continued to attend local meetings and wrote occasional letters to the *Era* on the subject of political reform.[4]

Sharon in the 1850s was not the isolated village it once had been. In 1853, the Ontario, Simcoe and Huron Union Railroad pushed its way north from Toronto through the village of Holland Landing, scarcely two miles to the west.[5] Thus, Sharon was at once connected to the wider world around it. Villagers could no longer consider themselves a largely autonomous community. News could travel faster than ever before, farm produce could be sent directly and quickly to city markets, and manufactured products could be obtained more easily from city stores and factories.

The Children of Peace came to be more closely linked with neighbouring villages through participation in new forms of municipal government, the boundaries of which far surpassed those of the community they had once hoped to establish along cooperative lines. Members of the sect took important roles in the secular affairs of East Gwillimbury Township, serving alongside elected officials from communities that had no religious affiliation with them. The Baldwin Act of 1849 had established a system of local government whereby citizens could elect members to serve on township councils.[6] Candidates such as Jesse Doan, who led the Sharon band for thirty years, were nominated and elected.[7] Hugh D. Willson, one of David Willson's sons, became particularly active in political affairs, chairing meetings of the East Gwillimbury Council and serving as township clerk.[8] Meetings of the township council were held for a time in the old 1819 meeting house.[9] Hugh Willson also became involved in secular affairs in his role as a custom house officer, an appointment he held for twenty years,[10] which was probably received as a political favour in return for his family's strong support of the prominent reform politician, Robert Baldwin. Involvement such as this – Children of Peace serving in municipal government, hosting meetings of the township council, and accepting patronage appointments – meant that the sect could no longer see itself as set apart from the world. They could no longer hope to establish the distinctive, cooperative community they had envisioned in the early 1830s. Involvement in municipal politics inevitably meant compromise and accommodation as members of the sect, who were but a small minority within the township's population, worked closely with other elected representatives who did not share their vision of a new church and a new society.

In education, the Children of Peace also gave up much of their autonomy during this period of change and reform in provincial affairs. In 1850, the colonial government established a comprehensive system of public schooling, placing the operation of schools in the hands of elected trustees[11] and effectively ending the need for religious groups to provide for the secular education of their children. In Sharon, the first trustees under this new system were Charles Haines, Reuben Lundy, and Willson Reid, all closely linked to the Children of Peace.[12]

As time passed, however, non-members were elected, distancing the sect from its former role in schooling. In 1859, classes that had been held at the 1819 meeting house were transferred to a new schoolhouse built with public funds at the south end of the village,[13] far removed from the shadow of the temple that stood at the heart of the community. Members of the Children of Peace did not suddenly abandon their interest in education any more than they did their involvement in politics. David Willson's son, John, who had taught at the earlier Sharon school, expanded his involvement by serving as a government examiner of schoolteachers, while continuing his role as clerk for the Children of Peace.[14] Such participation in the secular affairs of the broader community must inevitably have led the Willson brothers to bow to the ways of the world around them.

Politics and education were not the only interests that drew members of the Children of Peace away from the affairs of their sect. In the 1840s, the temperance movement swept through town and country, proclaiming the evils of drink and promising moral and social reform. It arose in response to a real problem: it has been estimated that Upper Canadians, like most North Americans, consumed roughly five times more alcohol than they do today. Addiction was a fact of life in many communities, leading to violence and upheaval.[15] Even as early as 1807, a committee had been formed by the Yonge Street Monthly Meeting of Friends to look into the problem of excess distilling and consumption of liquor by its members.[16] In the 1830s, records from Charles Doan's store indicate that large quantities of spirits were purchased at low prices and consumed by members of the Children of Peace.[17] David Willson's warnings against the habits of younger members who frequented taverns, and the creation in the 1830s of a committee to look into the operation of local places of public entertainment, indicate that drinking became a major concern of the community's leaders at an early date.[18] In the 1850s, there was fear in Sharon that liquor was destroying the once convivial atmosphere of feast days. A letter to the *Newmarket Era* in October 1856, signed by David Willson and ten prominent Children of Peace, railed against the "immoral and disgraceful practices" that disrupted their feasts when neighbouring taverns sold liquor without restriction to the many people who came to the village. Willson declared, "Strong drink moves the tongue – the tongue, the fist, till liquor and blood is mingled together in one cup, and given to spectators to behold."[19]

The temperance movement grew in response to such conditions. As social historians have argued, however, the movement may also have had its roots in other concerns of the day. The goal of its largely middle-class, Protestant supporters was not only to curb the abuse of alcohol, but to assert their own authority over an unruly working class, composed increasingly of people of non-Protestant background. Furthermore, the movement spent too much time and energy addressing the symptoms of social problems without attacking their cause. Excessive drinking was often a response to conditions of poverty, illness, isolation, inequality, and lack of opportunity – conditions that were more difficult to confront and solve.[20]

In Sharon, a division of the Sons of Temperance was organized in 1850 or 1851. The group built its own hall, originally at the north end of the village, but later moved to a site adjacent to the temple grounds.[21] The group may have formed out of concern that excessive consumption of liquor was threatening the peace and stability of the neighbourhood. Or, like many similar organizations, it may have grown out of a more general malaise and a feeling that old patterns of authority and social control were threatened by the disobedient ways of a new generation. No membership lists or other records have survived that might shed light on this question. It is significant, however, that such an organization took hold in Sharon at all. Previously, the Children of Peace had dealt with concerns about drinking within the context of their own meetings. By the 1850s, however, a separate organization outside their control arose as an alternative focal point. The Sons of Temperance also provided its own ritual and its own approach to mutual assistance in competition with those of the sect itself.

Another secular organization in competition with the traditional ways of the Children of Peace was the Masonic Lodge, organized in Sharon in 1858.[22] Like the Children of Peace, the Masons claimed links with ancient times and perpetuated those links in a rich material culture that included ceremonial clothing, banners, ritual signs and gestures, and elaborately decorated meeting halls that, like the Sharon temple, focused on a piece of furniture called an ark. The Masons, like the Children of Peace, often provided financial assistance to members who were in need.[23] Unlike the Children of Peace, however, the Masonic Lodge was part of a powerful, international movement whose members included some of the most prominent figures in the political and economic affairs of their day. In other words, it was part of the mainstream of life in the rapidly changing North America of the 1850s, whereas the Children of Peace remained a small, unique group outnumbered even in its own township. A group such as the Masons could command the allegiance of those who valued ritual, tradition, and the sense of brotherhood that arose from mutual assistance, but who also wanted to identify with the rising trends of entrepreneurship, economic growth, and urban expansion evident in the world around them.

Not only did the Children of Peace face competition in the secular world of the 1850s, they also witnessed the arrival of two other religious denominations in Sharon. The Methodists, who had been active in the area much earlier through their saddle-bag preachers and camp meetings, and whose hymnody, sermons, and love feasts inspired the Children of Peace during their earliest days, established their own meeting place just north of the village in the early 1850s. The congregation built its own chapel, described in the 1861 census as large enough to hold three hundred people. In 1867, the Methodists erected a new building in the centre of the village, boldly situated across Queen Street from the second meeting house. It was designed by John Stokes, who had once been a member of the Children of Peace.[24] By 1861, Stokes had become an Anglican. He and his family were prominent members of an Anglican congregation that was officially established in Sharon in 1866. Their church was built in 1869, south of the lands used by the Children of Peace.[25] Thus, by the 1860s, the Children of Peace faced competition not only from the Methodists, but from the once-despised Anglicans as well.

On 19 January 1866, David Willson died at the advanced age of eighty-seven years, seven months, and twelve days. His wife, Phebe, had died only five days before.[26] Willson's mantle of leadership fell on the shoulders of his oldest son, John, who was then in his seventieth year. John Willson conducted services for the next twenty years, reading his father's sermons and attempting to preserve as much of the old ways as possible,[27] despite declining numbers and an aging membership. While some Children of Peace continued faithfully in attendance at the meeting house and temple, sang in the choir or played in the band, others began attending services elsewhere. Some, such as Amos Hughes, whose diary provides one of the few first-hand accounts of the last years of the Children of Peace, continued their involvement with the sect while attending services with other denominations as well. Hughes recorded visits to Quaker meetings as well as to Presbyterian, Methodist, Anglican, Christian (Disciples of Christ), and Salvation Army services. He also wrote of meetings at the Temperance Hall and excursions of the choir and band to perform at gatherings throughout the neighbourhood.[28]

As a leading member of the Children of Peace, Hughes was given the task of investigating the advisability of incorporation in 1876. The Children of Peace opted for incorporation as The Children of Peace Charitable Society in order to administer their charity fund in the increasingly complicated financial world of the late-nineteenth century. Contained within their incorporation papers was a statement that shows they were growing closer to the mainstream of late-nineteenth-century Protestantism in doctrine as well as organization. They stated that "no confession of faith shall be required for admission into the Society, except a full belief in the Bible as the revealed Word of God, and Salvation through his Son, Jesus Christ."[29] Despite its assertion that "no confession of faith shall be required," this declaration broke with tradition. It ignored the teachings of David Willson and his early followers and their emphasis on the importance of the Inner Light. This statement brought the Children of Peace into line with the beliefs of orthodox Protestantism and reflected the influence that other denominations had on prominent members of the sect.

On occasions when John Willson was unable to conduct services, Amos Hughes took his place; however by the end of 1878, there were times when no one preached at all. This may have led some of the remaining members to grow restless and invite ministers from other denominations to speak to them.[30] The *Newmarket Era* reported on 18 June 1880: "Some of the younger members of the society have recently shown a disposition to depart from its teachings and have invited Rev. Mr. Frizzell, Presbyterian minister at Newmarket, to preach to them, which he does every Sunday; but the old members still adhere to their faith and seem happy and contented in their selection."[31] From this it would appear that division was growing among the Children of Peace between those who wished to follow the old ways and those who wished to hear preachers such as the Reverend Mr Frizzell. This division may not only have been between old and young, however, as the *Era's* correspondent suggested. William Willson, for instance, a cousin of David Willson and a senior member of the Sharon community, was among those who left to join the Presbyterian church.[32]

Amos Hughes was also attracted to the Presbyterians. In the spring of 1881, he contacted a lawyer to determine if it would be possible to form a Presbyterian congregation in Sharon and endow it with the lands and buildings then used by the Children of Peace. Evidently, a power struggle was starting to grow. On 17 May 1881, Hughes recorded that John Willson had taken possession of the meeting house. Willson and his brother, Hugh, claimed that they and their heirs, and not the trustees of the Children of Peace Charitable Society, had legal control over the lands and buildings and how they would be used. Their dispute ultimately went to Chancery Court in Toronto and was resolved in the Willsons' favour in April 1882. An account of the affair published in the Toronto *Globe* declared: "The suit really arises from a squabble between the Wilsons [sic] and the trustees, the former insisting on following the ways of old David, and continuing to read and sing from the Books of Sermons and Hymns composed by him, while the latter wishing to become more orthodox in their worship have invited different ministers, Presbyterian and others, to preach in their temple and meeting-house, and have, according to the Wilsons, become lax in the faith."[33] The Willsons' case was supported by the wording of David Willson's will, which had been written in 1858. That will gave two lots from his original 200-acre farm "whereupon the two Houses for worship are now erected, together with the Houses thereon" to the "Trustees of the alms society in Sharon ... to hold to them in trust for the worship of God."[34] The magistrate hearing the case interpreted this to mean that the trustees had only the use of the lands and buildings, while Willson's descendants retained ownership. Before this decision was handed down, the trustees and heirs arranged a temporary truce, allowing the fall feast and illumination to go ahead in September 1881. Following the court's ruling, however, Amos Hughes and others left the Children of Peace, diminishing the sect's numbers still further.[35]

John Willson continued to lead services following the patterns established by his father until the summer of 1886, when he became too ill and enfeebled to continue.[36] He was then in his ninetieth year. Thereafter, other members of the sect took charge of services, but the fall illumination and feast for 1886 were cancelled. After Willson's death on 14 March 1887, there was a brief attempt at reviving the fortunes of the Children of Peace. The fall illumination and feast were held again in 1887 and 1888, the choir and band continued their activities, and ministers from the Christian Church (Disciples of Christ) were invited to preach. In 1889, however, there was no illumination and no feast. On November 8, the *Newmarket Era* reported that "Elder Clarke of Brownhill, who has been conducting services in the Meeting House during the summer, has decided not to keep up the appointment here at present."

John Willson's heir, the owner of the property on which the temple and meeting house stood, was Absalom Willson (b. 1849), John's youngest son. Although his wife, Harriet Stokes, was an Anglican, Absalom became a follower of the Christian Church (the Disciples of Christ). After a meeting of the congregation, he determined to unite the Children of Peace with that denomination and transfer ownership of the meeting house and temple to the Ontario Christian Conference for the sum of one dollar. Those negotiations took place in the spring and summer of 1890 and were followed in early September by a highly successful illumination and feast. Elder Thomas Garbutt of the

Christian Church tried to build a new congregation in Sharon, but he was in poor health and competition from neighbouring Methodists and Anglicans was too strong. In July 1894, the Ontario Christian Conference relinquished ownership of the temple and meeting house and returned them to Absalom Willson.

Thereafter, the buildings were used only occasionally for meetings, garden parties, and services held by travelling evangelists. To help cover some of the costs of maintaining the temple, Absalom Willson charged a fee of twenty-five cents per person to the many visitors who still came to Sharon. In May 1912, Willson invited tenders for the dismantling of the 1842 meeting house, to be sold for the "75,000 feet of timber and lumber of the very best quality" that it contained. (The first meeting house had been sold for its lumber in May 1893.) Then in August 1912, Willson sold his land, including the temple, to Michael Ramsay. After 110 years, this land left the Willson family and was taken over by someone with no connection to the Children of Peace. Ramsay demolished the meeting house, but continued to allow public use of the temple. From 1915 to 1917, for instance, the Sharon band held concerts, garden parties, and illuminations there, while rumours spread through the community that the building might be purchased for a museum. Those rumours became a reality in the spring of 1918 when James L. Hughes, president of the York Pioneer and Historical Society, negotiated its purchase. Since that time, it has been open to the public as a museum.[37]

10 The Children of Peace and the World Around Them

The story of the Children of Peace began and ended in East Gwillimbury Township. It started amidst high expectations of a new church that would usher in an era of peace, but ended in courtroom challenges, declining membership, and extinction. The millennium did not come to East Gwillimbury. Yet the story of the Children of Peace extended beyond the bounds of a township. It was shaped by its broader environment – natural, social, religious, and political – as well as by the particular characteristics of its leaders. It drew deeply on the Quaker heritage of its members and on widespread religious concerns of its time. To observers more than a century later, parts of its story will seem curious and remote. Our more secular society may find the religious disputes of the nineteenth century difficult to comprehend. Yet even we do not have to look far to see the power of religious controversy: the fractious empires of televangelists are examples that quickly come to mind.

Understanding the Children of Peace begins with understanding the environment in which they lived. The physical setting that nurtured the growth of this sect was, in the beginning, a wilderness. A government-built road, Yonge Street, gave settlers access to this wilderness, but beyond its narrow bounds all was forest.[1] Trees needed to be cut before a settler could plant a crop, build a proper house, and start a farm. The land was free to those who came first and fulfilled certain duties to the satisfaction of the colonial government.[2] The real price of a farm, however, lay in months and years of hard and often dangerous work. Seeing the forest disappear year by year, as fields grew in size and houses were built, must have given a settler faith in the notions of progress, potential, and future abundance. Such circumstances also encouraged independence of spirit. Frederick Jackson Turner's "frontier thesis" made much of the experience a settler had in confronting the wilderness, claiming the traits of independence and self-reliance it induced as essential to the frontier character.[3] Some of Turner's conclusions hold true; however, the frontier experience may have equally engendered a need for cooperation and community, as settlers realized the complexity of their work and relied on family, neighbours, and hired hands to help them. "All help one; one help all" was a frontier-taught lesson just as important for survival as independent self-reliance.[4]

The wilderness, full of potential, was also a place of fear – "a howling wilderness," as some of the early Puritan settlers of New England called it.[5] It was a place that could cause feelings of apprehension and inadequacy. Such feelings were found in the writings of Upper Canadian author, Susanna Moodie, who told stories of failure as well as success. She wrote of the fear experienced by settlers isolated from human contact for weeks on end, shut into the confines of a tiny shelter during long periods of harshly cold weather.[6] This was the world where the first members of the Children of Peace lived. The natural environment of Upper Canada may have led them to thoughts of independence and progress, but it also impressed upon them the need for community and instilled a sense of awe at the task that lay ahead as they cleared their land and started their farms.

Into this wilderness environment came a group of people who were closely related by family ties as well as common religious beliefs. Many of them had been neighbours in the United States before moving north of the Oak Ridges in Upper Canada. They were an endogamous group, marrying others of the same religious background and geographic origins. They were also generally equal in wealth.[7] The sense of support and solidarity such close bonds of community must have given to these settlers, as they began the process of clearing land and making new homes for themselves, cannot be overestimated. Their social environment provided a sense of familiarity in unfamiliar, sometimes daunting circumstances. The fact that a significant number of settlers came from areas such as Lycoming County, Pennsylvania, which had been a largely uninhabited wilderness just a generation before, must have had important consequences too. These people had experienced first-hand the work of frontier settlers and could have advised and supported those who came from longer settled areas, such as the Delaware River valley. Thus, the challenges offered by their natural environment were tempered by their social environment, allowing the settlers on Yonge Street to quickly gain mastery over the land and establish important institutions, such as a formally constituted meeting for worship and a school to educate their children.[8]

Because of their common faith, the settlers' social and religious lives were closely connected. All these settlers were members of the Society of Friends, who believed that their God spoke directly to each one of them by means of the Inner Light. Their religion gave them a strong sense of individual worth and freedom. Being members of an interlocking network of meetings, however, they tempered their individuality with cooperation and interdependence and deferred to the authority of ministers, elders, and overseers who were believed to have special spiritual gifts.[9] As Quakers, they also possessed a strong sense of familial affection and a belief in the rights of women, which went beyond those of most other people of their day.[10] They adhered to a doctrine of plainness, which was intended to set them apart from the rest of the world in a tangible way to reinforce their sense of group identity, despite the individualistic tendencies of their theology.[11] While they emphasized personal religious experience, they developed a strong "tribalism" through their organizational structures for worship and business and their adherence to plainness in clothing, speech, and everyday living. If any among them challenged their discipline, they could be warned and even disowned. This gave a distinctive quality to Quaker settlements, placing religion at the forefront of community life and giving it an importance that surpassed even that of family loyalty.[12]

During the first years of the nineteenth century, Quaker hegemony in the Yonge Street settlement was challenged only by itinerant Methodists. These were people who shared the Quakers' emphasis on personal religious experience and espoused a similar doctrine of plainness. Yet their worship, in contrast with the Friends', included sermons by a paid preacher, hymns, love feasts, and an emotional vigour that the Quakers might not have experienced since the days of their founding in the seventeenth century.[13] In contrast with the "religion of experience" of the Quakers and Methodists was the "religion of order" exemplified by the Anglican church, which became the officially established church of the colony.[14] The power of the religious establishment in Upper Canada must at first have seemed remote since the Society of Friends had been encouraged to enter the colony by Lieutenant-Governor Simcoe himself, and their meetings had privileges, such as the right to solemnize marriages, that many other dissenting sects did not enjoy.[15]

The Quakers' complacency was challenged, however, when the Upper Canadian government began to treat them as the dissenters they actually were, by fining and imprisoning those who failed to take part in militia or military duty.[16] Such action flew in the face of Quaker pacifism and proved an early and direct assault on their religious freedoms. In this way, the religion of these early settlers came into opposition with the larger political environment in which they lived. The Quaker settlers of Yonge Street lived within twenty-five miles of the colonial capital on a road built by the government to help protect the capital in case of war. When war came in 1812, Quakers were persecuted for their pacifist religious beliefs, which stood at odds with the political and military agendas of the government. In later years, this same area north of the capital found its peace and stability threatened again as reform politicians such as William Lyon Mackenzie travelled north from the capital to gain support for a new political agenda.[17]

Another political dilemma faced the early settlers: they lived in a foreign country. At first that hardly mattered. They had come to Upper Canada in the company of family and neighbours from Pennsylvania, New York, and New England and brought much of their sense of home with them. On the way, they had followed valleys and waterways that provided natural links between the two areas.[18] When they got to Upper Canada, they were met by government officials who spoke the same language they did. In 1812, however, the border between the United States and the British North American colonies became a line of war. There could have been no proof stronger than war to tell them that they were now living in a foreign land with its own government and its own outlook on world affairs.

The new political environment of Upper Canada, which made itself obvious at that time, was rooted in principles that were different from those of the United States. While the American Declaration of Independence declared that governments are instituted in order to secure inalienable rights to "life, liberty, and the pursuit of happiness," the Constitutional Act that laid the groundwork for the political structure of the Canadas proclaimed "peace, welfare, and good government" among its primary objectives.[19] The Canadian document looked forward to the creation of a society modelled on that of England, with an established church, an enlightened aristocracy, and an emphasis on duties as well as rights. This society was intended to contrast favourably with what the British felt were the shortcomings of American republicanism.[20] Quakers, essentially apolitical because of their religious creed, may have admired British emphasis on order.

Quaker emphasis on equality and individuality through the doctrine of the Inner Light would, however, have prevented them from supporting British views on a deeper level.

In that complex natural, social, religious, and political environment was much that could bring people together or pull them apart. The Quaker community was bound to face difficulties during that early period. The direction those difficulties took – schism and the creation of a new religious movement – was owing largely to the presence of a few remarkable individuals. David Willson, first and foremost, was responsible for the creation of the Children of Peace. He was a charismatic speaker, imaginative, well-educated according to the standards of his day and, in contrast with his neighbours, a cosmopolitan figure who had lived for a time in New York City and sailed to the West Indies. Since he was a recent convert to Quakerism,[21] doctrines of plainness and simplicity may have meant less to him than they did to his neighbours. Despite Willson's espousal of elaborate ritual, music, and innovative architecture, his zeal for Quakerism continued in the unrelenting emphasis he placed on the importance of the Inner Light, even when some members of the Society of Friends moved toward an orthodox Protestant emphasis on Scripture and Christ's atonement for sin.

Central to Willson's role in creating a new sect was his training as a carpenter, which enabled him to translate his feelings about church reform into actual structures built under his guidance. Had he known nothing about carpentry, his followers, skilled as they were in the art of building, might not have been able to understand his directions or complete the work he felt called to do. Other details of Willson's background were important to the story as well. We can only speculate on how he must have felt after he rescued his wife and two young sons from drowning while they were on their way into York harbour. In the mind of an imaginative and religious man, this event would have seemed providential, strengthening his belief that he was called by God to perform an important mission. Certainly, it relates to the story told in his first vision of 1812, which was later painted on one of the banners the Children of Peace carried in processions.

Someone else of great importance was Ebenezer Doan. Unlike Willson, Doan was a Quaker of long standing. His family's defection to join the Children of Peace may have convinced others to follow. More importantly, Ebenezer Doan was a skilled craftsman who had been trained by one of the most celebrated builders of the mid-Atlantic states. His expertise probably outshone Willson's. Furthermore, he had likely been involved in large building projects during his apprenticeship, giving him the training necessary to coordinate the work of large numbers of people successfully. His brother, John, who had similar training and specialized in fine cabinetry, also brought exceptional skills with him. The Doan brothers possessed abilities that were unusual in their complexity and precision.[22] Without their support, Willson could not have given tangible expression to his vision of a new church to the extent that he ultimately did.

Another individual also played a vital role, although he was not of Quaker background and came on the scene seven or eight years after the original separation. This was Richard Coates, a talented musician, organ builder, and artist[23] whose work gave the worship of the Children of Peace distinctive qualities that set it apart from the ways of the Quakers. Had these remarkable people not been present, the Children of Peace would not have come into being and flourished as a sect. Like any other religious group, this sect was an organization created and led by individuals who were able to meet the needs of people in a particular environment. That environment – natural, social, religious, and political – nurtured sometimes conflicting ideals of individuality and cooperation. When those ideals were thrown out of balance, as they definitely were during the War of 1812, these leaders arose within the community to offer alternatives. What they and the Children of Peace created *was* new and different. Yet this new sect retained many of the ways of their Quaker past and unconsciously imitated many other religious movements of their time.

In considering the context in which the Children of Peace began and grew, it is important to go beyond the specific environment of Upper Canada. The community that the Children of Peace sought to build in East Gwillimbury had counterparts in Quaker communities both in England and the United States. Quaker theology not only emphasized the power of the Inner Light to guide and direct individuals, but also stressed equality by abandoning ostentatious forms of living and deferential terms of speech. Equality tempered individualism and led to the growth of cooperative villages in Wales and northwestern England, which became models for Quaker experiments in America.[24] Philadelphia – literally, the city of brotherly love – was founded by Quakers amidst high ideals of Christian love and community.[25] As Quakerism spread, members of the Society of Friends established communities that were known for their emphasis on extended family ties. Quaker parents were particularly successful in providing for the present and future well-being of their children. Their affectionate relationships, in contrast to stern parental authority, provided a model that broadly influenced later Victorian and twentieth-century ideals of family life.[26] Prosperity and a high standard of living were among the most striking outward signs of Quaker success.[27] These characteristics of Quaker community life must have inspired the Children of Peace in their quest to establish an ideal community in Upper Canada.

The balance between Quaker individualism and cooperation was never easy to maintain. Quaker theology was conducive to schism: any religion that emphasizes the concept that God speaks directly to individuals opens itself to the probability that individuals will feel directed in different ways. Ann Lee, who some saw as the female incarnation of Christ, was not the first member of the Society of Friends whose testimony was at odds with the beliefs of others in her community, but her case was among the most famous and influential. Jemima Wilkinson, The Publick Universal Friend, was another woman who challenged Quaker unity in late-eighteenth-century America. While her influence was far less than Mother Ann's, she too symbolized the disruption that could be caused by Quaker emphasis on the Inner Light.[28]

In 1828, North American Quakers were faced with even greater division when Orthodox and Hicksite Friends split into two distinct groups, each with its own network of meetings. The major theological cause for this division was differing opinions over the role of the Inner Light. Orthodox Quakers sought to emphasize the importance of Scripture and Christ's atonement for sin, whereas the Hicksite party wished to maintain Quaker emphasis on mysticism and intense spiritual contact with God.[29] The Society of Friends, which had no creed and emphasized the ministry of all believers, was poorly equipped to compete with the rising Protestant denominations of its day. Its *Disciplines* were statements of belief, but varied from one yearly meeting to another. Quakers had an organizational structure in their networks of meetings and recognized spiritually gifted members as ministers, but had little central direction or control. Their movement toward Protestant orthodoxy may have been an attempt to deal with these perceived shortcomings, but it ended by weakening the Society of Friends through schism.[30] By stressing credal and scriptural authority, as opposed to intense experiences with the Inner Light, Orthodoxy may have allowed Quakers to separate belief and behaviour so they could deal more easily with the secular world around them. That made Orthodoxy attractive to Quaker businessmen and entrepreneurs in urban areas and to farmers who produced for the marketplace. Hicksite Quakers, on the other hand, tended to include less prosperous urban dwellers and rural folk whose farms were small and often heavily mortgaged.[31] Since the strength of a religious sect often lies in its ability to resolve the frustrations of alienated individuals, Hicksite Quakerism appealed particularly to the poor because it emphasized that the Inner Light spoke to all people and put rich and poor on an equal level.

The links between the separation of the Children of Peace and the Orthodox/Hicksite schism of 1828 are obvious. While emphasizing music and ceremony in a way that would have offended many Hicksites, the Children of Peace similarly emphasized the Inner Light and minimized the role of Scripture and Christ's atonement. Both the Children of Peace and the Hicksite Quakers emphasized social and economic equality. Yet the Children of Peace broke away in 1812, rather than during the wider schism of 1828, in part because the War of 1812 gave focus to their concerns at an earlier date. The war brought physical and economic hardship through imprisonment, forced military duty, and fines. It also caused psychological hardship by forcing members of the Yonge Street community to consider family and friends in the United States as enemies. The War of 1812 called into question the ability of the Society of Friends to influence current affairs and promote its doctrine of peace. Events of the time made the Friends look weak and ineffective and opened the door for a new religious movement to arise.

Neither the separation of the Children of Peace in 1812, nor the Orthodox/Hicksite schism of 1828, was the end of division among the Quakers. Even the most orthodox Quakers could not give up their denomination's emphasis on personal religious experience and individual freedom. So it was that further divisions followed as controversies came to a head between Gurneyites and Wilburites in 1845[32] and between Progressives and Conservatives in 1881.[33] Among the Children of Peace, divisions arose at times when David Willson's leadership was questioned, when the Rebellion of 1837 seemed to offer a faster way to social reform, and when sect member fought over the question of adhering to the old ways or adopting new ones. Debates and divisions were endemic to any religious organization that emphasized personal contact with the Divine. However, while threatening and sometimes destroying the institutional unity of churches and sects, such controversies attested to the success of those organizations' efforts to inspire individual members to think deeply about spiritual questions. They also showed how closely religious issues were connected to changing social, economic, and political trends of their day.

Many Protestant groups in North America, not only Quakers and Children of Peace, felt the effects of schism through conflicting notions of religious authority and personal religious experience. During the Great Awakening of the 1740s and 1750s, New England Congregationalists, descendants of the Puritans, were split into Old Lights and New Lights. The Old Lights adhered to Calvinist doctrines of predestination and ecclesiastical authority. New Lights, however, sought an enlivened form of Calvinism that emphasized doctrines of human depravity and divine grace and stressed the need for Christians to undergo deep, transforming experiences of God's power as evidence of their salvation. In their emphasis on a 'religion of experience,' they were not unlike the later Hicksite Quakers. Both demanded a deeply felt contact with God.[34] In the early 1780s, Baptists also divided over similar religious disputes. They were followed by Old School and New School Presbyterians, who formally parted ways in 1837.[35] What begins as a source of strength and unity for a religious movement may lead to that movement's disruption. Quaker emphasis on the Inner Light ultimately led to disagreement and division as some were inspired in different ways than others. Similarly, Reformation-era Protestantism's emphasis on both individualism and predestination created theological entanglements that led to the old/new controversies. These were similar to the Orthodox/Hicksite dispute and entangled in all of them were conflicts between personal religious experience and religious authority.

Methodists also took part in this debate. In a sense, they were New Lights within Anglicanism, who eventually broke away from the Church of England to form their own denomination. They shared much with the Quakers in their emphasis on individual religious experience.[36] Originally a splinter group themselves, Methodists faced similar problems of schism in the second quarter of the nineteenth century. In the British North American colonies particularly, they were divided between Wesleyans, who came largely from England and followed a relatively cautious approach to church organization and evangelism, and members of the Methodist Episcopal Church, who came from the United States and favoured the highly emotional, individualistic style of saddle-bag preachers and camp meetings.[37]

Without going into great detail about the history of any one of these important religious movements and the internal divisions they faced, it is clear that the story of the formation of the Children of Peace may be read not only in the context of Quaker history, but also in the broader context of late-eighteenth and early-nineteenth-century Protestantism. All were part of a broad cultural debate on the issue of religious authority and freedom, a debate tied to the rethinking of political and social theory as well.[38] Sociologists and social historians who have studied eighteenth and nineteenth century religious movements have linked beliefs and controversies to the beginning of new social and economic systems. They have tied the rise of religious individualism and the questioning of denominational authority to the competitive, entrepreneurial spirit of nineteenth-century capitalism and the widespread acceptance of technological progress. They have argued that the same freedom of thought and initiative that built canals and textile mills demanded a system of religious belief that emphasized free will.[39]

Some have viewed this shift in outlook as a reactionary force, used by capitalists and entrepreneurs to gain power and control, to oppose outside interference, and to ignore considerations for the common good. Methodism, for example, has been characterized as a highly conservative, even repressive, force in eighteenth and nineteenth-century England, exploited by mill owners and industrialists to tame the growing working class through lessons in self-control and temperate behaviour.[40] In the Burned-Over District of upstate New York, the revivals of the 1820s and 1830s have been seen in similar terms, as movements led by economic and social elites who wanted to maintain control over a new proletariat.[41] As shops and factories grew in size, it has been argued, masters and employees could no longer live in close association, as they did in the days when hired journeymen, labourers, and apprentices lived in their employers' households. Employers supported the persuasive powers of evangelical religion and its ancillary array of associated movements, such as the crusades for temperance and sabbath observance, to compensate for the loss of older forms of authority and control.[42] A new theology that was liberating for some thus became repressive for others.

The story of the Children of Peace opposes the view that Protestant individualism by its very nature was conducive to economic independence, the rise of capitalism, and entrepreneurship. In fact, the Children of Peace used their belief in the importance of individual religious experience as a starting point for cooperative enterprise and a rallying cry for the poor. Any system of belief that declares that God speaks directly to all people can lead to belief in equality as well as individualism. English Methodism, called repressive by some, was also a revolutionary and liberating force that helped pave the way for important social and economic reforms.[43] Similarly, evangelical revivals in New York State, supported by some to maintain personal positions of power and authority, awakened Americans' interest in women's rights and the abolition of slavery.[44] The new Protestantism was much like the frontier in its combination of forces and effects: it could be liberating or restrictive and it could promote individualism or cooperation.

The very size of the North American frontier meant that all the many effects of religious enthusiasm could be tested. From the beginning of European settlement, North America was a laboratory for all shades and opinions of Christian belief. Among the most influential groups were the Puritans of New England, who founded Boston in 1630 as "a city on a hill," intended as an example of religious belief put into practice and a model for the rest of the world to follow.[45] Also important were the Roman Catholics of Lower Canada, who under the Sieur de Maisonneuve, founded the city of Montreal in 1649 as a model Catholic community in opposition to Protestant Boston.[46] In the eighteenth century, Moravians established communities such as Bethlehem, Pennsylvania (1741), and Salem, North Carolina (1753), along with missionary outposts among the Natives, including Fairfield, Upper Canada (1792).[47] Meanwhile, German Protestants led by Conrad Beissel began a monastic community in Ephrata, Pennsylvania.[48] During and after the American Revolution, numerous other religious communities were founded, including those of the Shakers and the Publick Universal Friend; the Harmony Society at Harmony and Economy, Pennsylvania, and New Harmony, Indiana; Separatists at Zoar, Ohio; Mormons in Nauvoo, Illinois, and Salt Lake City, Utah; the followers of William Kiel at Bethel, Missouri, and Aurora, Oregon; Inspirationist settlers at Amana, Iowa; and Perfectionist followers of John Humphrey Noyes at Oneida, New York. These are only a few of the several hundred religious communities founded in North America.[49]

Each of these communities had its own material culture, which was distinct from that of other groups by reason of differing religious beliefs and ethnic backgrounds. Puritan meeting houses, for example, were statements of Reformation theology, which placed emphasis on preaching and reading the scriptures,[50] whereas churches in Lower Canada were statements of Roman Catholicism, which stressed the mysteries of the Mass.[51] Puritan meeting houses also expressed the timber frame building traditions of East Anglia and the southwestern counties of England,[52] whereas the Catholic churches recalled their masonry ancestors in Normandy and the Ile de France.[53] Buildings erected in Moravian communities embodied religious traditions that emphasized music and provided for communal living or independent family life. Their half-timbered walls and distinctive rooflines were also reflections of northern European building traditions that differed from English and French practices in numerous details.[54]

The material culture of the Children of Peace likewise expressed religious beliefs and ethnic background. It is not surprising that the first meeting house and temple of the Children of Peace were like the worship places of Quakers and Puritans, who also emphasized preaching and the equality of all Christian believers. Nor is it a coincidence that the Children of Peace dressed plainly, like the Quakers and

Methodists, or built organs and a gallery for their musicians, like those of the Moravians. A long catalogue could be made of similarities between the material culture of the Children of Peace and numerous other religious sects. This catalogue would prove two things: that similar religious ideals and emphases led to similar material forms, and that similar ethnic backgrounds had influential effects.

In the late eighteenth and early nineteenth centuries, eager anticipation of a Christian millennium gave religious groups like the Children of Peace a distinctive quality. Most contemporary religious scholars believe that the original writers of the New Testament thought that the end of the world would come quickly, possibly within their own lifetimes.[55] As time passed, however, the church focused less on eschatology. It avoided precise predictions, but continued to remind the faithful of the coming apocalypse through oft-repeated statements of faith such as the Apostles' Creed or Nicene Creed. In the popular imagination, however, cataclysmic events such as plagues or violent storms were often taken as signs that the end might be near.[56] The social and political upheavals of the late eighteenth and early nineteenth centuries were also perceived as signals that the end of time was at hand. The American Revolution, the French Revolution, and the rise of Napoleon were linked in ingenious ways to events described in the book of Revelation and Old Testament prophecies.[57] Speculation about the timing of the apocalypse took the form of both premillennial and postmillennial theology. The former declared that Christ would return to earth before the thousand-year period of peace and prosperity described in Revelation 20 could begin, whereas the latter asserted that the millennium would be a moral or spiritual epoch *concluded* by Christ's appearance.[58] The complex and cryptic narrative of Revelation made many interpretations possible for generations of people who were living through times of change and were accustomed to viewing world history as a series of divinely guided events leading to a climactic end.

The Shakers were among those who took a premillennial view. They believed that, since Christ came to earth a second time in the body of Ann Lee, the millennium had already begun. They saw in their neatly ordered, celibate communities an earthly reflection of the heavenly life they believed would begin once the earthly millennium had passed. The prosperous and substantial communities they established, the great beauty of their architecture and furniture, their inventiveness, and the longevity of the church they founded all testify to the strength of Shaker convictions, regardless of how untenable those beliefs may seem to the modern world.[59]

The early Mormons, like the Shakers, sought to create a God-directed society. They sought to build a new Israel, a spiritual nation on North American soil, but did not believe that the Messiah had yet returned to earth. Shortly after their founding in 1830, Mormons arrived in Upper Canada with Joseph Smith, their founder, preaching their vision of a new world. Among the Mormons' earliest converts was John Taylor, a Toronto Methodist minister, who later became the third president of the Mormon church. Another Canadian Methodist, lay preacher Joseph Young, was a brother of Mormon leader Brigham Young and also a convert to Mormonism.[60]

Like the Mormons, followers of the Catholic Apostolic Church (generally known as Irvingites after their founder, the Reverend Edward Irving of London, England) proved disruptive to the Methodists in the 1830s. The Irvingites, who believed that Christ would soon return to earth to judge all nations, found an Upper Canadian convert in the Reverend George Ryerson. He was the elder brother of the Reverend Egerton Ryerson, editor of the influential Methodist periodical, the *Christian Guardian*.[61] The Irvingites were adherents of premillennial theology who foresaw the Second Coming of Christ as a dramatic event that all the world would witness. They believed the millennium would begin only after this great event had occurred and the earth in its present form was destroyed.

A more famous group who anticipated the millennium in this way were the followers of William Miller of New York State. Through a complex series of calculations, Miller believed that the world would come to an end in the year 1843. Before that time, Millerite followers toured the countryside of New York, New England, and the adjacent British North American colonies with their message.[62] In Toronto, a group of followers built an assembly hall and published their own newspaper. Reports circulated that Millerite farmers refused to plant crops that year, while Millerite artisans declined to take orders for work beyond the fateful day. When the end did not come, the Millerites fell into disarray. Meanwhile the press, particularly the papers of rival denominations, had a field day. The date was recalculated as 22 October 1844, supposedly through new research based on the Jewish calendar, but when the end again did not come at the appointed time, Millerism lost much of its remaining credibility.[63]

Within the context of millennial sects, the Children of Peace were closer to the Shakers than to the Mormons, Irvingites, or Millerites. This is because both the Children of Peace and the Shakers were offshoots from the Society of Friends. The Friends' emphasis on the Inner Light led them to think of significant religious events in inward, spiritual terms, rather than as tumultuous external happenings.

Friends were not usually associated with millennial and utopian movements of that period because of their Society's older roots; however, Quakerism has always lived on the faith that the world itself can become a utopia.[64] Following Quaker tradition, David Willson saw the Second Coming of Christ as a transforming event within the human heart and led his followers in the active pursuit of a just and prosperous earthly community. The imagery of Revelation was a powerful force in his mind: it coloured the visions that led him to build a new church; appeared on banners that were carried in processions; and inspired the "Armageddon" inscription painted with a setting sun on two sides of the temple. Yet at no time did Willson attempt to use the Bible to deduce a timetable for the destruction of the world. Like the Shakers, he and his followers spent much effort creating a neat and prosperous community as an outward sign that the millennium could already be seen on earth.

As the second half of the nineteenth century approached, there were signs that some of the more colourful and intense aspects of the "religion of experience" were in decline. This was owing, not only to the dramatic discrediting of the Millerites, but also to a combination of factors forming a pattern sometimes called "the routinization of charisma."[65] The evolution of the Society of Friends provides a good example of this process. The earliest Quakers were known for their sometimes bizarre behaviour: writhing on the floor when experiencing the Inner Light and running naked through village streets to publicize a cause. By the late seventeenth century, however, actions such as these were rare. Meetings for worship were orderly, and members were disciplined by a hierarchy of Friends, through a network of meetings that decided on more serious matters.[66] The Society of Friends did not necessarily become less spiritual through these changes, for if it was to continue its existence and hope to influence society as a whole, organization was necessary.

Methodism underwent a similar transformation. In its early days, meetings were known for their intense religious excitement, dramatic preaching, and near hysteria as sinners were awakened to the terrible prospect of Hell and brought to tearful repentance before their God. By the 1840s, many Methodists abandoned their old camp meeting techniques.[67] The Reverend James Caughey, who had served on the camp meeting circuit, complained that by the mid-nineteenth century, Methodists were building churches so elaborate that they rivaled those of the Anglicans, whom they had previously rejected. He railed against elaborately arched ceilings and decorative plasterwork that seemed to catch the preacher's voice and make it difficult to be heard.[68] Methodist services and even the remaining camp meetings and revivals held at that time became formal, carefully planned events. Changes in Methodism reflected the changing times. Growing urbanization demanded settled ministers, not itinerants, and churches, not camp meetings set in forest clearings. Higher standards of literacy and general education demanded more thorough training of ministers: religious zeal was no longer enough. Finally, a growing number of members, who had found salvation through the dramatic techniques used by Methodist preachers, now required regular care and sustenance that was best supplied by well-organized churches.[69]

The Children of Peace experienced similar changes over a period of nearly eighty years. At first, the sect was inspired by the dramatic visions of its founder and led by banners depicting half-naked women and children. It adopted elaborate rituals and built a temple and meeting house that expressed the spirit of equality its members espoused. By the 1840s, however, its Sunday services moved to a meeting house laid out more like a church, were members sang hymns from books and followed a liturgy little different from that of other Protestant denominations of that day. By the 1870s, sect members had forgotten much of their past. They invited ministers from other churches to preach to them and incorporated themselves as an organization adhering to orthodox beliefs that bore little resemblance to the radical views of their founder. As the century progressed, the Children of Peace became more and more like their earlier rivals.

Examining both the local and broader religious contexts helps put the story of the Children of Peace into perspective with certain conditions and events of their day. But is there a broader context still? If religion both shapes and is shaped by the wider culture around it, are there yet other ways of looking at this particular group? The community the Children of Peace established has been compared to Quaker communities elsewhere; however, Quakers were not the first people in North America to emphasize family ties and familial obligations as cornerstones of community development. Early Puritans were also known for creating communities where cooperation, rather than competition, was stressed and where parents took great pains to provide land and other resources for their children.[70] Studies of individual communities such as Dedham, Andover, or Rowley, Massachusetts, have found evidence of cooperation and consensus.[71] They have shown that some Puritan communities remained united in their allegiance to authority and provided well for their inhabitants into the third generation of their existence.

In the nineteenth century, some cooperative communities were based on largely secular beliefs. In Massachusetts, the famous Brook Farm experiment was founded by transcendentalists who, while spiritually-minded, were not religious in a conventional sense.[72] Owenite communities – such as New Lanark, Scotland; New Harmony, Indiana (after its purchase from the Harmony Society); and Maxwell, Upper Canada – were overtly secular, even though Owen himself had been influenced by the social experiments of the Quakers. Owen and his followers were determined to show that their cooperative communities grew out of sound principles of logic and humanitarianism, not out of religious creeds.[73] Similarly, the thirty Fourierist communities established in the United States between 1843 and 1858 were based on secular theories. Their mentor, Charles Fourier of France, substituted psychology for religion and sought collective luxury and "complete gratification of human passions."[74] However, these communities did not last as long as experiments based on religious ideals: it would seem that belief in spiritual authority was necessary if such communities were to prosper for more than a few years.[75] Even a cooperative community based on shared religious convictions generally had trouble maintaining the ideals of its founders beyond the third or fourth generation. As any religious community grows in size, and its children grow up and have children of their own, land and resources become scarcer. Competition for land increases, and people are forced to settle farther away from the spiritual centre of their community, its church. Breakdowns in community life result from a complex web of factors wherein religious ideals and economics are closely interwoven.[76]

North America set the stage for new beginnings, not only for religious and secular communities, but for social and political experiments of much wider scope. For many, the American Revolution seemed to initiate a *secular* millennium. Tom Paine's *The Rights of Man* (1791) and *The Age of Reason* (1794) saw the Revolution as an momentous event, fundamental to humanity's social and political progress – the harbinger of a new way of life that would soon sweep the world.[77] How closely Americans came to see themselves as the modern heirs of Revelation was demonstrated in America's first epic poem, Timothy Dwight's *Conquest of Canaan* (1785), which linked the revolutionaries to the Israelites of old.[78] In Upper Canada, Canadians saw *their* side as true heirs of justice and truth. Loyalists who settled in the colony during its earliest days were praised as the real heroes of the revolution, models of sacrifice and nobility. They too were compared with the ancient Israelites, an oppressed people seeking their promised land.[79] When Lieutenant-Governor Simcoe arrived as the first administrator of the new colony, he saw its existence in providential terms and hoped that its society would stand as a model to entice the wayward Americans back to the British fold.[80] Trying to remain aloof from politics, Quakers and Children of Peace were not caught up in the rhetoric of Revolutionaries or Loyalists to the extent that others were. Yet David Willson himself was convinced that British institutions were preferable to American ones: he too compared Britain's constitutional monarchy to the government of ancient Israel.

North Americans of the late eighteenth and early nineteenth centuries believed that a better society could be created on their new continent. That vision was coloured by Christian imagery, but directed by secular as well as theological impulses. It was sustained by a faith in widespread material and technological progress that stood as a secular counterpart to millennial theology.[81] Year by year, forests gave way to farms and towns. Steam engines replaced the power of water and wind, and locomotives replaced the horse for long-distance travel. As new inventions seemed to conquer nature, faith in human ability to conquer social problems by secular means grew apace. Beyond the limited sphere of model religious and secular utopias or even the broader context of national dreams, institutions such as prisons, asylums, and hospitals were built in the nineteenth century as new types of model communities. Where they had existed at all in earlier times, their major purpose had been confinement. In the nineteenth century, however, belief in progress contributed to a new way of thinking, which held that people who had committed crimes not punishable by death could be reformed, while those who suffered from illness could be treated and possibly cured. These beliefs were no doubt influenced by changing religious doctrines that no longer emphasized predestination. Ultimately, they took on a life of their own, bolstered by scientific and pseudo-scientific research.[82]

To accomplish their goals of rehabilitation and cure, reformers began searching for both material and non-material solutions to the problem of treating prison, asylum, and hospital inmates.[83] Architecture was used not only to improve the physical well-being of patients, but also to stress the social importance of these new institutions. At a time when art and architecture were widely regarded as having power to uplift and inspire, buildings played an active role in the treatment process itself.[84] New architectural solutions were sought for other secular problems as well. By the mid-nineteenth century, feminist writers began calling for domestic reforms ranging from improved kitchen layouts in private homes to entire apartment complexes designed with communal facilities for cooking and laundry.[85] What the Children of Peace accomplished in East Gwillimbury did not have the far-reaching effects of any of these other experiments. Nonetheless, all were part of a broad reform impulse inspired by secular and religious convictions, which found tangible expression in material culture and cooperative community life.

The buildings erected by the Children of Peace, along with the clothes they wore, the furniture they made, and the community they established, were all metaphors for spiritual and secular beliefs. The use of material things to express non-material ideas is as old as civilization itself, but it seems to have reached new heights in the nineteenth century. In North America, a continent of religious diversity, there was great variety in the material culture of religion. At one end of the spectrum were Plain People such as the Quakers, who espoused a doctrine of plainness and simplicity that was complex and could allow for a wide range of personal expression.[86] At the other end of the spectrum were the Ecclesiologists, High Church Anglicans and Episcopalians who placed great emphasis on reforming church architecture and ritual. Beginning in the 1840s, the ecclesiological movement sought to remove all "pagan," classically inspired architecture and ornament from churches and instead follow the Gothic style, which they believed to be expressive of Christian beliefs and the only proper style for churches.[87] On the surface, the Plain People and the Ecclesiologists had little in common; however, both of them placed great emphasis on the role that material culture played in the lives of believers. The Quaker *Disciplines* and the Ecclesiologists' tracts both were adamant that material culture was of the utmost importance as an expressive religious force. Both saw material culture as a vital tool in helping believers to distance themselves from secular concerns so that they might achieve spiritual freedom and enlightenment and come closer to God. It was the means, not the end, that separated the two views.

An illustration of the links between such seemingly different schools of thought is found in the career of George Washington Doane, Episcopalian bishop of New Jersey, who was a nephew of John and Ebenezer Doan of the Children of Peace. George Washington Doane was the son of Jonathan Doan. He grew up in a Quaker household,[88] but in later life added an *e* to the end of his name and became one of the leading proponents of the ecclesiological movement in America. Doane was a patron of such notable architects as John Notman and Richard Upjohn. His church, St Mary's (1846–48), in Burlington, New Jersey, was the first American church convincingly patterned after a specific English model.[89] It is radically different from the temple his uncles helped to build for the Children of Peace, yet it stems from the same conviction that material culture plays a vital role in communicating and extending religious belief.

Quakerism and Ecclesiology were not as far apart from the mainstream of North American thinking as might at first be supposed. During the nineteenth century, material culture was commonly used to express both secular concepts and religious beliefs. At the beginning of the century, for instance, plainness was not only a doctrine of the Quakers, but also a republican virtue.[90] At first, republicanism preached frugality and restraint out of necessity. Popular theatrical productions, such as Royall Tyler's *The Contrast* (1787), linked American plainness and simplicity with honesty and virtue and condemned European luxury and extravagance.[91] By the 1820s, however, American technological progress seemed to offer the prospect of great prosperity for everyone, making the old republican values less attractive. Material abundance was reinterpreted: it too could be a metaphor for republicanism provided that, in theory at least, it was available to all.[92]

By the 1840s, houses and house-building were seen in vividly metaphorical ways. The writings of A.J. Downing differed from earlier treatises on domestic architecture in their conviction that houses were not only structures erected by builders who followed certain architectural rules and conventions: they could also represent the highest aspirations of their occupants.[93] Catherine Beecher followed a similar line of thinking when she wrote about housework and home management. Drawing on her strong New England Congregationalist background, she described the role of the housewife and mother as that of a Christian minister, giving the house itself great sanctity and purpose.[94] Other writers extended the metaphor, arguing that the furniture of each room and even the pattern of carpets and wallpaper could teach valuable lessons in Christian love and conduct.[95] Even the elaborate rules of etiquette, which concerned everything from table manners to formal calls, were said to reflect Christian principles.[96]

It was in this context that the Children of Peace developed their own material culture of religion, building a temple that represented their faith and mission and taking part in ritual acts that symbolized abstract beliefs and convictions. They differed from the majority of North Americans in the metaphors they used, but shared their culture's widespread belief that both secular and religious truths could be embodied in artifacts and in prescriptive codes of behaviour. The decline of the Children of Peace is linked to the local arrival of new organizations – the Sons of Temperance, the Masonic Lodge, the Methodist Church, and the Anglican Church – whose metaphoric use of material culture and ritual were more in keeping with the changing world around them. It may also be linked to a general shift away from using objects and patterns of behaviour to represent moral truths and values toward greater emphasis on the power of material things to lead to self-fulfillment and personal happiness. The advertising industry, which thanks to new means of printing, distribution, and transportation, grew hand in hand with the consumption-oriented culture of the late nineteenth century, stressed personal, rather than group, expression. It emphasized the therapeutic values of material goods; their ability to make life more comfortable; and their promise of ease, happiness, beauty, and esteem. In the changing world of late-nineteenth-century consumer culture, material things took on values that were quite different from the messages of the past.[97]

From time to time in this study, the presence of the political border between Canada and the United States has been emphasized. Certainly it was important in 1812 and helped lead to the crisis in the Yonge Street Quaker community that spawned the formation of the Children of Peace. It also played an important role in the political thinking of David Willson, who favoured Upper Canada's British institutions, linked them to those of ancient Israel, and disliked the republican ways of his neighbours to the south. At other times, however, the political border was of little significance. Willson's dispute with the Quakers went beyond the bounds of Upper Canada and reflected broad issues of religious controversy that involved not only the Friends, but many other Christian denominations as well. His religious outlook and hope for social reform were based on secular notions of progress as well as widespread interest in the coming of a Christian millennium. Even his use of material culture to express abstract religious beliefs reflected broader tendencies of his time. The story of the Children of Peace shows that communities and movements that espoused a particular religious outlook and established a cooperative social structure could exist successfully on either side of the border. They are not exclusively a product of the American frontier or republican character. Willson's own Loyalist history and preference for monarchial government in themselves support this view.

Willson and his followers were transplanted Americans. Could their American background have been a vital key to their success? After all, no other comparable group survived very long in Upper Canada. The Owenite community at Maxwell failed after only a few months. Inspirationist communities, about which very little is known, were founded at Kenneberg and Canada Ebenezer, but soon disbanded to join their American counterparts in Amana.[98] Despite the camp meetings of the Methodists and the enthusiasms of the Millerites, Upper Canada seems to have been a calmer, more conservative place than the nearby Burned-Over District in New York. Some early writers felt they could detect differences between the temperaments of Upper Canadians and Americans that, if true, could help explain this phenomenon. A Methodist observer from England wrote in the 1840s: "On the American side, the people are all life, elasticity, buoyancy, activity; on the Canadian side, we have a people who appear subdued, tame, spiritless, as if living much more under the influence of fear than hope. Again: on the American territory, we behold men moving as if they had the idea that their calling was to act, to choose, to govern, – at any rate, to govern themselves; on the Canadian soil, we see a race, perhaps more polite than the other, but who seem to live under the impression that their vocation is to receive orders, and obey."[99]

What this writer took as evidence of American "life, elasticity, buoyancy, activity," others took as signs of rudeness and fanaticism. Of the experiences of a British traveller in the United States during the early-nineteenth century, a Canadian observer wrote: "Being accustomed to civil behaviour, even from the lower class of people amongst his own countrymen, the first remark that struck him in the United States, was the uncommon brutality or rudeness he experienced in conversing with its citizens, from the governors and magistrates, down to the lowest mechanics and petty farmers ... The political as well as the religious fanaticism prevails in all the provinces of the United States where sects and parties are equally tolerant; there being hardly an example of a Federalist or an anti-Federalist, of a presbyterian or a Church of England man, visiting, much less permitting their families to intermarry ..."[100]

Both writers exaggerated, but similar observations were made by others too. There is no doubt that the two places and their people appeared to be different. When visitors travelled across the border from Upper Canada to New York State, they were conscious of being in a different country. However, the differences observed probably related to differing stages of economic development, rather than inherently different characteristics of their people. For example, Joseph Pickering observed the following after crossing the Niagara River on a visit to New York in the late 1820s: "On the United States side [there are] large towns springing up; the numerous shipping, with piers to protect them in harbour, coaches rattling along the road, and trade evidenced by waggons, carts and horses, and people on foot, in various directions. On the Canadian side, although in the immediate vicinity, an older settlement, and apparently better land, there are only two or three stores, a tavern or two, a natural harbour without piers, but few vessels, and two temporary landing places."[101] Of the same area a decade later, another traveller wrote: "On the American territory, all along the shores of the lakes the country is being cleared, houses and villages built, works put up, incipient ports opened, and trade begun. On the Canada shore, unbroken forest appears for miles, while the small openings which have been made present themselves to view in a very infantile and feeble state of progress."[102] The more rapid economic growth of New York State must have had an important influence on the impressions travellers had since they compared people and societies at two different stages of economic development. Perhaps the comparisons they made between Americans and Upper Canadians were similar to what they might have written had they contrasted urban dwellers and country folk or entrepreneurs and farmers.

Whitney R. Cross's study of the Burned-Over District of New York has shown that two of the key factors that permitted the extensive growth of religious movements there were a relatively homogeneous population and rapid economic development. In those counties of upstate New York where religious revivals and innovations flourished, the majority of the population were New England Congregationalists, descendants of the Puritans, who were already accustomed to viewing their world in religious terms and placing great importance on church affiliation. In counties where these people were not in the majority and where settlers had come from a wider variety of places, religious enthusiasm was less important.[103] In most areas of Upper Canada to which Loyalist, other American, and British immigrants came, the population consisted of a more varied mixture of people than in the Burned-Over District. These people brought with them a wider range of religious opinions.[104] When a new religious movement took hold, as it did among the settlers of Yonge Street north of the Oak Ridges, it did so in an atypical area, where many settlers came from the same place and shared common religious views before their migration.

The relatively slow economic advancement of Upper Canada made it difficult for ideas, as well as goods and services, to travel across the new land.[105] In upstate New York, the 1825 opening of the Erie Canal, which linked the Great Lakes with the Hudson River, New York City, and the Atlantic Ocean, brought rapid growth to towns and villages. With that growth came new social organizations and institutions, newspapers, books, periodicals, and the beginnings of an efficient postal service. In Upper Canada, communication was more difficult. When David Willson published his first pamphlets, he went to the United States to do so, partly because he wanted to appeal to the Society of Friends internationally, but also because facilities for printing in Upper Canada were limited.[106] Poor roads also hampered communication. Yonge Street was among the few good roads built during the first three decades of the colony's existence, although even it caused complaints. Because of its location around Yonge Street north of the capital, the Quaker community was in closer contact with the rest of the world and its ideas than most other people in Upper Canada. Thus, it was able to share in some of the widespread religious debates of its time more readily than most Upper Canadian communities could. An ability to communicate easily with others and a homogeneous population with an established tradition of viewing the world in religious terms seem to have been essential ingredients in the success of revivalism and religious innovation. In most parts of Upper Canada, these factors were lacking. In the Burned-Over District of New York, they were clearly present.[107]

In the end, the question must be asked: were the Children of Peace important? Were they simply a group of sincere, talented, but misguided people who failed to achieve their mission of creating a new church and a new society? Were they caught up in a delusion and nothing more?

The temple, David Willson's study, the banners and organs built by Richard Coates, the Ebenezer Doan house, furniture made by John Doan, and other surviving artifacts linked to the Children of Peace declare that these people led a rich spiritual and material life. Like any group, they experienced disputes and failures; however, they established a successful community known for its emphasis on education, charity, music, innovative architecture, ritual, and religious belief. The fact that their distinctive way of life vanished by the end of the nineteenth century need not be seen as failure. All institutions and ways of life vanish, or at least change, over time. The Society of Friends, the Methodist church, and the government of Canada all changed too. Unlike the Children of Peace, these institutions have continued in some way into the present day; however, they would be unrecognizable to the people of Upper Canada who knew them 150 years ago.

Perhaps the Children of Peace possessed what Dolores Hayden, in her study of American communal societies, termed "premature truths." Hayden wrote: "Historic communal societies offer more than odd architecture: they represent a history of organizing and building processes. Here there are "premature truths" to be grasped. Social and economic reorganization must be the basis of any environmental reorganization. A new architecture expressing liberation can come only from a liberated group of people, not from an idealistic planner sitting at a drawing board."[108] The achievements of the Children of Peace, all the more remarkable because they took place in a wilderness, were the work of people who, for a time, achieved a sense of unity and purpose inspired by spiritual beliefs and a dream of starting the world anew.

Their buildings for worship represented not only the work of one or two designers, but a collective belief that God could guide and direct the lives of all people. Their material culture successfully met two very basic human needs: the need to feel connected to others and the need for individual expression. Their involvement in worship and community life did not threaten the privacy of their family-centred home activities. Through plainness and simplicity, they set themselves apart from the world around them, reinforcing community identity in a tangible way. By the late nineteenth century, however, the Children of Peace could no longer remain aloof from change outside their community. People with different beliefs and values now surrounded them. There was no more land available nearby for grandsons and great-grandsons of the founding generation to farm. New options for collective involvement began to appear through secular organizations and other churches. New prospects for individualism opened up as railways provided a link with other communities and faraway places.

Today's competitive urban/industrial society, which those options and prospects foreshadowed, is now being questioned and, some would say, is on the brink of its own destruction. Increasing pollution and depleted natural resources, the by-products of the kind of society created in many parts of North America during the past century, have become major threats to civilization. Urban planners, architects, and environmentalists are now trying to solve the problems that face our cities and countryside. Their success may depend, not on still newer forms of technology, but on the *collective will and vision* of the people they serve. Like the material culture of the Children of Peace, the material culture of our own world can only reflect the beliefs of the people who create it. Perhaps the cooperative community life and rich material culture of the Children of Peace did express some "premature truths" that are applicable to some of the problems of our own world. That is testimony enough to the success of the vision of the Children of Peace.

Notes

ABBREVIATIONS

ACYM	Archives of the Canada Yearly Meeting of the Society of Friends, Pickering College, Newmarket, Ontario
ADHS	Aurora and District Historical Society, Aurora, Ontario
AO	Archives of Ontario, Toronto, Ontario
BCC	Bucks County Conservancy, Doylestown, Pennsylvania
BCCH	Bucks County Court House, Doylestown, Pennsylvania
BCHS	Bucks County Historical Society, Doylestown, Pennsylvania
MTRL	Metropolitan Toronto Reference Library, Toronto, Ontario
NJSA	New Jersey State Archives, Trenton, New Jersey
OGS	Ontario Genealogical Society, Toronto, Ontario
STM	Sharon Temple Museum, Sharon, Ontario
STMA	Sharon Temple Museum Archives, Pickering College, Newmarket, Ontario

WL   D.B. Weldon Library
      University of Western Ontario, London, Ontario

PREFACE

1 McFaddin, "Buildings of the Children of Peace."
2 McIntyre, *Early Writings of David Willson*; and "David Willson and Politics," 2–15.
3 In illustrating the diffusion of American vernacular architectural forms, for example, scholars have divided maps of the United States into several folk culture regions and then drawn arrows outward from these regions to suggest movement. Almost invariably, these arrows stop at the Canadian border, and no arrows are shown leading downward from Canada. See, for instance, Glassie, *Material Folk Culture*, 38, although elsewhere Glassie does allude to movement to and from Canada.
4 Deetz, *In Small Things Forgotten*, 24.
5 Ibid.
6 Hayden, *Seven American Utopias*.
7 Nordhoff, *Communistic Societies*.
8 Bestor, *Backwoods Utopias*; and Holloway, *Heavens on Earth*.
9 Kanter, *Commitment and Community*; and Erasmus, *In Search of the Common Good*.
10 Bauman, *Let Your Words Be Few*.
11 Levy, *Quakers and the American Family*.
12 Glassie, "Delaware Valley Folk Building," 29–57.
13 Lemon, *The Best Poor Man's Country*.
14 Westfall, *Two Worlds*.

CHAPTER 1

1 Berchem, *The Yonge Street Story*, 56–7.
2 Gourlay, *Statistical Account of Upper Canada*, 1:459–60.
3 John Graves Simcoe to Phineas Bond, 7 May 1792, in Cruikshank, ed., *John Graves Simcoe*, 1:151.
4 Dorland, *Quakers in Canada*, 91–2; and Reaman, *Trail of the Black Walnut*, 83–4, 103–4.
5 Hovinen, "Quakers of Yonge Street," 54–5; and Dorland, *Quakers in Canada*, 2–5.
6 Hovinen, The "Quakers of Yonge Street," 13.
7 Dorland, *Quakers in Canada*, 53–8.
8 Webb, "Recollections of an Immigrant," 10.
9 Stradley, *Economic History of Pennsylvania*, 59–60.
10 Lemon, *The Best Poor Man's Country*, 24, 40, 43, 88, 91, 175.

11 BCCH, deed from Scholfield to Doan.
12 Levy, *Quakers and the American Family* 127–8, 135, 152.
13 Lemon, *The Best Poor Man's Country*, 86, 224.
14 Higgins, *Joseph Gould*, 25.
15 BCHS, letter from Doan to Paxson.
16 Hovinen, "Quakers of Yonge Street," 19.
17 Wood, "The Settlers and the Land," 115.
18 Biographical data concerning David Willson come from three sources: Willson, "Reminiscences 9–26; Mann, "Legends and Folk Tales," 11–17; and Carolyn Mann's genealogy of the Willson family, Sharon Temple Museum. The late Carolyn Mann based her research on the account by her ancestor, Richard Titus Willson (1793–1878); stories told by her grandmother, Rachel Syllindia Willson (b. 1837); and documentary research in Dutchess County, New York, and in Carrickfergus, Belfast, and Dublin Castle in Ireland. It is now known that the William H. Willson family, also early settlers in East Gwillimbury and active members of the Children of Peace, were related. The Willson genealogy is further complicated by the fact that Catherine Willson, David's widowed mother, was married a second time to a John Willson, apparently unrelated to her first husband, also John Willson.
19 Gerry, "Beliefs of David Willson," 33–4; and Dorland, *Quakers in Canada*, 104–5.
20 Genealogical data, names, and dates regarding members of the Doan (or Doane) family are taken from Doane, comp., *The Doane Family* 15, 26, 53, 80–1, 226–31.
21 Mercer, "The Doanes Before the Revolution," 176–8; BCHS, Atkinson, History of Wrightstown Index; and BCCH, Will and inventory of Daniel Doan.
22 SRC, "Grandfather Doane to his youngest brother, Ebenezer, during their apprenticeship."
23 NJSA, 1570AM, 1573AM, 1813AM, 1841AM, 1844AM, and 3200AM and Cohen, "State House of New Jersey" John Notman made extensive additions and alterations to Doan's original building in 1845.
24 Deed from Scholfield to Doan; and BCHS, Solebury Township tax records.
25 Davis, *History of Bucks County*, 393; and Lemon, *The Best Poor Man's Country*, 88–91.
26 Robinson, *History of Toronto*, 2:447.
27 AO, Minutes of Yonge Street Monthly Meeting, 3, 32.

CHAPTER 2

1 Armstrong, *The Affecting Presence*, 31.
2 AO, Minutes of Yonge Street Monthly Meeting, 42.

3 Newlands, "A Meeting House," 25.
4 McFall, "Elmer Starr," 42.
5 Morrison, *Early American Architecture*, 518; and Richman, *Pennsylvania's Architecture*, 14–16.
6 Stilgoe, *Landscape of America*, 45–50.
7 Lemon, *The Best Poor Man's Country*, 102, 131.
8 Newlands, "A Meeting House," 27.
9 AO, Minutes of Yonge Street Monthly Meeting, 38, 39, 42.
10 Newlands, "A Meeting House," 27.
11 AO, Minutes of Yonge Street Monthly Meeting, 77.
12 Bacon, *Mothers of Feminism*, 21–3.
13 George Fox, quoted in Barry Levy, "The Birth of the 'Modern Family' in Early America: Quaker and Anglican Families in the Delaware Valley, Pennsylvania, 1681–1750," in Zuckerman, *Friends and Neighbours*, 38–9.
14 Dorland, *Quakers in Canada*, 10–18; and Bacon, *Mothers of Feminism*, 24–5.
15 Bacon, *Mothers of Feminism*, 24–5.
16 Tolles, *Quakers and the Atlantic Culture*, 10–15.
17 Sawdon, *The Woodbridge Story*, 44.
18 STMA. This volume is inscribed with the name, "Eleazar Lewis," and with historical notes by a descendant, Anna Pauline Ewen. See also: AO, Eleazer Lewis Papers, Indenture of Apprenticeship of Eleazar Lewis with Reuben Burr, 15 June 1809.
19 Hamlin, *Greek Revival Architecture*, 64.
20 Bauman, *Let Your Words Be Few*, 50, 95.
21 Barclay, *True Christian Divinity*, 11–12.
22 Ibid., 4.
23 From William Penn, *The Written Gospel Labours of John Whitehead*, quoted in Wright, *Literary Life*, 64.
24 Bauman, *Let Your Words Be Few*, 136–53.
25 Quoted in Tolles, *Quakers and the Atlantic Culture*, 81–2.
26 Ibid., 84–9.
27 Garfinkel, "Discipline, Discourse, and Deviation", 45–7, 94, 123.
28 AO, Minutes of the Yonge Street Monthly Meeting, 16.
29 MacRae and Adamson, *Hallowed Walls*, 39–42.
30 Peter Benes, "Sky Colors and Scattered Clouds: The Decorative and Architectural Painting of New England Meeting Houses, 1738–1834," in Benes, ed., *New England Meeting House*, 51–69.
31 AO, Minutes of the Yonge Street Monthly Meeting, 3, 32.
32 AO, Miscellaneous Marriage Records Collection, Marriage certificate of Doan and Paxson.
33 Lévi-Strauss, *Structural Anthropology*, 246.
34 Moir, *The Church in the British Era*, 88.

35 Manly, *Wesleyan Methodism*, 10.
36 Wise, *Objections to Methodism*, 48.
37 Barclay, *True Christian Divinity*, 7–8.
38 MacRae and Adamson, *Hallowed Walls*, 28–34.
39 Stevens, *Nathan Bangs*, 47.
40 Goffman, *The Presentation of Self*, 15–20.
41 Bauman, *Let Your Words Be Few*, 84–9.
42 Stevens, *Nathan Bangs*, 15, 25, 34, 99–100.
43 Ibid., 149.
44 Ibid., 108.
45 Ibid., 149.
46 Ibid., 152.
47 Westfall, "Order and Experience," 5–24.

CHAPTER 3

1 Schau, "Sharon's Musical Past," 17; and Harper, *A People's Art*, 36–7.
2 AO, *Upper Canada Gazette*, 17 Nov. 1825.
3 A description of a political procession during which the Children of Peace carried other banners may be found in AO, *The Colonial Advocate*, 20 and 27 Feb. 1834.
4 Willson, *Life of David Willson*, 4.
5 STMA, uncataloged MS, 28–9. (Identified hereafter as "uncataloged MS," this manuscript material was discovered in a compartment in the altar in the temple on 1 May 1990.) An account of this vision later appeared in Willson, *The Practical Life*, 17–18.
6 Ibid., 19–20.
7 Ibid., v.
8 Willson, *The Rights of Christ*, 3.
9 STMA, uncataloged MS, 5, 14–16.
10 Dorland, *Quakers in Canada*, 106–7.
11 Willson, *The Rights of Christ*, 5.
12 Dorland, *Quakers in Canada*, 107.
13 Schrauwers, *Awaiting the Millenium*, Appendix 1.
14 STMA, MS X987.8.1a,b. and Willson, *The Practical Life*, 21–2.
15 Martin, *Revelation*, 9.
16 M.-L. von Franz, "The Process of Individuation," in Jung, ed., *Man and His Symbols*, 177.
17 Joseph L. Henderson, "Ancient Myths and Modern Man," in Jung, ed., *Man and His Symbols*, 122–3.
18 Dorland, *Quakers in Canada*, 245.
19 Webb, "Recollections of an Immigrant," 14.
20 STMA, MS L24, entry dated 15 Feb. 1815.

21 Jones, *History of Agriculture*, 37–8; and Trewhella, *Town of Newmarket*, 49–50.
22 Schrauwers, *Awaiting the Millenium*, 29, Appendix 1.
23 AO, Graham, *Recollections*.
24 STMA, MS 985.5.15.
25 STMA, MS 985.5.22,23.
26 Ryan, ed., "Mathias Hutchinson's Notes, 41.
27 STMA, uncataloged MS, 17.
28 Dorland, *Quakers in Canada*, 134–5.
29 Willson, *An Address*, 10, 24–5, 41, 47.
30 Dorland, *Quakers in Canada*, 160.
31 Doherty, *The Hicksite Separation*, 26.
32 STMA, MS 986.3.1, David Willson, "A Short Account of the origin and principles of the people that constitute the worship of God and almsgiving in Sharon, East Gwillimbury," 2.
33 Wilson, *Philadelphia Quakers*, 84–5.
34 Dorland, *Quakers in Canada*, 130–1; and Ryan, ed., "Mathias Hutchinson's Notes," 36–43.
35 Doherty, *The Hicksite Separation*, 34–5; and J. William Frost, "Years of Crisis and Separation: Philadelphia Yearly Meeting, 1790–1860," in Moore, ed., *Friends in the Delaware Valley*, 65–9. Doherty stresses economic and social divisions between the Orthodox and Hicksite Quakers. Frost believes that evangelicalism was used by the Orthodox party in an attempt to revitalize the Society of Friends at a time when other Protestant groups were making numerous converts in an area where Friends had once been dominant.
36 Bauman, *For the Reputation of Truth*.
37 Schrauwers,"The Politics of Schism," 31–52.
38 Willson, *An Address*, 41.
39 Harrison, *The Second Coming*, 58–77, 86–8.
40 Ibid., 61, 80–1.
41 Sandeen, *The Roots of Fundamentalism*.
42 Watson, "Moraviantown," 125–6.
43 AO, *Upper Canada Gazette*, 17 Nov. 1825.
44 Hayden, *Seven American Utopias*, 65–7.
45 Cross, *The Burned-Over District*, 33–4; and Wisbey, *Pioneer Prophetess*.
46 Harrison, *The Second Coming*, 96–111, 132.
47 Levy, *Quakers and the American Family*, 25, 53, 193.
48 Edward Hicks, quoted in Dorland, *Quakers in Canada*, 131.
49 Furnas, *The Americans*, 489.
50 Sarah Grimke, quoted in Smith-Rosenberg, *Disorderly Conduct*, 125.
51 See Sklar, *Catherine Beecher* and Ryan, *Cradle of the Middle Class*, chapters 2 and 3.

52 STMA, MS 975.441.1, 174–80.
53 Schrauwers, *Awaiting the Millennium*, 43.
54 STMA, MS 985.5.2.
55 Schrauwers, *Awaiting the Millennium*, Appendix 1.
56 Ryan, ed., "Mathias Hutchinson's Notes," 41.

CHAPTER 4

1 Dorland, *Quakers in Canada*, 107.
2 STMA, uncataloged MS, 38–9; and ACYM, journal of Timothy Rogers, 103.
3 Jones, *History of Agriculture*, 37–8; and Trewhella, *Town of Newmarket*, 49–50.
4 STMA, MS X975.441.1.
5 Ibid., 184–6, 187, 192–4.
6 Willson, *An Address*, 41.
7 STMA, MS X975.441.1, 180–2, 187–9, 248.
8 Ibid., 182–4.
9 STMA, MS 985.5.6; and MS 985.5.114.
10 Reference to this school may be found in Bacon, *Mothers of Feminism*, 82.
11 Newlands, "Yonge Street Friends School," 12–14.
12 Schrauwers, *Awaiting the Millennium*, Appendix 1.
13 McArthur, *Children of Peace*.
14 Garvan, "The Protestant Plain Style," 12.
15 Pierson, *American Buildings*, 55.
16 Donnelly, "New England Meeting Houses," 92–7.
17 Morrison, *Early American Architecture*, 79–81.
18 Mallary, *New England Churches*, 48.
19 See Deetz, *Invitation to Archaeology*, 45–52, and *In Small Things Forgotten*, 108–13.
20 Wilson, *Philadelphia Quakers*, 18. The Friends meeting house built in 1748 at Fourth and West Streets in Wilmington, Delaware, was also square in shape and had a cupola at the apex of its hipped roof. (See Ibid., 31.)
21 Ibid., 7; and Moore, ed., *Friends in the Delaware Valley*, cover illustration and notes.
22 Wilson, *Philadelphia Quakers*, 19.
23 Armstrong, *The Affecting Presence*, 31.
24 McArthur, *Children of Peace*; and Schau, "Sharon's Musical Past," 16.
25 Fraser, "Diary," 80–125.
26 AO, *Weekly Register*, 17 Nov. 1825.
27 STMA, MS 959.84.3, 37–8.
28 Ibid., 39.
29 Ibid., 39.
30 STMA, MS 986.3.2.

31 STMA, letter from Jacob to Mary Albertson. I am indebted to Albert Schrauwers for drawing this letter to my attention.
32 AO, *Weekly Register*, 17 Nov. 1825.
33 AO, *Recorder*, 31 Oct. 1861. Again I am indebted to Albert Schrauwers for this reference.
34 STMA, MS 971.28.57.
35 Bauman, *Let Your Words Be Few*, 30.
36 STMA, MS 985.5.22, 23.
37 Mackenzie, *Sketches of Canada*, 119.
38 Willson, *An Address*, 41.
39 STMA, MS 985.5.1, 63–5.
40 See Blunt, *Artistic Theory in Italy*, 1–22.
41 The Reverend H.H. O'Neill, quoted in Allen, *Notes on St. James'*.
42 Postscript to Willson, *A Friend to Britain*, 314, bound with Willson, *Impressions of the Mind* and signed "for the Village of Hope" by Murdoch McLeod, Sr; William Reid, Sr; John Doan, Sr; Samuel Hughes; and Ebenezer Doan.
43 Willson, *Life of David Willson*, 8.
44 Shirreff, *A Tour Through North America*, 107.
45 STMA, MS X975.434.1, 279–80.
46 STMA, MS 986.3.2, entry dated 9 May 1831.
47 Mann, "Legends and Folk Tales, 5.
48 Higgins, *Joseph Gould*, 26.
49 Rempel, *Building With Wood*, 104.
50 STMA MS 986.3.2.
51 McArthur, *Children of Peace*.
52 Ibid.
53 STMA, MS 986.3.2.
54 Ibid.
55 Architectural historian Anthony Adamson has suggested that the altar was originally made as a model of a building that the Children of Peace intended to build and became an altar only as an afterthought. He has speculated that it might have been a model for the 1819 meeting house, but proved too expensive to build; or that it represented an early design for the temple, but proved to be too small for the congregation when it came time to start construction. This is just speculation, however. No documentation survives to support his theories. See Adamson, "The Ark," 28–30.
56 See Downs, *American Furniture*, pl. 185.
57 Morrison, *Early American Architecture*, 455.
58 Morris, ed., *Encyclopedia of American History*, 548–9; and Grinstein, *Rise of the Jewish Community*.
59 Shirreff, *A Tour Through North America*, 107.

60 STMA, MS 986.3.2, entry dated 15 Nov. 1831.
61 STMA, MS X975.434.1, 279; and MS 986.3.2, entries dated 17 Sept. 1830 and 13 June 1831.
62 Ibid. entry dated 24 June 1831.
63 McArthur, *Children of Peace*.
64 AO, *Recorder*, 31 Oct. 1861.
65 McArthur, *Children of Peace*.
66 Shirreff, *A Tour Through North America*, 106.
67 See Wright, *Architecture of the Picturesque*, 20–36.
68 McArthur, *Children of Peace*.
69 AO, Davidite Records, series A, vol. 1.
70 The Reverend H.H. O'Neill, quoted in Allen, *Notes on St. James'*.
71 Smith, *Canadian Gazetteer*, 169; and McArthur, *Children of Peace*.
72 STMA, MS 986.3.2, entry dated 14 July 1834.
73 AO, Davidite Records, series A, vol. 2.
74 Ibid.; and AO, Davidite Records, series A, vol. 1.
75 Smith, *Canadian Gazetteer*, 169.
76 AO, *Recorder*, 31 Oct. 1861.
77 McArthur, *Children of Peace*.
78 See, for example, a multi-sided music stand displayed in the Red Lion Inn Courtyard setting, The Henry Francis du Pont Winterthur Museum.
79 McArthur, *Children of Peace*. A sketch of the interior (Fig. 15), however, shows the organ in a corner off to one side.
80 Shirreff, *A Tour Through North America*, 106.
81 Archaeological Services, *Heritage Resource Assessment*. An alternative to a continuous stone foundation would have been large boulders placed at the corners and at regular intervals to support the sills, as at the Yonge Street meeting house. There is no evidence that either of these methods was followed.

CHAPTER 5

1 Sibbald, "A Few Days," 31.
2 STMA, MS 986.3.2, entry dated 22 Dec. 1831.
3 Mackenzie, *Sketches of Canada*, 118–19.
4 MacRae and Adamson, *Hallowed Walls*, 117.
5 Willson, *The Rights of Christ*, 51–4.
6 STMA, MS 986.3.1, 1–2.
7 Willson, *Life of David Willson* and *The Practical Life*.
8 "Brief Memoir of the Life of John Pemberton," 57.
9 Willson, *Impressions of the Mind*, 139–40.
10 Ibid., 119.

11 Gerry, "David Willson," 19–43.
12 I am indebted to Jane Zavitz Bond, archivist of the Canada Yearly Meeting, for this reference from the minutes of the Yonge Street Monthly Meeting of the Society of Friends.
13 Gerry, *David Willson*, 189–91.
14 David Willson, "Observations to the Reader" in Willson, *Impressions of the Mind*.
15 Ibid. 139.
16 David Willson, quoted in Hughes, *Sketches of the Sharon Temple*, 14–15. I am indebted to Albert Schrauwers for establishing the date of this vision as 1828.
17 See Dorland, *Quakers in Canada*, 112–56.
18 Hughes, *A Vision*.
19 STMA, MS 986.3.2.
20 Henry, *The Emigrants' Guide*, 124. This book appears to have been a pirated reprint of Hume, *Canada As It Is*.
21 Sibbald, "A Few Days," 31.
22 Willson, *Letters to the Jews*, 19.
23 Ibid., 7.
24 Ibid., 26.
25 Ibid., 10.
26 Ibid., 21.
27 Willson, *Life of David Willson*, 6.
28 Postcript in Willson, *Impressions of the Mind*, 270, written by Murdoch McLeod, Sr; William Reid; John Doan, Sr; Samuel Hughes; and Ebenezer Doan, Sr.
29 STMA, uncataloged MS, 41.
30 Ibid.; and Dorland, *Quakers in Canada*, 107.
31 *Discipline of the Yearly Meeting*. This book (in the archives of the Canada Yearly Meeting, Pickering College, Newmarket) bears the inscription, "Queenstreet preparative meeting."
32 Mackenzie, *Sketches of Canada*, 124.
33 Postcript in Willson, *Impressions of the Mind*, 270.
34 STMA, MS 985.5.2.
35 Dorland, *Quakers in Canada*, 6.
36 STMA, uncataloged MS, 45.
37 Ibid., 41.
38 See references to monthly meetings in AO, Davidite Records, series A, vol. 1.
39 Dorland, *Quakers in Canada*, 6.
40 STMA, MS 985.5.2.
41 AO, Davidite Records, series A, vol. 2, entry dated 9 Aug. 1832.
42 Dorland, *Quakers in Canada*, 4–5.
43 AO, Davidite Records, series A, vol. 2, entry dated 9 Aug. 1832.

44 Ibid.
45 Ibid.; and Dorland, *Quakers in Canada*, 4. From the beginning, yearly meetings had been planned, but may not have seemed necessary as the sect continued to be based in East Gwillimbury and did not establish additional monthly meetings elsewhere. (See STMA, uncataloged MS, 44.
46 AO, Davidite Records, Series B, undated entry.
47 AO, *Newmarket Era*, Obituary of John D. Willson, 18 March 1887.
48 AO, Davidite Records, Series B, undated entry.
49 See, for example, STMA, MS 986.3.2, entries dated 19 Dec. 1831, 22 Dec. 1831, 3 Jan. 1832.
50 STMA, MS X975.441.1, 182–4.
51 STMA, MS 986.3.1, entry dated 31 May 1845.
52 STMA, MS X975.441.1, 187.
53 Ibid., 211–14.
54 McArthur, *Children of Peace*.
55 See Ibid.; and Schau, "Sharon's Musical Past," 17.
56 See advertisements by Coates in AO, *Upper Canada Gazette*, 20 Jan. 1825, 22 July 1826.
57 Schau, "Sharon's Musical Past," 17–20.
58 STMA, from Jacob to Mary Albertson.
59 AO, *Weekly Register*, 17 Nov. 1825.
60 AO, *Colonial Advocate*, 3 Sept. 1829.
61 AO, Davidite Records, series A, vol. 1.
62 See Semmel, *The Methodist Revolution*.
63 These are: Willson, *Hymns and Prayers*, *Hymns of Praise Adapted*, and *Hymns of Praise*.
64 Mackenzie, *Sketches of Canada*, 125.
65 Stevens, *Nathan Bangs*, 44.
66 Schrauwers, "An Itinerant Sect," 32–3.
67 McArthur, *Children of Peace*.
68 STMA, MS 986.3.2, entry dated 14 July 1835. The cookhouse where the feasts were prepared has now been moved to the grounds of Sharon Temple Museum.
69 Davidite Records, series A, vol. 1.
70 See Rock, "Mechanics of New York City," 367–94; and Katz, *The People of Hamilton*, introduction.
71 STMA, MS 986.3.2, entry dated 24 June 1831.
72 AO, *Weekly Register*, 17 Nov. 1825.
73 STMA, MS 986.3.2, undated entry, probably from early 1831.
74 STMA, MS 973.33.1, 16–17.
75 STMA, MS 986.3.2, undated entry, probably from early 1831.
76 Ibid., undated "statement signed on behalf of the Brethren" by Murdoch McLeod, John Doan, and Ebenezer Doan.

77 STMA, MS 986.3.1, 1–2.
78 Hayden, *Seven American Utopias*, 68–71.
79 See Coffey, "From Shanty to Log House 61–75; and Schrauwers, *Awaiting the Millennium*, Appendix 2.
80 AO, Graham, *Recollections*, photocopied ms in STMA.
81 STMA, MS 985.5.1, 266.
82 McArthur, *Children of Peace*.
83 Ibid.
84 Ibid.
85 Ibid.
86 Schrauwers, *Awaiting the Millennium*, 171.
87 McFall, "The Last Days," 22. Here an 1865 extract from the *Newmarket Era* is cited, noting that "Mr. David Willson conducted Divine Service in the Temple, as usual."
88 AO, *Colonial Advocate*, 6 Oct. 1831; and AO, *The Advocate*, 21 Aug. 1834, 16 Oct. 1834.
89 Ibid., 20 Feb. 1834.
90 Wilkie, *Sketches of a Summer Trip*, 203–6.
91 From Francis Higginson, *A Brief Relation of the Irreligion of the Northern Quakers* (London, 1653), quoted in Bauman, *Let Your Words Be Few*, 78.
92 Westfall, *Two Worlds*, 35.
93 Caswall, *America*, 12.
94 Bauman, *Let Your Words Be Few*, 78.

CHAPTER 6

1 STMA, uncataloged MS, 208.
2 See, for example, an 1853 reference to "David's Town" in Backhouse, *Journal and Letters*, 159; Smith, *Canadian Gazetteer*, 168–9; and *Canada*, 285.
3 Rolling, *East Gwillimbury*, 53.
4 Duncumb, *The British Emigrant's Advocate*, 272–3.
5 AO, *Recorder*, 26 Sept. 1861. This description is signed, "PLOUGHBOY" and dated at Newmarket, 21 Sept. 1861.
6 Hardy, *Alternative Communities*, 126–7.
7 Fogarty, *Communal and Utopian History*, 88–9.
8 Shirreff, *A Tour through North America*, 107.
9 Burrowes, *Maxwell and Henry Jones*, 15–16; Morrison, "'The Toon 'o Maxwell'," 1–12; and Ontario, *Historical Sketches*, 35–6.
10 Hume, *Canada As It Is*, 123.
11 AO, *Weekly Register*, 17 Nov. 1825.
12 AO, Diary of Mary O'Brien, entry dated 26 Feb. 1829.
13 Rolph, *A Brief Account*, 184.

14 STMA, MS 986.3.2, entry dated 17 Sept. 1830. Because he has not found evidence in records of land transactions that these and other guidelines were carried out precisely, Matthew Cooper has questioned the degree to which the Children of Peace acted on their beliefs in cooperation. While it is true that they were neither "communistic" nor "communal" in the way of some American sects, it is clear that the principles these terms imply were evident in their early community life. (See Cooper, "Living Together," 3–18.)
15 Levy, *Quakers and the American Family*, 135.
16 Susan S. Forbes, "Quaker Tribalism," in Zuckerman, ed., *Friends and Neighbors*, 171.
17 STMA, MS 986.3.2, entry dated 17 Sept. 1830.
18 Ibid., entry dated 2 April 1831.
19 AO, East Gwillimbury, Index of Deeds, vol. 1.
20 Ibid.
21 BCCH, deed, from Doan to Doan, deed from Scholfield to Doan; and deed from Doan to Ely. See also BCHS, Solebury Township tax records.
22 AO, East Gwillimbury Abstract Index. As Albert Schrauwers has shown, purchases recorded in the Abstract Index may not always tell the whole story. Township and personal papers provide a more complete picture regarding the details of transactions and methods of payment. See Schrauwers, *Awaiting the Millennium*, 97–9.
23 BCHS, letter from Doan to Paxson.
24 AO, York County Surrogate Court Records, Will of Ebenezer Doan (d. 3 Feb 1866).
25 AO, East Gwillimbury Abstract Index.
26 Doane, *The Ebenezer Doane Family*, 58.
27 AO, East Gwillimbury Abstract Index.
28 BCCH, deed from Doan to Doan.
29 AO, East Gwillimbury Abstract Index.
30 Schrauwers, *Awaiting the Millennium*, 101.
31 STMA, MS 985.5.3.
32 AO, East Gwillimbury Census, 1851.
33 Hume, *Canada As It Is*, 122–3.
34 Shirreff, *A Tour Through North America*, 107.
35 McFall, "The Last Days," 22.
36 STMA, MS 986.3.2, entry dated 3 Dec. 1831.
37 AO, East Gwillimbury Census, 1851.
38 STMA, MS 986.3.2, undated entry from 1832.
39 AO, East Gwillimbury Assessment roll, 1834; and STM, Carolyn Mann's genealogy of the Willson family. The obituary of Charles Doan (AO *Aurora Banner*, 21 June 1895) indicates that he once was in partnership with Willson's son, Hugh.
40 East Gwillimbury (north half), Assessment roll, 1825.

41 Trewhella, *Town of Newmarket*, 31, 35.
42 AO, Sharon Temple Papers. Written inside the account book is the inscription, "David Doan Day Book 1837" in a later hand. This is a misattribution since David Doan, born in 1820, a son of Ebenezer, would have been only seventeen when the book was begun. He is known to have been a farmer, not a storekeeper. Albert Schrauwers has attributed it, without explanation, to William H. Willson. (See Schrauwers, *Awaiting the Millennium*, 176–7.) The earliest entries were covered by newspaper clippings when the book was used as a scrapbook in the late-nineteenth century. Uncovered entries date from 10 July 1837 to 4 Feb. 1839.
43 AO, East Gwillimbury Census, 1851.
44 Hume, *Canada As It Is*; and Henry, *The Emigrant's Guide*, 122.
45 Shirreff, *A Tour Through North America*, 108.
46 AO, Davidite Records, series A, vol. 2.
47 Hume, *Canada As It Is*, 123.
48 Wilkie, *Sketches of a Summer Trip*, 203.
49 AO, *Colonial Advocate*, 29 July 1830.
50 STMA, MS 986.3.2, entry dated 16 Aug. 1832; and AO, *Colonial Advocate*, 22 Aug. 1832.
51 AO, Davidite Records, series A, vol. 2.
52 STMA, MS 986.3.2, entry dated 3 Nov. 1832.
53 AO, Ebenezer Doan Papers, MS 47, in Sharon Temple Papers, MS 834.
54 AO, Davidite Records, series B.
55 Susan S. Forbes, "Quaker Tribalism," in Zuckerman, ed., *Friends and Neighbors*, 148.
56 *Discipline of the Yearly Meeting*, 81.
57 Susan S. Forbes, "Quaker Tribalism," in Zuckerman, ed., *Friends and Neighbors*, 149.
58 STMA, MS 985.5.6, MS 985.5.99, and MS 985.5.114; and AO, Ethel Willson Trewhella Papers, letter from Julia Brown to Ethel Trewhella, 27 Aug. 1949.
59 AO, Letter from Jacob to Mary Albertson.
60 Rolph, *A Brief Account*, 183.
61 WL, Petition, purporting to be from David Willson, to the House of Assembly.
62 McArthur, *Children of Peace*.
63 Mackenzie, *Sketches of Canada* 119. His descriptions of the Children of Peace had appeared earlier in his newspaper, the *Colonial Advocate*.
64 One non-traditional skill added to the curriculum was the use of firearms. The traveller, George Henry Hume, recorded that "They, together with all the women belonging to the sect, used to be drilled to the use of fire-arms, probably in case of extremity, to defend themselves; on

one occasion, however, one of their muskets burst, after which they declined the practice." (Hume, *Canada As It Is*, 124–5.)

65 STMA, MS X975.441.1, 158–64.
66 STMA, MS 986.3.2, entry dated 13 July 1832.
67 STMA, MS 971.20.28.
68 Hume, *Canada As It Is*, 122–3.
69 Shirreff, *A Tour Through North America*, 108.
70 STMA, MS 986.3.2, entry dated 3 Jan. 1832.
71 Gummere, *The Quaker*, 7.
72 ACYM, *Discipline of the Yearly Meeting*, 64–8.
73 See Susan S. Forbes, "Quaker Tribalism," in Zuckerman, ed., *Friends and Neighbors*, 145–6.
74 ACYM, *Discipline of the Yearly Meeting*, 67.
75 Ibid., 65.
76 Bauman, *Let Your Words Be Few*, 43–4, 55.
77 AO, Graham, *Recollections*, 4.
78 Duncumb, *The British Emigrant's Advocate*, 273–4.
79 Hume, *Canada As It Is*, 122–3.
80 Shirreff, *A Tour Through North America*, 107.
81 See, for example, Willson's reply to Methodist Peter Conger, dated "5th of 1st mo. 1815" (STMA, MS X975.441.1).
82 See BCHS, letter from Doan to Paxson.
83 AO, York County Surrogate Court Records, Will of Thomas Dunham (d. 19 Sept. 1850).
84 Archaeological Services, *Heritage Resource Assessment*.
85 See Garfinkel, Discipline, Discourse and Deviation, 47, 94, 123.
86 AO, Graham, *Recollections*.
87 Smith, *Canadian Gazetteer*, 169.
88 STMA, MS 986.3.2.
89 Mackenzie (pseud. Patrick Swift), *New Almanac*, 8.
90 Wood, "The Settlers and the Land," 117.
91 See Katz, *The People of Hamilton*, introduction and chapter 1.
92 AO, East Gwillimbury Assessment Roll, 1834.
93 AO, East Gwillimbury Assessment Roll, 1860.
94 AO, East Gwillimbury Assessment Roll, 1861.
95 O'Mara, "The Seasonal Round," 103–10. While dealing with the farming practices of the Sibbalds and Johnsons, "gentry farmers," the author concludes that these practices were largely typical of the norm.
96 For comparative statistics from Pennsylvania, see Lemon, *The Best Poor Man's Country*, 154–64, 216.
97 AO, York County Surrogate Court Records, Will of Ebenezer Doan (d. 3 Feb. 1866).
98 Lemon, *The Best Poor Man's Country*, 178.

99 AO, York County Surrogate Court Records, Inventory of Jacob Lepard (d. 24 Oct. 1850).
100 Jones, *History of Agriculture*, 79–80.

CHAPTER 7

1 AO, *Recorder*, 26 Sept. 1861.
2 AO, East Gwillimbury Abstract Index.
3 "Restoring House of Ebenezer Doan," 14.
4 Wood, "The Settlers and the Land," 117.
5 Coffey, "From Shanty to Log House," 70–1.
6 AO, East Gwillimbury Assessment Rolls, 1825, 1834; and AO, East Gwillimbury Census, 1851.
7 Norris, "Vetting the Vernacular," 80–3.
8 Glassie, *Material Folk Culture*.
9 The Abdon Hibbs house, built c.1820, is located at Washington Crossing (formerly Taylorsville) in Bucks County, Pennsylvania, and has been restored by the Pennsylvania Historical and Museum Commission.
10 Richie, *Of Stone and Dreams*.
11 Glassie, "Delaware Valley Folk Building," 37.
12 BCHS, United States Direct Tax Lists, 470–83.
13 BCC, Upper Makefield Tax List. The date 1795/96 is based on detailed research by Jeff Marshall of the Conservancy. For information regarding Benjamin Doan (1734–1809), see Doane, *The Doane Family*, 122.
14 See Moxon, *Mechanick Exercises*. See also Roger W. Moss, Jr, "The Origins of the Carpenters' Company of Philadelphia," in Peterson, ed., *Building Early America*, 39–41.
15 Richie, *Of Stone and Dreams*.
16 See Glassie, *Material Folk Culture*, 49, 54, and "Delaware Valley Folk Building," 43–7.
17 See Glassie, *Material Folk Culture*, 48, 50–1, and "Continental Log House," 32–9. See also Swank, "The Architectural Landscape," in Swank *et al.*, *Arts of the Pennsylvania Germans*, 31–4.
18 Doane, *The Ebenezer Doane Family*, 5.
19 Davis, *History of Bucks County*, 393.
20 Rempel, *Building With Wood*, 16–18, 60–1. The Stong houses today form the nucleus of Black Creek Pioneer Village, Toronto.
21 Doane, *The Doane Family*; and Mercer, "The Doanes Before the Revolution," 173.
22 Cooper, "A Quaker-Plan House," 14–34, and "Postscript to 'A Quaker-Plan House'," 143–50; Shurtleff, *The Log Cabin Myth*, 123–6; and Waterman, *Dwellings of Colonial America*, 41, 43, 79, 125, 158–9. For a more recent interpretation of the origins of the "Quaker plan" and the 1684

promotional pamphlet, see Carson *et al.*, "Impermanent Architecture," 141, 144, footnote 21. For an account of the three-room plan as interpreted in North Carolina, see Bernard L. Herman, "Continuity and Change in Traditional Architecture: The Continental Plan Farmhouse in Middle North Carolina," in Swain, ed., *Carolina Dwelling*.

23 See Allen, *In English Ways*, 11; Jenkins, "Early Welsh Settlers", 397–401; and Worrall, *Quakers in the Colonial Northeast*, 5.

24 Brunskill, *Vernacular Architecture* 60–1; Hilling, *Historic Architecture of Wales*, 93; Jenkins, *Tradition in Rural Wales*, 118; Peate, *The Welsh House*; Reid, *Shell Book of Cottages*, 134; and Smith, *Houses of the Welsh Countryside*, 172, 175.

25 See purchase by Ebenezer Doan, Jr, from Benjamin Scholfield, 1801 (BCCH, Office of the Recorder of Deeds, Book 37, p. 416), and purchase by Thomas Rose from Samuel Scholfield, 1797 (BCCH, Office of the Recorder of Deeds, Book 37, p. 188). The Solebury house differs from Doan's house in East Gwillimbury in several respects. Most obviously, it is built of stone, but there are subtler differences as well. The small back room on the first floor of the Solebury house appears to have been accessible only through the front room and not through the hall/kitchen. Also, its roof frame is different from preferred Anglo-American types. It is more complex than the roof structure of the Doan house, which has common rafters joined at the apex by pegged mortice-and-tenon joints.

26 Minhinnick, *At Home in Upper Canada*, 57, 60.

27 CA, York County Surrogate Court Records, Probate inventory of John Doan, 1862.

CHAPTER 8

1 AO, *The Advocate*, 27 Feb. 1834.
2 Craig, *Upper Canada*, 213–19.
3 AO, *The Advocate*, 27 Feb. 1834.
4 Berrin, "Henry Blackstone," 25.
5 AO, *The Advocate*, 13 March 1834.
6 Wilkie, *Sketches of a Summer Trip*, 206.
7 The Reverend H.H. O'Neill, quoted in Allen, "Notes on St. James.'"
8 Willson, *The Rights of Christ*, 19–30.
9 STMA MS X975.441.1, p.194. Peter Conger, a Methodist itinerant, also appears to have accused Willson of breaking the law. (See MS STMA, X975.441.1, pp.192–3)
10 Read, "The Rebellion of 1837", 6.
11 Willson, *A Friend to Britain*, 280–1.
12 Ibid., 284.
13 Mann, "Legends and Folk Tales," 14.

14 Willson, *A Friend to Britain*, 298.
15 Ibid., 288.
16 Cruikshank, ed., *John Graves Simcoe*, 1:27.
17 See Craig, *Upper Canada*, 188–209.
18 Johnson, "Simcoe's Yonge Street," 35.
19 Dorland, *Quakers in Canada* 14; and Groh, "Disabilities of the Dissenters," 22–7.
20 AO, *Colonial Advocate*, 27 Jan. 1831.
21 AO, Davidite Records, series A, vol. 2.
22 Quoted in Mann, "Newly Discovered Records," 39.
23 Dorland, *Quakers in Canada*, 14.
24 Willson, *A Friend to Britain*, 302.
25 Ibid., 310.
26 AO, *Colonial Advocate*, 16 July 1829; and genealogical notes from Carolyn Mann.
27 AO, *Colonial Advocate*, 17 March 1831.
28 Quoted in Craig, *Upper Canada*, 212.
29 AO, Diary of Mary O'Brien, entry dated 18 Jan. 1832.
30 AO, *Colonial Advocate*, 27 Jan. 1831.
31 AO, Mackenzie-Lindsey Papers, unidentified newspaper clipping, dated 9 Oct. 1840.
32 STMA, MS 986.3.2, entry dated 19 Dec. 1831.
33 Ibid., entry dated 22 Dec. 1831.
34 Ibid., entry dated 3 Jan. 1832.
35 Craig, *Upper Canada*, 213.
36 STMA, MS 986.3.2, entry dated 5 Feb. 1832.
37 Craig, *Upper Canada*, 215–16.
38 STMA, MS 986.3.2, entry dated 23 Nov. 1833.
39 Ibid., entries dated 22 and 23 Jan. 1834.
40 Ibid., entry dated 14 July 1834.
41 Ibid., entry dated 31 Oct. 1835.
42 Ibid., entry dated 30 Jan. 1836.
43 Craig, *Upper Canada*, 232–5.
44 Walsh, *The Christian Church*, 182.
45 STMA, MS 986.3.2, entry dated 4 Nov. 1836.
46 Ibid., entry dated 28 July 1837.
47 Read, The Rebellion of 1837, 10.
48 Craig, *Upper Canada*, 228–32, 237–8.
49 Higgins, *Joseph Gould*, 96.
50 STMA, MS 986.3.2, entry dated 1 Aug. 1837.
51 Ibid., entry dated 7 Aug. 1837.
52 Craig, *Upper Canada*, 240, 244–6.
53 Read and Stagg, eds., *The Rebellion of 1837*, xxxviii.

54 Ibid., xl.
55 AO, Rebellion Papers, Charles Doan's sworn statement, taken 15 Dec. 1837.
56 Robinson, *History of Toronto*, 2:491-2; AO, Mackenzie-Lindsey Papers, letter from Maria Waite to Murdoch McLeod, 8 Feb. 1840; and Schrauwers, "Letters," 36.
57 OGS, *Rebels Arrested*.
58 Sibbald, "A Few Days," 32.
59 J.H.S. Drinkwater to Sir Francis Bond Head, 16 Dec. 1837, in Read and Stagg, *Rebellion of 1837*, 338.
60 Arthur Carthew to John Joseph, 2 May 1838, Ibid., 423.
61 ADHS, 989.25.1.
62 ADHS, 989.25.2.
63 OGS, *Rebels Arrested*, 19.
64 Ibid., 13.
65 Ibid., and genealogical data from Mrs. Marjorie Richardson.
66 See Gay, *Education of the Senses*, 244-52.
67 STMA, MS 983.5.3 letter from Mary to Charles Doan, 19 Jan. 1838.
68 Illustrated in Stewart, "The Little Boxes," 39.
69 STMA, MS X976.10.3 letter from Elizabeth to John Graham, 6 May 1838.
70 Casey, *Letters*, 53.
71 STMA, MS 959.84.3, p.52.
72 STMA, MS 986.3.2, following entry dated 20 Nov. 1837.
73 STMA, MS 973.33.1, entries dated 15 Aug. and 5 Sept. 1838.
74 Ibid., entries dated 27 and 31 Dec. 1838.
75 AO, Davidite Records, series A, vol. 2.
76 Craig, ed., *Lord Durham's Report*, i-x; and Read *The Rebellion of 1837*, 22.
77 STMA, broadside L1230, David Willson, *To the Memory of David Lepard*.
78 AO, Mackenzie-Lindsey Papers, Newspaper clipping from *The Mirror*, n.d. [Sept. 1840].
79 AO, Mackenzie-Lindsey Papers, unidentified newspaper clipping, dated April 1841.
80 Careless, *Union of the Canadas*, 46-51.
81 MTRL, Letter from David Willson to Robert Baldwin, 9 Aug. 1841.
82 Letter, same to same, 7 March 1844.
83 Letter, same to same, 5 Oct. 1844.
84 Letter, same to same, 27 Oct. 1844.
85 STMA, broadside L1228, David Willson, *The Sharon Meeting*.
86 AO, Davidite Records, series A, vol. l.
87 This was not an entirely new development. Early in the sect's history, a "Youths Meeting of the Children of Peace" had existed and may then have challenged Willson's authority. (See chapter 4, p.77.)
88 STMA, MS 986.3.1, entries dated 5 and 31 May 1845.

89 STMA, MS 973.33.2, entry dated 2 Aug. 1848.
90 Ibid., entry dated 5 Nov. 1850.
91 Ibid., following entry dated 21 Dec. 1850.
92 See Careless, *Union of the Canadas*, 194.

CHAPTER 9

1 OA, East Gwillimbury Census 1851, 1861, and 1871.
2 AO, *Newmarket Era*, 12 June 1857.
3 These included Willson, *Life of David Willson, Sacred Impressions, Hymns of Praise, Mysteries of the Mind,* and *Life of the Author*.
4 See, for example, AO, *Newmarket Era*, 25 Jan. 1856, wherein Willson urges reformers in his riding to unite.
5 Rolling, *East Gwillimbury*, 27.
6 Careless, *Union of the Canadas*, 226.
7 See AO, *Newmarket Era*, 25 Dec. 1868. Obituary of Jesse Doan, reeve of East Gwillimbury Township and active on the municipal council during the preceding ten years.
8 AO, *Newmarket Era*, 25 Jan. 1856; and Rolling, *East Gwillimbury*, 228.
9 Ibid., 228.
10 Robinson, *History of Toronto*, 2:498.
11 Careless, *Union of the Canadas*, 176.
12 Rolling, *East Gwillimbury*, 205.
13 Ibid., 53, 205.
14 AO, *Newmarket Era*, 18 March 1887. Obituary of John D. Willson.
15 Clemens, "Temperance Literature," 143.
16 AO, Minutes of the Yonge Street Monthly Meeting, 16.
17 AO, Sharon Temple Papers, MS 834, Account book. Whiskey was cheapest, selling at 9d a quart or 2s 9d a gallon. Brandy and wine both sold for 2s 6d a quart, while gin sold for 3s 3d per bottle of unspecified capacity.
18 AO, Davidite Records, series A, vol. II, entry dated 9 Aug. 1832.
19 AO, *Newmarket Era*, 10 Oct. 1856.
20 See, for example, Clemens, "Taste Not; Touch Not; Handle Not," 142–60; Boyer, *Urban Masses*, chapter 1; and Singleton, "Protestant Voluntary Organizations," 47–8.
21 AO, Sons of Temperance Grand Division of Ontario, *Proceedings*, 1850–1851; and Rolling, *East Gwillimbury*, 52.
22 Ibid., 178.
23 Ibid., 179.
24 Ibid., 49–50; and East Gwillimbury Census, 1861.
25 Rolling, *East Gwillimbury*, 50.
26 OA, *Newmarket Era*, 22 Jan. 1866. Obituary of David Willson.
27 OA, *Newmarket Era*, 18 March 1887. Obituary of John D. Willson.

28 Jean McFall, "The Last Days," 24.
29 Ibid., 25; and Wills, "The Frayed Years," 34.
30 McFall, "The Last Days," 25–6.
31 AO, *Newmarket Era*, 18 June 1880.
32 OA, *Newmarket Era*, 14 July 1882. Obituary of William Willson.
33 McFall, "The Last Days," 28–30; and Wills, "The Frayed Years," 34–5.
34 AO, York County Surrogate Court Records, Will of David Willson.
35 McFall, "The Last Days," 28–30; and Wills, "The Frayed Years," 34–5.
36 AO, *New Market Era*, 18 March 1887. Obituary of John D. Willson.
37 This account of the period 1886 to 1918 follows McFall, "The Last Days," 32–3; and Wills, "The Frayed Years," 36–40.

CHAPTER 10

1 Berchem, *The Yonge Street Story*, 56–7.
2 Craig, *Upper Canada*, 24–5.
3 Turner, "The Significance of the Frontier," 38–9.
4 Unruh, "The Way West," 306–18. See also Boorstin, *The Americans*, chapter 2.
5 Jones, *O Strange New World*, 61–70; and Stilgoe, *Landscape of America*, chapter 1.
6 Moodie, *Roughing It in the Bush*, 163–5. Mrs. Moodie's book was first published in London in 1852.
7 Hovinen, "Quakers of Yonge Street," 54–5; and Dorland, *Quakers in Canada*, 91–3.
8 Dorland, *Quakers in Canada*, 95; and Newlands, "Yonge Street Friends School," 12–14.
9 Dorland, *Quakers in Canada*, 1–10.
10 Levy, "The Birth of the 'Modern Family' in Early America: Quaker and Anglican Families in the Delaware Valley, Pennsylvania, 1651–1750" in Zuckerman, ed., *Friends and Neighbors*, 26–61; and Levy, *Quakers and the American Family*, 25–53. See also Bacon, *Mothers of Feminism*, 54.
11 ACYM, *Discipline of the Yearly Meeting*, 64–8. See also Bauman, *Let Your Words Be Few*, 22–30; Garfinkel, "Discipline, Discourse and Deviation," 123; Gummere, *The Quaker*, 71; and Tolles, *Quakers and the Atlantic Culture*, 84–9.
12 Susan S. Forbes, "Quaker Tribalism," in Zuckerman, ed., *Friends and Neighbors*, 145–73; and Lemon, *The Best Poor Man's Country*, 116.
13 Stevens, *Nathan Bangs*, 99–100, 107–8, 149–54. See also Clark, *Church and Sect*, 94; and Semmel, *The Methodist Revolution*, 8.
14 Westfall, "Order and Experience, 5–24.
15 John Graves Simcoe to Phineas Bond, 7 May 1792, in Cruikshank, ed., *John Graves Simcoe* 1:151; and Dorland, *Quakers in Canada*, 14.

16 Dorland, *Quakers in Canada*, 317.
17 Ibid.; and Craig, *Upper Canada*, 317.
18 Reaman, *Trail of the Black Walnut*, 83–4, 103–4.
19 See Syrett, ed., *American Historical Documents*, 82; and Reid, et al. eds., *A Source-Book*, 64.
20 Jane Errington, "Loyalists in Upper Canada: A British American Community" in Wise et al., eds., "'None was ever better...'" 64.
21 Willson, *Reminiscences*, 9–26.
22 Doane, comp., *The Doane Family*, 15, 26, 53, 80–1, 226–31.
23 Schau, "Sharon's Musical Past," 17; and Harper, *A People's Art*, 36–7.
24 Davis, *Utopia and the Ideal Society*, 335–8, 351; Hardy, *Alternative Communities*, 126–7; and Levy, *Quakers and the American Family*, 25.
25 Bacon, *The Quiet Rebels*, 50; and Wilson, *Philadelphia Quakers*, 9–15.
26 Levy, *Quakers and the American Family*, 193, 267.
27 Lemon, *The Best Poor Man's Country*, 68, 216.
28 Wisbey, *Pioneer Prophetess*, 12–28.
29 Dorland, *Quakers in Canada*, 127–56.
30 J. William Frost, "Years of Crisis and Separation: Philadelphia Yearly Meeting, 1790–1860" in Moore, ed., *Friends in the Delaware Valley*, 68–9.
31 See Doherty, *The Hicksite Separation*, chapters 3 and 4.
32 Bacon, *Mothers of Feminism*, 95; and Hamm, *Transformation of American Quakerism*, 34–48.
33 Dorland, *Quakers in Canada*, 233–54.
34 Bushman, *From Puritan to Yankee*, 196–7; and Nye, *The Cultural Life*, 221–2.
35 Ibid., 227–8.
36 Manly, *Wesleyan Methodism*, 10–12.
37 Walsh, *The Christian Church*, 140–1.
38 See, for example, Bushman, *From Puritan to Yankee*. Bushman argues that the religious revivals of the mid-eighteenth century, with their emphasis on individual quests for salvation by God's grace and their questioning of all earthly authority, weakened control by both the churches and the secular governments of the time and reinforced a spirit of individualism, which already was growing in economic and social spheres.
39 A major influence on many studies has been the work of Max Weber. See, for example, Max Weber, "The Protestant Sects and the Spirit of Capitalism" in Gerth and Mills, *From Max Weber*.
40 Thompson, *English Working Class*, 362–3, 368.
41 Johnson, *A Shopkeeper's Millennium*, 138. Here Johnson declares, "The religion that [the revival] preached was order inducing, repressive

and quintessentially bourgeois ... We must conclude that many workmen (the number varied enormously from town to town) were adopting the religion of the middle class, thus internalizing beliefs and modes of comportment that suited the needs of their employers."

42 See, for instance, Laurie, *Working People*, chapter 2; and Wallace, *Rockdale*, chapter 3.
43 Semmel, *The Methodist Revolution*, 7–8.
44 Bacon, *Mothers of Feminism*, 73. See also Thomas, "Romantic Reform," 656–81; and Waters, *American Reformers*. Both Thomas and Walters see reform movements in this period as having their origins in a religious impulse that was politically and socially conservative. Reformers hoped to restore order to a society in which the traditional powers of the church and clergy were diminishing.
45 John Winthrop, "A Model of Christian Charity," Miller and Johnson, in *The Puritans*, 1:195–9. See also Hawke, *The Colonial Experience*, 132–3.
46 Eccles, *France in America*, 46–8.
47 Watson, "Moraviantown," 125–31; and Wright, *The Cultural Life*, 61–2.
48 Wright, *The Cultural Life*, 194.
49 An excellent comparative study is Hayden, *Seven American Utopias*. See also Fogarty, *Communal and Utopian History*; and Kanter, *Commitment and Community*, 246–7.
50 Donnelly, "New England Meeting Houses," 85–99; and Philip D. Zimmerman, "The Lord's Supper in Early New England: The Setting and the Service" in Benes, ed., *New England Meeting House*, 124–34.
51 Kalman, *Pioneer Churches*, 16–32.
52 Cummings, *Framed Houses*, 3–17.
53 Kalman, *Pioneer Churches*, 16–26.
54 Hayden, *Seven American Utopias*, 24; Morrison, *Early American Architecture*, 541–42; and Richman, *Pennsylvania Architecture*, 8–11.
55 Macquarrie, *Christian Theology*, 313.
56 Grelot, "Apocalyptic," 17–18.
57 Sandeen, *The Roots of Fundamentalism*, chapters 1 and 2.
58 Westfall, *Two Worlds*, 265–6.
59 Hayden, *Seven American Utopias*, 65–71.
60 Westfall, *Two Worlds*, 166–7; and O'Dea, *The Mormons*, 78, 92.
61 Westfall, *Two Worlds*, 167, 171–2.
62 Clark, *Church and Sect*, 308–13; and Barkun, *Crucible of the Millennium*, 31–46.
63 *Christian Guardian*, 29 April 1843, 6 March 1844, 10 April 1844, and 24 April 1844.
64 Hedges, "John Woolman," *American Experience*, 87–102.

65 This phrase is used in Bauman, *Let Your Words Be Few*. Note the chapter, "Where Is the Power that Was at First? The Prophetic Ministry and the Routinization of Charisma," 137–53.
66 Bauman, *Let Your Words Be Few*, 84–9, 136; Vann, *English Quakerism*, 200; Bacon, *The Quiet Rebels*, 84–5; and Dorland, *Quakers in Canada*, 113–16.
67 Bush, "The Reverend James Caughey," 231.
68 Wise, *Earnest Christianity Illustrated*, 397–402.
69 Arthur, *Toronto*, 229; and Westfall, *Two Worlds*, 142–5.
70 Morgan, *The Puritan Family*, 65–86. See also Demos, *A Little Commonwealth*.
71 Lockridge, *A New England Town*, 3–22. See also Greven, *Four Generations*. A useful commentary on the work of Lockridge and Greven and on other community studies is Beeman, "The New Social History," 422–43. See also Allen, *In English Ways*, chapter 3.
72 Horton and Edwards, *American Literary Thought*, 112–21, 225.
73 Manuel and Manuel, *Utopian Thought*, 581–9; Burrowes, *Maxwell and Henry Jones*, 15–16; Fogarty, *Communal and Utopian History*, 88–9; and Hardy, *Alternative Communities*, 126–7.
74 Hayden, *Seven American Utopias*, 149. See also Olson, *Millennialism*, 248.
75 Hayden, *Seven American Utopias*, 349–53; and Holloway, *Heavens on Earth*, 225.
76 A general outline of this evolutionary process is provided in Lockridge, "New England Society," 62–80.
77 Otto F. Kraushaar, "America," 11–29. See also May, *The Enlightenment*, chapter 3.
78 Silverman, *A Cultural History*, 187.
79 Errington, "Loyalists in Upper Canada," in Wise, et al., ed., "'None was ever better ...',*" 60–2.
80 Craig, *Upper Canada*, 20–1.
81 Marx, *The Machine in the Garden*, 194–208.
82 Thomas, "Romantic Reform," 656–81.
83 Ibid., 82–3.
84 Rothman, *Discovery of the Asylum*, chapter 3; Loth and Sadler, *The Only Proper Style*, 44; and Arthur, *Toronto*, 140–1.
85 See Hayden, *The Grand Domestic Revolution*.
86 Garfinkel, "Discipline, Discourse and Deviation", 47, 94, 123.
87 Loth and Sadler, *The Only Proper Style*, 56–67.
88 Doane, *George Washington Doane*, 11–23; and *The Biographical Encyclopaedia*, 389.
89 Loth and Sadler, *The Only Proper Style*, 60–1.
90 Kasson, *Civilizing the Machine*, chapter 1.
91 Nye, *The Cultural Life*, 264–5.

92 See Potter, *People of Plenty*.
93 Lynes, *The Domesticated Americans*, 77–9; and Clark, *The American Family Home*, 19.
94 Beecher and Stowe, *The American Woman's Home*, 18–20.
95 Ware, *Home Life*, 2.
96 Young, *Our Deportment*, 17.
97 Lears, "From Salvation to Self-Realization," 4. See also Lears, *No Place of Grace*, chapter 1; Gay, *Education of the Senses*, 438 ff.; and Campbell, *The Romantic Ethic*, 135–7.
98 Hayden, *Seven American Utopias*, 227.
99 Dixon, *Methodism in America*, 90.
100 Parkinson, *A Tour in America*, 1:661.
101 Pickering, *Emigration, or No Emigration*, 37.
102 Dixon, *Methodism in America*, 122.
103 Cross, *The Burned-Over District*, 4–6, 67.
104 Craig, *Upper Canada*, 227–32; and Harris and Warkentin, *Canada Before Confederation*, 128.
105 Craig, *Upper Canada*, 131; and Harris and Warkentin, *Canada Before Confederation*, 142–5.
106 Rutherford, *Canadian Media*, 2–3.
107 Cross, *The Burned-Over District*, 98–102.
108 Hayden, *Seven American Utopias*, 349–50.

Bibliography

PRIMARY SOURCES

ARCHIVES OF THE CANADA YEARLY MEETING
Journal of Timothy Rogers (typescript copy).

AURORA AND DISTRICT HISTORICAL SOCIETY
989.25.1,2

ARCHIVES OF ONTARIO
Account book, Doan store, 1837–9 (Sharon Temple Papers, MS 834, microfilm).
Aurora Banner.
East Gwillimbury Township, Census, 1851 (C–11761, microfilm).
East Gwillimbury Township, Census, 1861 (C–1087, microfilm).
East Gwillimbury Township, Census, 1871 (C–9965, microfilm).
David Graham, "Recollections of the Early Settlement of the Township of East Gwillimbury and Its Pioneer Inhabitants," 1908 (Sharon Temple Papers, MS 834, microfilm).
Davidite Records, series A, vol. 1, 1832–44, acc. 15119 (microfilm).
Davidite Records, series A, vol. 2, 1832–45, acc. 15119 (microfilm).
Davidite Records, series B, 1833–57 and n.d., acc. 15119 (microfilm).
Diary of Mary O'Brien (typescript).
East Gwillimbury Township, Abstract Index of Deeds, vol. 1, 1805–1911 (microfilm).

238 Bibliography

East Gwillimbury Township (north half), Assessment Roll, 1825 (R.G. 21, microfilm).
East Gwillimbury Township, Assessment Roll, 1834 (R.G. 21, microfilm).
East Gwillimbury Township, Assessment Roll, 1860 (R.G. 21, microfilm).
East Gwillimbury Township, Assessment Roll, 1861 (C-1087, microfilm).
Ebenezer Doan Papers (Sharon Temple Papers, MS 47, microfilm).
Eleazar Lewis Papers (MU 1737).
Ethel Willson Trewhella Papers (MU 2138).
Mackenzie-Lindsey Papers. Newspaper clipping file.
Marriage certificate of Ebenezer Doan and Elizabeth Paxson, 15 April 1801 (Miscellaneous Marriage Records Collection).
Minutes of Yonge Street Monthly Meeting of Friends (C-3-97A, microfilm).
Newmarket Era.
Rebellion Papers.
Recorder (Brockville).
Sharon Temple Papers (MS 834, microfilm).
The Advocate (Toronto).
The Colonial Advocate (York).
The Mirror (Toronto).
The Reverend Canon W.R. Allen, "Notes on St. James,' Sharon" (Misc. Coll. 1949, typescript).
Upper Canada Gazette (York).
Weekly Register (York).
York County Surrogate Court Records, Estate Files (microfilm).

BUCKS COUNTY CONSERVANCY
Upper Makefield Township, Bucks County Tax list [1795/96].

BUCKS COUNTY COURT HOUSE
Deed, Benjamin and Martha Schofield to Ebenezer Doan, Jr, 30 March 1801.
Deed, Samuel Schofield to Thomas Rose, 1797.
Deed, Jonathan and Mary Doan to Ebenezer Doan, 14 Feb. 1789.
Deed, Joseph and Mary Doan to John Ely, 1 April 1808.
Will and inventory, Daniel Doan, 1743.

BUCKS COUNTY HISTORICAL SOCIETY
Buckingham Monthly Meeting Certificates of Removal, 1778-1821 (photocopies).
D. Watson Atkinson, History of Wrightstown Index.
Letter, Oliver Doan to Howard Paxson, 11 May 1830.
Solebury Township, Bucks County Tax records, 1801-5 (microfilm).
United States, Direct Tax lists for Pennsylvania, 1798. vol. 283: 470-83 (microfilm).

NEW JERSEY STATE ARCHIVES
1570AM, 1573AM, 1813AM, 1841AM, 1844AM, and 3200AM.

PRIVATE COLLECTIONS
Mrs. Marjorie Richardson, Vandorf, Ontario.
Mr. and Mrs. Stewart Rogers, Sharon, Ontario.

SHARON TEMPLE MUSEUM
Carolyn Mann, genealogy of the Willson family.

SHARON TEMPLE MUSEUM ARCHIVES
Letter, Jacob to Mary Albertson, 20 Oct. 1820 (photocopy).
David Graham, "Recollections of the Early Settlement of the Township of East Gwillinbury and its pioneer inhabitants," 1908 (photocopied MS).
Catalogued manuscripts: L1228; L1230; L24; MS 959.84.3; MS 971.20.28; MS 971.28.57; MS 975.434.1; MS 975.441.1; MS 985.5.1, 2, 6, 15, 22, 23, 99, 114; MS 986.3.1, 2; MS X987.8.1ab.
Uncatalogued manuscripts.

METROPOLITAN TORONTO REFERENCE LIBRARY
Christian Guardian (Toronto).
Correspondence, David Willson to Robert Baldwin, 18 April 1841 to 18 May 1849 (Baldwin Papers).
John Ross Robertson Collection.

D.B. WELDON LIBRARY
Petition to the House of Assembly of Upper Canada, n.d.

PUBLISHED SOURCES

Adamson, Anthony. "The Ark of the Children of Peace." *The York Pioneer* 72, no. 1 (Spring 1977): 28–30.
Allen, David Grayson. *In English Ways: The Movement of Societies and the Transferral of English Local Law and Custom to Massachusetts Bay in the Seventeenth Century*. New York: W.W. Norton for the Institute of Early American History and Culture 1982.
Andrews, Edward Deming. *The Gift to Be Simple*. New York: Dover 1962.
Archaeological Services "Heritage Resource Assessment, B. Ramsay Property, Sharon, Ontario." Report to the Sharon Temple Committee of the York Pioneer and Historical Society, October 1985.
Armstrong, Robert Plant. *The Affecting Presence: An Essay in Humanistic Anthropology*. Urbana: University of Illinois Press 1971.

Arthur, Eric. *Toronto: No Mean City*. 2nd ed. Toronto: University of Toronto Press 1974.
Backhouse, Hannah Chapman. *Extracts from the Journal of Hannah Chapman Backhouse*. N.p. 1858.
Bacon, Margaret Hope. *The Mothers of Feminism: The Story of Quaker Women in America*. San Francisco: Harper and Row 1986.
– *The Quiet Rebels: The Story of Quakers in America*. New York: Basic Books 1969.
Barclay, Robert. *An Apology for the True Christian Divinity, As the same is Held Forth, and Preached, by the People called, in scorn, Quakers*. London: n.p. 1736.
Barkun, Michael. *Crucible of the Millennium: The Burned-Over District of New York in the 1840s*. Syracuse, NY: Syracuse University Press 1986.
Bauman, Richard. *For the Reputation of Truth: Politics, Religion, and Conflict Among the Pennsylvania Quakers*. Baltimore: Johns Hopkins Press 1971.
– *Let Your Words Be Few: Symbolism of Speaking and Silence Among Seventeenth-Century Quakers*. Cambridge: Cambridge University Press 1983.
Beecher, Catherine E., and Harriet Beecher Stowe. *The American Woman's Home*. 1869. Reprint. Watkins Glen, NY: American Life Foundation 1979.
Beeman, Richard R. "The New Social History and the Search for 'Community' in Colonial America." *American Quarterly* 29, no. 4 (Fall 1977): 422–43.
Benes, Peter, ed. New England Meeting House and Church: 1630–1850. *The Dublin Seminar for New England Folk Life Annual Proceedings* 4 (1979).
Berchem, F.R. *The Yonge Street Story, 1793–1860*. Toronto: McGraw-Hill Ryerson 1977.
Berrin, Ralph. "Henry Blackstone or How Henry Died." *The York Pioneer* 59 (1964): 24–6.
Bestor, Arthur, Jr. *Backwoods Utopias, The Sectarian and Owenite Phases of Communitarian Socialism in America: 1663–1829*. Philadelphia: University of Pennsylvania Press 1950.
Biographical Encyclopaedia of New Jersey of the Nineteenth Century. Philadelphia: Galaxy Publishing Co. 1877.
Blunt, Anthony. *Artistic Theory in Italy, 1450–1600*. 1940. Reprint. London: Oxford University Press 1968.
Boorstin, Daniel J. *The Americans: The National Experience*. New York: Random House, 1965.
Boyer, Paul. *Urban Masses and Moral Order in America, 1820–1920*. Cambridge, Mass.: Harvard University Press 1972.
"Brief Memoirs of the Life of John Pemberton." *Friends' Miscellany* 8, no. 2 (January 1836): 48–96.
Brodie, Fawn M. *Thomas Jefferson: An Intimate History*. New York: W.W. Norton 1974.
Brunskill, R.W. *Vernacular Architecture of the Lake Counties*. London: Faber and Faber 1974.

Burrowes, Helen. *Maxwell and Henry Jones: Lambton's Communal Settlement.* Sarnia, Ont.: Lambton County Historical Society 1986.

Bush, Peter. "The Reverend James Caughey and Wesleyan Methodist Revivalism in Canada West, 1851–1856." *Ontario History* 79, no. 3 (September 1987): 231–50.

Bushman, Richard L. *From Puritan to Yankee: Character and the Social Order in Connecticut, 1690–1765.* New York: W.W. Norton 1967.

Campbell, Colin. *The Romantic Ethic and the Spirit of Modern Consumerism.* Oxford: Basil Blackwell 1987.

Careless, J.M.S. *The Union of the Canadas: The Growth of Canadian Institutions, 1841–1857.* Toronto: McClelland and Stewart 1967.

Carson, Cary et al. "Impermanent Architecture in the Southern American Colonies." *Winterthur Portfolio* 16, no. 2/3 (Summer/Autumn 1981): 135–96.

Casey, John. *Letters, Addressed to Several Philanthropic Statesmen.* Buffalo: Lazell and Francis 1826.

Caswall, the Reverend Henry. *America, and the American Church.* London: n.p. 1839.

Clark, Clifford Edward, Jr. *The American Family Home, 1800–1960.* Chapel Hill: University of North Carolina Press 1986.

Clark, S.D. *Church and Sect in Canada.* Toronto: University of Toronto Press 1948.

Clemens, James M. "Taste Not; Touch Not; Handle Not: A Study of the Social Assumptions of the Temperance Literature and Temperance Supporters in Canada West Between 1839 and 1859." *Ontario History* 64, no. 3 (September 1972): 142–60.

Coffey, Brian. "From Shanty to Log House: Log Construction in Nineteenth Century Ontario." *Material Culture* 16, no. 2 (Summer 1984): 61–75.

Cohen, Zara. "A Comprehensive History of the State House of New Jersey and Recommendations for its Continuation as a Historic Site." MA Newark State College 1969.

Cooper, Matthew. "Living Together: How Communal Were the Children of Peace?" *Ontario History* 79, no. 1 (1987): 3–18.

Cooper, Patricia Irvin. "A Quaker-Plan House in Georgia." *Pioneer America* 10, no. 1 (June 1978): 14–34.

– "Postscript to 'A Quaker-Plan House in Georgia'." *Pioneer America* 11, no. 2 (August 1979): 143–50.

Craig, Gerald M. *Upper Canada: The Formative Years, 1784–1841.* Toronto: McClelland and Stewart 1963.

Craig, Gerald M., ed. *Lord Durham's Report.* Toronto: McClelland and Stewart 1963.

Crèvecoeur, Hector St Jean de. *Letters from an American Farmer.* 1782. Reprint. London: J.M. Dent and Sons 1962.

Cross, Whitney R. *The Burned-Over District: The Social and Intellectual History of Enthusiastic Religion in Western New York, 1800–1850*. Ithaca, NY: Cornell University Press 1950.

Cruikshank, E.A., ed. *The Correspondence of Lieutenant Governor John Graves Simcoe*. Toronto: Ontario Historical Society 1923.

Cummings, Abbott Lowell. *The Framed Houses of Massachusetts Bay, 1625–1725*. Cambridge, Mass.: Harvard University Press 1979.

Davis, J. C. *Utopia and the Ideal Society: A Study of English Utopian Writing, 1516–1700*. Cambridge: Cambridge University Press 1981.

Davis, William A. *History of Bucks County, Pennsylvania, from the Discovery of the Delaware to the Present Time*. 2nd ed. Pipersville, Pa.: A.E. Lears 1975.

Deetz, James. *In Small Things Forgotten: The Archaeology of Early American Life*. Garden City, NY: Anchor Books 1977.

– *Invitation to Archaeology*. New York: Natural History Press 1967.

Demos, John. *A Little Commonwealth: Family Life in Plymouth Colony*. New York: Oxford University Press 1970.

Diceman, Janette. *The Occupational, Agricultural and Demographic Circumstances of the Children of Peace in East Gwillimbury Township, 1851 to 1889*. MA, University of Western Ontario 1984.

Discipline of the Yearly Meeting of the Society of Friends, Held in New-York, For the State of New York, and Parts Adjacent: As Revised and Adopted, in the Sixth Month, 1810. New York: Collins and Perkins 1810.

Dixon, James. *Methodism in America: With the Personal Narrative of the Author, During a Tour Through a Part of the United States and Canada*. London: the author 1849.

Doane, Alfred Alder, comp. *The Doane Family and Their Descendants*. 1902. Reprint. Boston: Doane Family Association of North America 1960.

Doane, Gilbert Jones. *The Ebenezer Doane Family: Supplement to A.A. Doane's Genealogy of Deacon John Doane and His Descendants, Published in 1902*. Ottawa, the author 1961.

Doane, William Crosswell. *A Memoir of the Life of George Washington Doane, DD, LLD, Bishop of New Jersey*. New york: D. Appleton and Co. 1860.

Doherty, Robert W. *The Hicksite Separation*. Rahway, NJ: Rutgers University Press 1967.

Donnelly, Marian Card. "New England Meeting Houses in the Seventeenth Century." *Old-Time New England* 47 (April/June 1957): 85–99.

Dorland, Arthur Garrat. *The Quakers in Canada: A History*. 2nd ed. Toronto: Ryerson Press 1968.

Douglas, Ann. *The Feminization of American Culture*. New York: Alfred A. Knopf 1977.

Downs, Joseph. *American Furniture: Queen Anne and Chippendale Periods*. New York: Macmillan 1952.

Duncumb, Thomas. *The British Emigrant's Advocate*. London: n.p. 1837.

Eccles, W.J. *France in America*. New York: Harper and Row 1972.
Egle, William H. *Pennsylvania Archives*. 3rd series, vol. 13. Harrisburg: State Printer of Pennsylvania 1897.
Erasmus, Charles J. *In Search of the Common Good: Utopian Experiments Past and Future*. New York: Macmillan 1977.
Erikson, Erik H. *Young Man Luther: A Study in Psychoanalysis and History*. New York: W.W. Norton 1974.
Fogarty, Robert S. *Dictionary of American Communal and Utopian History*. Westport, Conn.: Greenwood Press 1980.
Fraser, William. "Diary of William Fraser, August 1834–July 1835." London and Middlesex County Historical Society *Transactions* 14 (1930): 80–125.
Furnas, J.C. *The Americans: A Social History of the United States, 1587–1914*. New York: G.P. Putnam's Sons 1969.
Garfinkel, Susan Laura. "Discipline, Discourse, and Deviation: The Material Life of Philadelphia Quakers 1762–178. MA, University of Delaware 1986.
Garvan, Anthony N.B. "The Protestant Plain Style Before 1630." *Journal of the Society of Architectural Historians* 9, no. 3 (October 1950): 4–13.
Gay, Peter. *The Bourgeois Experience, Victoria to Freud*. New York: Oxford University Press 1984.
– *Education of the Senses*. New York: Oxford University Press 1984.
Gerry, Thomas. "The Religious Beliefs of David Willson and the Children of Peace." *The York Pioneer* 80 (1985): 32–44.
– *David Willson (1778–1866): Canadian Visionary Writer and Hymnodist*. PhD, University of Western Ontario 1983.
Gerth, H.H., and C. Wright Mills, eds. *From Max Weber: Essays in Sociology*. New York: Oxford University Press 1946.
Glassie, Henry. "A Central Chimney Continental Log House." *Pennsylvania Folklife* 18, no. 2 (Winter 1968/69): 32–9.
– "Eighteenth-Century Cultural Process in Delaware Valley Folk Building." *Winterthur Portfolio* 7 (1972): 29–57.
– *Pattern in the Material Folk Culture of the Eastern United States*. Philadelphia: University of Pennsylvania Press 1968.
Goffman, Erving. *The Presentation of Self in Everyday Life*. Garden City, NY: Doubleday 1959.
Gourlay, Robert F. *Statistical Account of Upper Canada, Compiled with a View to a Grand System of Emigration*. London: Simpkins and Marshall 1822.
Grelot, Pierre. "Apocalyptic." In *Encyclopedia of Theology: The Concise Sacramentum Mundi*, edited by Karl Rahner, 17–18. New York: Seabury Press 1975.
Greven, Philip J., Jr. *Four Generations: Population, Land and Family in Colonial Andover, Massachusetts*. Ithaca, NY: Cornell University Press 1970.
– *The Protestant Temperament: Patterns of Child Rearing, Religious Experience, and the Self in Early America*. New York: Alfred A. Knopf 1977.

Grinstein, Hyman B. *Rise of the Jewish Community of New York, 1654–1860*. New York 1945.

Groh, Ivan. "Disabilities of the Dissenters, Part 1: Solemnization of Marriages." *Canadian-German Folklore* 2 (1967): 22–7.

Gummere, Amelia Mott. *The Quaker: A Study in Costume*. Philadelphia: Ferris and Leach 1901.

Hamlin, Talbot. *Greek Revival Architecture in America*. 1944. Reprint. New York: Dover 1964.

Hamm, Thomas D. *The Transformation of American Quakerism: Orthodox Friends, 1800–1907*. Bloomington: Indiana University Press 1988.

Hardy, Dennis. *Alternative Communities in Nineteenth Century England*. London: Longman 1979.

Harper, J. Russell. *A People's Art: Primitive, Naïve, Provincial and Folk Painting in Canada*. Toronto: University of Toronto Press 1974.

Harris, R. Cole, and John Warkentin. *Canada Before Confederation: A Study in Historical Geography*. New York: Oxford University Press 1974.

Harrison, J.F.C. *The Second Coming: Popular Millenarianism 1780–1850*. New Brunswick, NJ: Rutgers University Press 1979.

Hawke, David. *The Colonial Experience*. Indianapolis, Ind.: Bobbs-Merrill 1966.

Hayden, Dolores. *Seven American Utopias: The Architecture of Communitarian Socialism, 1790–1975*. Cambridge, Mass.: MIT Press 1976.

– *The Grand Domestic Revolution: A History of Feminist Designs for American Homes, Neighbourhoods, and Cities*. Cambridge, Mass.: MIT Press 1981.

Hedges, William L. "John Woolman and the Quaker Utopian Vision." In *Utopias: The American Experience*, edited by Gardiner B. Moment and Otto F. Kraushaar, 87–102. Metuchen, NJ: Scarecrow Press 1980.

Henry, George. *The Emigrants' Guide, or Canada As It Is*. Quebec: n.p. n.d.

Heininger, Mary Lynn Stevens, et al. *A Century of Childhood, 1820–1920*. Rochester: Margaret Woodbury Strong Museum 1984.

Herman, Bernard L. "Continuity and Change in Traditional Architecture: The Continental Plan Farmhouse in Middle North Carolina." In *Carolina Dwelling*, edited by Doug Swaim. Raleigh: North Carolina State University 1978.

Higgins, W.H. *The Life and Times of Joseph Gould*. 1877. Reprint. Belleville, Ont.: Mika Silk Screening 1972.

Hilling, John B. *The Historic Architecture of Wales*. Cardiff: University of Wales Press 1976.

Holloway, Mark. *Heavens on Earth: Utopian Communities in America, 1680–1880*. London: Turnstile Press 1951.

Horton, Rod W., and Herbert W. Edwards. *Backgrounds of American Literary Thought*. New York: Appleton-Century-Crofts 1967.

Hovinen, Elizabeth J. "The Quakers of Yonge Street." York University Department of Geography, *Discussion Paper*, no. 17 (May 1978).

- "The Quakers of Yonge Street." *Canadian Geographic Journal* (January/February 1976): 54–5.
Hughes, James L. *Sketches of the Sharon Temple and of its Founder, David Willson.* Toronto: n.p. n.d.
Hughes, Samuel. *A Vision Concerning the Desolation of Zion: or, the Fall of Religion among the Quakers, Set Forth in a Similitude or Vision of the Mind: Particularly Dedicated to the Captives, or Scattered Tribes of that Body; Now Commonly Called Orthodox and Hicksites.* Toronto: J.H. Lawrence 1835.
Hume, George Henry. *Canada As It Is, Comprising Details Relating to the Domestic Policy, Commerce and Agriculture, of the Upper and Lower Provinces.* New York: William Stoddart 1832.
Jenkins, Howard W. "Early Welsh Settlers." In *A Collection of Papers Read Before the Bucks County Historical Society.* Vol. 1, 397–401. Riegelsville, Pa.: B.F. Fackenthal, Jr for the Bucks County Historical Society [c.1910].
Jenkins, J. Geraint. *Life and Tradition in Rural Wales.* London: J.M. Dent and Sons 1976.
Johnson, Leo A. "Simcoe's Yonge Street and the Laying Out of the York County Reserve Lands." *The York Pioneer* 69 (1974): 33–7.
Johnson, Paul E. *A Shopkeeper's Millennium: Society and Revivals in Rochester, New York, 1815–1837.* New York: Hill and Wang 1978.
Jones, Howard Mumford. *O Strange New World: American Culture, The Formative Years.* New York: Viking 1952.
Jones, Robert Leslie. *History of Agriculture in Ontario, 1613–1880.* 1946. Reprint. Toronto: University of Toronto Press 1977.
Jung, Carl G., ed. *Man and His Symbols.* New York: Doubleday 1964.
Kalman, Harold. *Pioneer Churches.* Toronto: McClelland and Stewart 1976.
Kanter, Rosabeth Moss. *Commitment and Community: Communes and Utopias in Sociological Perspective.* Cambridge, Mass.: Harvard University Press 1972.
Kasson, John F. *Civilizing the Machine: Technology and Republican Values in America, 1776–1900.* New York: Grossman 1976.
Katz, Michael B. *The People of Hamilton, Canada West: Family and Class in a Mid Nineteenth Century City.* Cambridge, Mass.: Harvard University Press 1975.
Kniffen, Fred. "Folk Housing: Key to Diffusion." *Annals of the Association of American Geographers* 55, no. 4 (December 1965): 549–77.
Kraushaar, Otto F. "America: Symbol of a Fresh Start." In *Utopias: The American Experience,* edited by Gardiner B. Moment and Otto F. Kraushaar, Metuchen, NJ: Scarecrow Press 1980, 11–29.
Laurie, Bruce. *Working People of Philadelphia, 1800–1850.* Philadelphia: Temple University Press 1980.
Lears, T.J. Jackson. "From Salvation to Self-Realization: Advertising and the Therapeutic Roots of the Consumer Culture, 1880–1930." In *The Culture of Consumption: Critical Essays in American History, 1880–1930,* edited by

Richard Wrightman Fox and T.J. Jackson Lears. New York: Pantheon Books 1983.
- *No Place of Grace: Anti-modernism and the Transformation of American Culture, 1880–1920.* New York: Pantheon Books 1981.
Lehr, John. "Ukrainian Vernacular Architecture in Alberta." Alberta Culture Historic Sites Service, *Occasional Paper,* no. 1 (1976).
Lemon, James T. *The Best Poor Man's Country: A Geographical Study of Early Southeastern Pennsylvania.* Baltimore: Johns Hopkins Press 1972.
Levy, Barry. *Quakers and the American Family: British Settlement in the Delaware Valley.* New York: Oxford University Press 1988.
Lévi-Strauss, Claude. *Structural Anthropology.* Translated by Claire Jacobson and Brooke Grundfest Schoepf. New York: Basic Books 1963.
Lockridge, Kenneth A. "Land, Population, and the Evolution of New England Society, 1630–1790." *Past and Present* 39 (1968): 62–80.
- *A New England Town: The First Hundred Years.* New York: W.W. Norton 1970.
Loth, Calder, and Julius Trousdale Sadler, Jr. *The Only Proper Style: Gothic Architecture in America.* Boston: New York Graphic Society 1975.
Lynes, Russell. *The Domesticated Americans.* New York: Harper and Row 1963.
Mackenzie, William Lyon [Patrick Swift, pseud.]. *New Almanac for Canadian True Blues.* Toronto: n.p. 1834.
- *Sketches of Canada and the United States.* London: n.p. 1833.
Macquarrie, John. *Principles of Christian Theology.* London: SCM Press 1966.
MacRae, Marion, and Anthony Adamson. *Hallowed Walls: Church Architecture of Upper Canada.* Toronto: Clarke, Irwin and Co. 1975.
Mallary, Peter T. *New England Churches and Meeting Houses, 1680–1830.* Secaucus, NJ: Chartwell Books 1985.
Manly, John G. *The Nature, Progress, Present State, and Character of Wesleyan Methodism.* Kingston, Ont.: T.H. Bentley 1840.
Mann, Carolyn. "Legends and Folk Tales of Sharon, Part III." *The York Pioneer* 74, no. 1 (Spring 1979): 5–9.
- "Legends and Folk Tales of Sharon." *The York Pioneer* 73, no. 1 (Spring 1978): 11–17.
- "Newly Discovered Records of the Children of Peace." *The York Pioneer* 65 (1970): 33–43.
Mannion, John J. *Irish Settlements in Eastern Canada: A Study of Cultural Transfer and Adaptation.* Toronto: University of Toronto Press 1974.
Manuel, Frank E., and Fritzie P. Manuel. *Utopian Thought in the Western World.* Cambridge, Mass.: Harvard University Press 1979.
Martin, James P. "Revelation: Bad News or Good News?" Paper presented at the Canadian Christian Festival, Calgary, Alberta 1986.
Marx, Leo. *The Machine in the Garden: Technology and the Pastoral Ideal in America.* New York: Oxford University Press 1964.

May, Henry F. *The Enlightenment in America*. New York: Oxford University Press, 1976.
McArthur, Emily. *History of the Children of Peace*. 1898. Reprint. Toronto: York Pioneer and Historical Society 1967.
McFaddin, Charles E. "A Study of the Buildings of the Children of Peace, Sharon, Ontario." MA, University of Toronto 1953.
McFall, Jean. "Elmer Starr of Yonge Street." *The York Pioneer* 54 (1959): 42–50.
– "The Last Days of the Children of Peace." *The York Pioneer* 68 (1973): 22–33.
McIntyre, W. John. "David Willson and Government, Politics and Society in Upper Canada." *The York Pioneer* 68 (1973): 2–17.
– *The Early Writings of David Willson: A Forgotten Voice from Upper Canada*. Toronto: York Pioneer and Historical Society 1974.
Mercer, Henry C. "The Doanes Before the Revolution." In *A Collection of Papers Read Before the Bucks County Historical Society*, vol. 1. Riegelsville, Pa.: B.F. Fackenthal, Jr for the Society [c.1910], 173–81.
Miller, Perry, and James H. Johnson, eds. *The Puritans: A Sourcebook of Their Writings*. Rev. ed. New York: Harper and Row 1963.
Minhinnick, Jeanne. *At Home in Upper Canada*. Toronto: Clarke, Irwin and Co. 1970.
Moir, John S. *The Church in the British Era*. Vol. 2, A History of the Christian Church in Canada, edited by John Webster Grant. Toronto: McGraw-Hill Ryerson 1972.
Moodie, Susanna. *Roughing It in the Bush*. 1852. Reprint. Toronto: McClelland and Stewart 1962.
Moore, John B., ed. *Friends in the Delaware Valley: Philadelphia Yearly Meeting, 1681–1981*. Haverford, Pa.: Friends Historical Association 1981.
Morgan, Edmund S. *The Puritan Family*. Rev. ed. New York: Harper and Row 1966.
Morris, Richard B, ed. *Encyclopedia of American History*. New York: Harper and Brothers 1953.
Morrison, Hugh. *Early American Architecture from the First Colonial Settlements to the National Period*. New York: Oxford University Press 1952.
Morrison, John. "The 'Toon 'o Maxwell' – An Owen Settlement in Lambton County, Ontario." *Ontario Historical Society Papers and Records* 12 (1914): 1–12.
Moxon, Joseph. *Mechanick Exercises or the Doctrine of Handy-Works, Applyed to the Art of House Carpentry*. London: the author 1679.
New York Yearly Meeting of Friends. *Discipline of the Yearly Meeting of Friends, Held in New-York, For the State of New York, and Parts Adjacent: As Revised and Adopted, in the Sixth Month, 1810*. New York: Collins and Perkins 1810.
Newlands, D.L. "A Meeting House for Friends." *Rotunda* 7, no. 4 (Fall 1974): 24–9.

– "The Yonge Street Friends School, 1806–1828." *The York Pioneer* 71, no. 2 (Fall 1976): 12–16.

Nordhoff, Charles. *The Communistic Societies of the United States.* 1875. Reprint. New York: Dover 1966.

Norris, Darrell A. "Vetting the Vernacular: Local Varieties in Ontario's Housing." *Ontario History* 74, no. 2 (June 1982): 66–94.

Nye, Russel Blaine. *The Cultural Life of the New Nation, 1776–1830.* New York: Harper and Row 1960.

O'Dea, Thomas F. *The Mormons.* Chicago: University of Chicago Press 1957.

O'Mara, James. "The Seasonal Round of Gentry Farmers in Early Ontario: A Preliminary Analysis." In *Canadian Papers in Rural History*, vol. 2, edited by Donald H. Akenson. Gananoque, Ont.: Langdale Press 1980.

Olson, Theodore. *Millennialism, Utopianism, and Progress.* Toronto: University of Toronto Press 1982.

Ontario Genealogical Society. *Rebels Arrested in Upper Canada, 1837–1838.* Toronto: Toronto Branch of the Society 1987.

Ontario Ministry of Culture and Recreation. *Historical Sketches of Ontario.* Toronto: Province of Ontario 1976.

Parkinson, Richard. *A Tour in America in 1798, 1799, and 1800.* 2 vols. London: the author 1805.

Peate, Iorweth C. *The Welsh House: A Study in Folk Culture.* Liverpool: Hugh Evans and Sons 1946.

Peterson, Charles E., ed. *Building Early America.* Radnor, Pa.: Chilton Book Company 1976.

Pickering, Joseph. *Emigration or No Emigration: Being the Narrative of the Author (an English Farmer) from the Year 1824 to 1830.* London: Longman, Rees, Orme, Brown, and Green 1830.

Pierson, William H., Jr. *American Buildings and Their Architects: The Colonial and Neoclassical Styles.* Garden City, NY: Doubleday 1970.

Pocius, Gerald L. "Architecture on Newfoundland's Southern Shore: Diversity and the Emergence of New World Forms." In *Perspectives in Vernacular Architecture*, edited by Camille Wells. Annapolis, Md.: Vernacular Architectural Forum 1982.

Potter, David M. *People of Plenty: Economic Abundance and the American Character.* Chicago: University of Chicago Press 1954.

Read, Colin. "The Rebellion of 1837 in Upper Canada." Canadian Historical Association *Booklet* no. 46 (1988).

Read, Colin, and Ronald J. Stagg, eds. *The Rebellion of 1837 in Upper Canada.* Toronto: The Champlain Society in Cooperation with the Ontario Heritage Foundation 1985.

Reaman, G. Elmore. *The Trail of the Black Walnut.* Toronto: McClelland and Stewart for the Pennsylvania German Society 1957.

Reid, J.H. Stewart et al. *A Source-Book of Canadian History: Selected Documents and Personal Papers.* Rev. ed. Toronto: Longmans 1964.

Reid, Richard. *The Shell Book of Cottages.* London: Michael Joseph 1977.

Rempel, John I. *Building With Wood and Other Aspects of Nineteenth Century Building in Ontario.* Toronto: University of Toronto Press 1967.

"Restoring the House of Ebenezer Doan, Master Builder of the Temple." *The York Pioneer* 59 (1957): 11–14.

Richie, Margaret Bye. *Of Stone and Dreams: A History of Bucks County Houses.* Doylestown, Pa.: Bucks County Community College 1980.

Richman, Irwin. *Pennsylvania's Architecture.* Pennsylvania History Studies, no. 10. University Park, Pa.: Pennsylvania Historical Association 1969.

Robinson, C. Blackett. *History of Toronto and the County of York, Ontario.* 2 vols. Toronto: the author 1885.

Rock, Howard B. "The American Revolution and the Mechanics of New York City: One Generation Later." *New York History* 57, no. 3 (July 1976): 367–94.

Rolling, Gladys M. *East Gwillimbury in the Nineteenth Century.* Sharon, Ont.: East Gwillimbury Township Council 1967.

Rolph, Dr Thomas. *A Brief Account Together with Observations Made During a Visit in the West Indies and a Tour through the United States of America in Parts of the Year 1832–3, Together with a Statistical Account of Upper Canada.* Dundas, Ont.: n.p. 1836.

Rothman, David J. *The Discovery of the Asylum: Social Order and Disorder in the New Republic.* Boston: Little, Brown and Co. 1971.

Rutherford, Paul. *The Making of the Canadian Media.* Toronto: McGraw-Hill Ryerson 1978.

Ryan, Mary P. *Cradle of the Middle Class: The Family in Oneida County, New York, 1790–1865.* Cambridge: Cambridge University Press 1981.

Ryan, Pat M., ed. "Mathias Hutchinson's Notes on a Journey (1819–20)." *Quaker History* 69 (1950): 27–34.

Sandeen, Ernest R. *The Roots of Fundamentalism: British and American Millenarianism, 1800–1930.* Chicago: University of Chicago Press 1970.

Sawdon, Herbert. *The Woodbridge Story.* N.p. 1960.

Schau, Ann. "Sharon's Musical Past." *The York Pioneer* 80, no. 1 (Spring 1985): 17–31.

Schrauwers, Albert. "An Itinerant Sect." *The York Pioneer* 81 (Summer 1986): 29–37.

– "Letters to the Children in Prison, 1838." *The York Pioneer* (1987): 29–36.

– *Awaiting the Millennium: The Children of Peace and the Village of Hope, 1812–1889.* Toronto: University of Toronto Press 1993.

– *Awaiting the Millennium: The Children of Peace, East Gwillimbury, 1812–1837.* MA, University of Toronto 1988.

- "The Politics of Schism: The Separation of the Children of Peace, 1812." *Ontario History* 80, no. 1 (March 1988): 31–52.
Semmel, Bernard. *The Methodist Revolution*. New York: Basic Books 1973.
Shirreff, Patrick. *A Tour Through North America; Together With a Comprehensive View of the Canadas and United States as Adapted for Agricultural Emigration*. Edinburgh: n.p. 1835.
Shurtleff, Harold R. *The Log Cabin Myth: A Study of the Early Dwellings of the English Colonists in North America*. Cambridge, Mass.: Harvard University Press 1939.
Sibbald, Capt. Thomas. "A Few Days in the United States and Canada with Some Hints to Settlers." Reprint. Women's Canadian Historical Society *Transactions* 16 (1916–17): 28–34.
Silverman, Kenneth. *A Cultural History of the American Revolution*. New York: Thomas Y. Crowell 1976.
Singleton, Gregory H. "Protestant Voluntary Organizations and the Shaping of Victorian America." In *Victorian America*, edited by Daniel Walker Howe. Philadelphia: University of Pennsylvania Press 1976.
Sklar, Kathryn Kish. *Catherine Beecher: A Study in American Domesticity*. New Haven: Yale University Press 1973.
Smith, Peter. *Houses of the Welsh Countryside*. London: Her Majesty's Stationery Office 1975.
Smith, William H. *Canada: Past, Present and Future*. 1852. Reprint. Belleville, Ont.: Mika Silk Screening 1973.
- *Smith's Canadian Gazetteer*. 1846. Reprint. Toronto: Coles 1970.
Smith-Rosenberg, Carroll. *Disorderly Conduct: Visions of Gender in Victorian America*. New York: Alfred A. Knopf 1985.
Stevens, Abel. *Life and Times of Nathan Bangs, DD*. New York: Carlton and Porter 1863.
Stewart, Janet. "The Little Boxes of 1837." *The York Pioneer* 82 (1987): 37–42.
Stilgoe, John R. *Common Landscape of America, 1580–1845*. New Haven: Yale University Press 1982.
Stradley, Leighton P. *Early Financial and Economic History of Pennsylvania*. New York: Commerce Clearing House 1942.
Swaim, Doug, ed. *Carolina Dwelling*. Raleigh: North Carolina State University 1978.
Swank, Scott T. et al. *Arts of the Pennsylvania Germans*. New York: W.W. Norton for the Henry Francis du Pont Winterthur Museum 1983.
Syrett, Harold C., ed. *American Historical Documents*. Rev. ed. New York: Barnes and Noble 1965.
Thomas, John L. "Romantic Reform in America, 1815–1865." *American Quarterly* 17, no. 1 (Winter 1965): 656–81.
Thompson, E.P. *The Making of the English Working Class*. New York: Vintage Books 1966.

Tolles, Frederick B. *Quakers and the Atlantic Culture*. New York: Macmillan 1960.
Trewhella, Ethel Willson. *History of the Town of Newmarket*. N.p. n.d.
Turner, Frederick Jackson. "The Significance of the Frontier in American History." In *Frontier and Section: Selected Essays of Frederick Jackson Turner*, edited by Ray Allen Billington. Englewood Cliffs, NJ: Prentice Hall 1961.
Unruh, John D., Jr. "The Way West." In *The Social Fabric: American Life from 1607 to 1877*, vol. 2, edited by John H. Cary and Julius Weinberg. Boston: Little, Brown, and Co. 1987.
Upton, Del. "Traditional Timber Framing." In *Material Culture of the Wooden Age*, edited by Brooke Hindle. Tarrytown, NY: Sleepy Hollow Press 1981, 35–93.
Vann, Richard T. *The Social Development of English Quakerism, 1655–1755*. Cambridge, Mass.: Harvard University Press 1969.
Wallace, Anthony F. C. *Rockdale: The Growth of an American Village in the Early Industrial Revolution*. New York: W.W. Norton 1972.
Walsh, H. H. *The Christian Church in Canada*. Toronto: Ryerson Press 1956.
Ware, John F.W. *Home Life: What It Is, and What It Needs*. Boston: William V. Spencer 1866.
Waterman, Thomas Tileston. *The Dwellings of Colonial America*. Chapel Hill: University of North Carolina Press, 1950.
Waters, Ronald G. *American Reformers, 1815–1860*. New York: Hill and Wang 1978.
Watson, O. K. "Moraviantown." *Ontario Historical Society Papers and Records* 28 (1932): 125–31.
Webb, Clayton. "Recollections of an Immigrant." In *Recollections on the Pioneer Settlement of Newmarket by Two Yonge Street Quakers*. Newmarket Historical Society *Occasional Papers*, vol. 1, no. 2. N.d.
Westfall, William. "Order and Experience: Patterns of Religious Metaphor in Early Nineteenth Century Upper Canada." *Journal of Canadian Studies* 20, no. 1 (Spring, 1985): 5–24.
– *Two Worlds: The Protestant Culture of Nineteenth-Century Ontario*. Kingston and Montreal: McGill-Queen's University Press 1989.
Wilkie, D. *Sketches of a Summer Trip to New York and the Canadas*. Edinburgh: n.p. 1837.
Wills, Harold A. "The Frayed Years, 1866–1918." Chronicles of the Sharon Temple Series, part 6. *The York Pioneer* 77, no. 1 (Spring 1982): 16–17, 34–40.
Willson, David. *A Collection of Items of the Life of David Willson*. Newmarket, Ont.: G.S. Porter 1852.
– *A Friend to Britain*. Toronto: J.H. Lawrence 1835.
– *A Lesson of Instruction*. Reading, Pa.: George Getz 1816.
– *A Present to the Teachers and Rulers of Society*. N.p. 1821.
– *A Testimony to the People Called Quakers*. N.p. 1816.

- *An Address to the Professors of Religion.* New York: George Largin 1817.
- *Hymns and Prayers for the Children of Sharon: To be Sung in Worship on Sabbath Days.* Newmarket: G.S. Porter 1846.
- *Hymns of Praise Adapted to the Worship of God in Sharon.* Newmarket: G.S. Porter 1849.
- *Hymns of Praise containing Doctrine and Prayer Adapted to the Worship of God in Sharon.* Newmarket: Jackson and Henderson 1853.
- *Sacred Impressions of the Mind in Praise and Prayer, Devoted to God in Worship by the Children of Peace in Sharon.* Newmarket: Jackson and Henderson 1853.
- *Letters to the Jews.* Toronto: W.J. Coates 1835.
- *Mysteries of the Mind; or, Operations of Grace.* Toronto: Leader and Patriot Steam Press 1858.
- *The Impressions of the Mind.* Toronto: J.H. Lawrence 1835.
- *The Practical Life of the Author, from the Year 1801 to 1860.* Newmarket: Erastus Jackson 1860.
- *The Rights of Christ.* Philadelphia: n.p. 1815.

Willson, Richard Titus. "Reminiscences." *Newmarket Historical Society Occasional Papers,* vol. 1, no. 1. N.d.

Wilson, Robert W. *Philadelphia Quakers, 1681–1981.* Philadelphia: Philadelphia Yearly Meeting of the Religious Society of Friends 1981.

Wisbey, Herbert A., Jr. *Pioneer Prophetess: Jemima Wilkinson, the Publick Universal Friend.* Ithaca, NY: Cornell University Press 1964.

Wise, Daniel. *Earnest Christianity Illustrated; or, Selections from the Journal of the Rev. James Caughey.* 9th ed. Toronto: Wesleyan Book Room 1856.

- *Popular Objections to Methodism Considered and Answered.* 3rd. American ed. Toronto: G.R. Sanderson 1856

Wise, S.F. et al., eds. "'None was ever better ...' The Loyalist Settlement of Ontario." *Proceedings of the Annual Meeting of the Ontario Historical Society* (June 1984) Cornwall, Ont.: Stormont, Dundas and Glengarry Historical Society 1984.

Wood, J. David. "The Settlers and the Land: Pioneer Experience in the Home District." *Families* 14, no. 4 (Fall 1975): 108–25.

Worrall, Arthur J. *Quakers in the Colonial Northeast.* Hanover, NH: University Press of New England 1980.

Wright, Janet. *Architecture of the Picturesque in Canada.* Ottawa: Government of Canada 1984.

Wright, Louis B. *The Cultural Life of the American Colonies, 1607–1763.* New York: Harper and Row 1957.

Wright, Luella M. *The Literary Life of the Early Friends.* New York 1932.

Young, John H. *Our Deportment; or the Manners, Conduct and Dress of the Most Refined Society.* Paris, Ont.: John S. Brown 1883.

Zuckerman, Michael, ed. *Friends and Neighbors: Group Life in America's First Plural Society.* Philadelphia: Temple University Press 1982.

Index

Albertson, Jacob and Mary, 57, 93, 122
altar/ark, 60–1, 72–3, 97, 108, 162, 171, 181
American Revolution, 5, 6, 11, 43, 44, 153, 166, 171, 196, 197, 201–2
Anglicans, 21, 50, 51, 82, 156–60 passim, 164, 194; and Constitutional Act (1791), 24, 157; and "religion of order," 29, 106, 188; in Sharon, 182, 184, 185, 204
Anthony, Susan B., 45
Apocalypse, 33, 64, 96, 197. *See also* millennium, Revelation
architecture: Anglican churches, 21, 203–4; influence of, 14, 202–3, 204; Methodist churches, 25, 199–200. *See also* Biddle, Owen; construction; Doan, Ebenezer; Doan, John; Doan, Jonathan; Georgian style; Gothic style; meeting houses; neoclassical style; temple

ark. *See* altar/ark
Armageddon, 64, 67, 75, 199
Armitage, Amos and Martha, 13, 15, 16, 49, 89

Baldwin, Robert, 174–5, 179
Baldwin Act (1849), 179
Bangs, Nathan, 26–7
banners, 30–4, 56–7, 95, 103, 104, 151, 152, 181, 190, 199, 200; imagery in poetry, 38–9, 54–6, 97
Baptists, 194
Barclay, Robert, 19, 25, 40
Baskerville, Benjamin [?], 135
Beecher, Catherine, 45, 204
Beissel, Conrad, 196
Beman, Eli, 117
Bible: authority of, 27; and Children of Peace, 183; and the Jews, 88; and Orthodox/Hicksite schism, 40, 192–3; on speaking and silence, 63; and preaching, 106; in temple altar/ark, 73;

Willson's imagery from, 39, 67, 73; Willson's views on, 35, 39, 42, 48, 82–3, 88, 183. *See also* Apocalypse, millennium, Revelation, Solomon's temple
Biddle, Owen, 18
Birmingham, Eliza, 134
Blackstone, Henry, 153
Blackstone, William, 153
Blake, William, 42, 84
Boehme, Jacob, 84
Bolton, Attorney General, 163
Bond, Thomas G., 115
Bournville, 110
Brammer, George and Ellen, 133
Briggs, Caleb and Mary, 133, 134
British Constitution, 152, 153, 157, 165, 191; symbolized by banner, 151, 152
Brodie, Robert and Phebe Ann, 133
Brook Farm, 200
Brothers, Richard, 42
Buckingham, monthly

meeting, 8, 13. *See also* meeting houses
Bucks County, 6, 8, 9, 12, 13, 39, 41, 46, 143–50 passim
building. *See* construction
Burned-Over District, 195, 205, 207–8
Burr, Reuben, 15, 18

cabinet-making. *See also* Doan, John; furnishings
Calvinists, 158, 194. *See also* predestination, Presbyterians
Cane, William, 135
carpentry. *See* construction
Caswall, Rev. Henry, 106
Caughey, Rev. James, 199
charity, 91, 93, 98, 120–2, 164, 176, 182. *See also* Orphan House, Poor House
children: death of, 169–70; education of, 49, 122–3; and "grandfather Willson," 116; in Willson's visions, 31–4, 36, 38
Children of Peace: decline 178–85; disownment by Quakers, 35, 37; first meetings, 47, 89–90; incorporation (1876), 182–3; membership, 132–4; organization, 90–1, 120, 176, 182–3; origin of name, 41. *See also* choirs, community life, dissent, economic organization, elders, family life, farming practices, meeting houses, music/musicians, temple
choirs, 92, 93, 96, 102, 103–4, 182, 184
cholera epidemic (1832), 121, 124, 163
churches. *See* architecture, meeting houses, temple

Christ: beliefs of Children of Peace, 183; Orthodox and Hicksite beliefs, 40, 48, 192–3; Willson's beliefs, 35, 38, 39–40, 42, 82–3, 88, 101, 183. *See also* millennium
Christian Church. *See* Disciples of Christ
Christmas observance, 101
Church of England. *See* Anglicans
Church of Scotland. *See* Presbyterians
clergy reserves, 154, 157–9 passim, 177
clothing: of Children of Peace, 97–8, 123–8; Methodist, 25–6; Quaker, 22–3, 25–6; store-bought, 118
cloth production, 119, 136, 138
Coalbrookdale, 110
Coates, Richard, 30, 41, 54, 76, 79, 92–3, 94, 97, 102, 191
Colborne, Sir John, 164
community life, 110–13, 115–22, 139, 187–8, 195, 200. *See also* charity
Conger, Peter, 47
Congregationalists. *See* Puritans
Constitutional Act (1791), 24, 157, 189
construction: of boxes by prisoners, 168–71; Doan family, 12–13, 66, 143–6; of Doan house, 142–9; of first meeting house, 49–50; and plainness, 20–1; of second meeting house, 78, 81; of temple, 58–9, 60, 62, 65–71; Willson as carpenter, 11, 66; of Willson's study, 75; of Yonge Street meeting house, 4, 15–22 passim
consumer culture, 118–19, 204–15

Corbett, Benjamin [?], 134
Cory, Daniel, 102
Crone, Nelson and Mary, 133
crown reserves, 158

David (King), 39, 42, 67, 73, 88, 89, 100
Davidites, 109. *See also* Children of Peace
Davidtown, 109. *See also* Hope/Sharon
decoration: of first meeting house, 54; in houses, 57; and plainness, 20–3, 57; of temple, 59–60; of Willson's study, 76; of Yonge Street meeting house, 21–2
Delaware River valley, xiv, 13, 70, 110, 187
Dennis, Enos and Sarah, 133
Disciples of Christ, 182, 184–5
dissent among Children of Peace: defection of Doan and Hughes, 78, 172; over Rachel Lundy scandal, 46, 48, 49; over Rebellion of 1837, 160–7 passim, 171; over second meeting house, 77–8; in Uxbridge, 48; over Willson's estate, 183–4; over Willson's leadership, 163, 172, 175–6; among youth, 48, 175–6, 183
Doan, Abraham, 114, 132, 133, 135, 142
Doan, Ann, 133, 134
Doan, Benjamin, 144
Doan, Charles, 78, 116, 138, 166–71
Doan, Daniel, 12
Doan, Daniel, Jr, 12
Doan, David, 114, 136, 142
Doan, David Willson, 169
Doan, David Willson (2nd), 170
Doan, Deacon John, 12

Doan, Ebenezer: early life, 12–13, 190–1; farming practices, 136–7; house, 133, 140–50; land transactions, 113–15; marriage to Elizabeth Paxson, 23; master builder of temple, 68, 70; resignation, 102, 115, 173; and second meeting house, 78; and temple worship, 98
Doan, Ebenezer Sr, 12, 113, 119
Doan, Eli and Josephine, 133, 134
Doan, Elias, 113, 114, 133, 142
Doan, Eliza, 133
Doan, Elizabeth, 133
Doan, Elizabeth (Paxson), 23, 114, 133, 136, 141
Doan, Elizabeth [Stockdale], 168
Doan, George Washington, 203
Doan, Hannah, 114, 142
Doan, Hester Ann, 136
Doan, Ira, 113, 114, 142
Doan, Jesse, 132, 135, 167–8, 171, 179
Doan, John: and ark, 72–3; as cabinet-maker, 129–30, 168; early life, 12–13, 190–1; in 1851, 134; inventory (1862), 130–1, 137, 148; land transactions, 113; and second meeting house, 78; and Yonge Street meeting house, 15, 16, 24; and temple worship, 98
Doan, John, Jr, 130, 134
Doan, Jonathan, 12–13, 114
Doan, Joseph, 12, 113
Doan, Joseph, Jr, 13
Doan, Judah and Anna, 133, 134
Doan, Lemuel, 135
Doan, Mahlon, 13, 113, 134
Doan, Mary, 13

Doan, Mary Willson, 170
Doan, Oliver, 9, 113, 114, 133, 134, 142
Doan, Rebecca, 134
Doan, Sarah, 114, 142
Doan, Wait, 133
Doan, Wait Ann, 133
Doan, William, 13
Doan, William, 138
Downing, A.J., 204
dreams. *See* visions
Drinkwater, J.H.S., 166
drunkenness: concerns of Children of Peace, 180–1; concerns of Quakers, 21, 180. *See also* temperance movement
Duncumb, Thomas, 109, 128
Dunham, Benjamin and Anna, 133
Dunham, Thomas and Mary, 130
Durham, Lord, 172, 173
Durham Meeting, 172–3
Dwight, Timothy, 201

East Gwillimbury Township government, 179
Ecclesiologists, 203
economic disparity: and political unrest, 160, 164; and religious issues, 47, 48, 104, 110, 124, 154
economic organization: building contributions, 76; study as "counting room," 78
Edmonstone, William Graham, 169
education. *See* school
elders: among Children of Peace, 78, 82, 90, 91, 97, 116, 120, 121, 161–2; among Quakers, 20
Elgin, Lord, 176
Elmer, William and Mary, 133
Emerson, Ralph Waldo, 84

Ephrata Cloister, 43
Episcopalians. *See* Anglicans

Fairfield, 196
Family Compact, 152, 160
family life: among Children of Peace, 113–16, 134–5, 148–9; among Quakers, 8, 191
farming practices, 113–15, 119, 136–8
feasts, 77, 94–5, 100, 117, 118, 178, 180, 184
Ferris, Joseph, 11
Fletcher, Silas, 166
food and drink, 118, 136–8, 164, 180–1. *See also* drunkenness, feasts
Foster, Abby Kelley, 45
Foster, George, 135
Fourier, Charles. *See* Fourierist communities
Fourierist communities, 201
Fox, George, 16, 17, 19, 39, 84
Fray, Sabra, 13
French Revolution, 42, 171, 197
Friends. *See* Quakers
Fries's Rebellion, 8
Frizzell, Rev., 183
frontier thesis, 187
furnishings: Delaware valley, 70, 73; in homes, 123, 124, 129–32, 204; in meeting houses, 18, 21, 54; and plainness, 20–1; from second meeting house, 80; in temple, 60–1, 72–3, 97, 98; in Willson's study, 76

Georgian style, 18, 106, 123, 143, 146
Gillvrie, Andrew, 133, 134, 138
Gillvrie, Hester, 133, 134
Gothic style, 203
Gould, Joseph and family, 7, 8, 69, 165

government: American, 156; British, 154–6; Upper Canadian, 157
Graham, David, 128, 132, 138
Graham, Jane 170
Graham, Jeremiah, 167
Graham, John and Elizabeth, 170
Graham, Richard, 167, 170
Graham, William and Elizabeth, 133, 138
Great Awakening, 193
Great Migration, 6
Grimké, Sarah and Angelina, 45
Gurneyite Quakers, 193

Hagerman, Solicitor General, 158, 161, 163
Haines, Anna, 133
Haines, Charles, 133, 138, 179
Haines, Israel, 114
Hall, F., 93, 95, 111
Harmony Society, 43, 196, 201
Harrison, Hiram, 114
Harrison, Joshua and Sarah, 133
Harrison, Peter, 74
Hartman, John and Mary, 7
Head, Sir Francis Bond, 164, 167
Henderson, Ellen, 134
Henderson, James, 167
Hicks, Edward, 41, 45
Hicks, Elias, 40, 41
Hicksite Quakers, 102, 194. *See also* Bible, Christ, Orthodox/Hicksite schism
Higginson, Francis, 104
Hilborn family, 7
Holland Landing, 153
Holy Communion: feasts and Communion House, 77, 95
Hope/Sharon: founding of, 49; life in and around, 108–39; name changed to "Sharon," 109; political events in, 173–5; and railroad, 178–9
households, composition of, 133–5
houses: in Bucks County, 143–50 passim; in Hope/Sharon, 109, 123, 133–4, 142; three-room plan, 144–6; Victorian attitudes toward, 204; in York County, 142
Hughes, Amos, 121
Hughes, Amos, 182–4
Hughes, James L., 185
Hughes, Job and Elizabeth, 133, 134
Hughes, Samuel, 78, 87, 90, 120–1, 172
Huguenots, 52–3
Hume, George Henry, 111, 115, 120, 129
Hutchinson, Mathias, 39, 46
hymns, 94, 96, 97, 101, 102, 104–5, 200

illuminations, 100–1, 117, 162, 184
Inner Light: of millenarian sects, 44; and Orthodox/Hicksite schism, 40, 82, 192; of Quakers 17, 28, 54, 82, 83, 92, 94, 101, 105, 127, 149, 188, 190, 194, 199; and Willson's beliefs, 48, 54, 63, 80, 86, 102, 183, 190; and Willson's visions, 31, 42, 108
Inspirationalists, 196, 205
Irving, Capt. John, 175
Irving, Rev. Edward. *See* Irvingites
Irvingites, 198
Israelites. *See* Jews/Judaism

Jacksonian democracy, 156

Jews/Judaism: and American revolution, 201–2; Ark of the Covenant, 73; and British government, 155, 156, 202, 205; British interest in, 42; and Children of Peace, 67, 73, 75, 95, 101; Sephardim, 74; synagogue design, 74; Willson's interest in, 33, 86–9, 162; at worship, 96. *See also* Solomon's temple
Jones, Henry, 110

Kavanaugh, James, 134, 167
Kester, George, 133, 138
Kester, Martha, 133
Kiel, William, 196
King Township, 132, 133

Lafontaine, Louis-Hippolyte, 174
Lee, Mother Ann. *See* Shakers
Lepard, Benjamin and Moriah, 133
Lepard, David, 172–3
Lepard, Emarilla, 134
Lepard, Jacob, 134, 137
Lepard, Mary, 133, 134
Lepard, Peter, 117
Leppard, Peter and Elizabeth, 133
Leppard, Savina, 133
Lewis, Eleazar, 18
Linsted, William and Martha, 133, 138
Linvill, Thomas, 15
Lloyd, Jesse, 166
Lord's Supper. *See* Holy Communion
Lount, Samuel, 166
Loyalists, 6, 11, 156, 159, 201–2, 205. *See also* American Revolution
Lundy, Hannah, 133
Lundy, Israel, 46, 78, 90
Lundy, Jacob, 114, 133

Lundy, Judah and Elizabeth, 133
Lundy, Mary, 133
Lundy, Rachel, 35, 46, 48, 49, 90, 133
Lundy, Reuben, 133, 138, 179
Lundy, Samuel, 5
Lundy, Sarah, 159
Lutherans, 158

McArthur, Alexander, 135
Mackenzie, William Lyon: on Children of Peace, 56, 64, 71, 82, 90, 93, 94, 104, 110, 120, 123, 132; and Rebellion of 1837, 152, 160–7 passim, 189
McLeod, Alexander, 167
McLeod, Murdoch, 78, 90, 98, 121, 167
McLeod, William D. and Martha, 133
Maguire, John and Grace, 133
Mallow, William and Rebecca, 133
Markham, 94, 103, 121, 158
marriage: among Children of Peace, 115, 158–9; Marriage Bill (1831), 158, 161; among Quakers, 9, 17, 158, 159, 187, 188
Masonic Lodge, 32, 181–2, 204
Maxwell, 110–11, 201, 205
meeting houses: Bank, 52–3; Bristol, 51; Buckingham, 23–4; Burlington, 52; Deerfield, 51; first meeting house, 49–57, 101, 179, 180, 185; Merion, 52; New Haven, 51; New Paltz, 52; Newport, 51; Old Ship, 51; Pine Orchard, 15; Salem, 51; second meeting house, 77–81, 101, 185; Woburn, 51; Yonge Street, 4, 14–24, 188. *See also* square plans

meetings. *See* monthly meetings, yearly meetings
Mennonites, 145
Methodism/Methodists: camp meetings, 27–8, 100, 199–200, 205; dispute with Willson, 47; doctrine, 25, 194; historians' views of, 195; love feasts, 94–5; music, 94; plainness, 25–6, 197; and "religion of experience," 29; in Sharon, 182, 185, 204; and women preaching, 45; at worship, 24–5, 199–200; on Yonge Street, 24–8, 188. *See also* Bangs, Nathan; Caughey, Rev. James; Conger, Peter; Irvingites; Methodist Episcopal Church; Ryerson, Rev. Egerton; Ryerson, Rev. George; Young, Rev. Joseph
Methodist Episcopal Church, 194
migration: reasons for, 7–8; route to Upper Canada, 7
millennium: 44; historical interest in, 42, 64, 197, 205; for Irvingites, 198; for Millerites, 198; for Mormons, 198; for Quakers, 198–9; secular attitudes, 201–2; for Shakers, 43, 197; and temple design, 64; for Willson, 40, 42, 48, 64, 154, 198–9
Miller, William. *See* Millerites
Millerites, 198, 205
ministry: among Children of Peace, 90, 98; among Methodists, 26–7; among Quakers, 19–20; of Willson, 91–2. *See also* preaching

monarchy, 154–6, 174
Montgomery's Tavern, 166–7
monthly meetings: of Children of Peace, 90; of Quakers, 6
Moodie, Col. Robert, 166
Moodie, Susanna, 187
Moore, Daniel, 134
Moravians, 43, 94, 101, 196, 197
Mormons, 196, 198
Morris, Anna, 135
Morris, John and Eliza, 133
Mott, Lucretia, 45
Moxon, Joseph, 144
music/musicians: among Children of Peace, 31, 54, 80, 92–3, 95–7, 101, 103–4, 151, 173, 174–5, 179, 182, 184, 185; among Methodists, 25, 27, 94; among Quakers, 93–4. *See also* choirs; Coates, Richard; hymns; organ
mysticism, 84–5, 88

neoclassical style, 18, 21, 148
New Brunswick, 159
New Harmony, 110, 196, 201
New Jersey: bishop of, 203; Quaker settlers from, 6; St Mary's Church, Burlington, 203; Willson's stepfather from, 159; Doans' work in, 13
New Lanark, 110, 201
New Lights/New School, 194
New York City: journey to, 46; Methodists, 106; processions in, 95–6; publication in, 48, 103; Sephardic Jewish community, 74; Willson's life in, 11, 190
New York State: Quaker settlers from, 6; travellers' observations,

206–7; and Upper Canada, 205–8; visitor from, 31. *See also* Burned-Over District, Nine Partners
Nine Partners, 10, 11, 52
Notman, John, 203
Noyes, John Humphrey, 196
numerology, 72

O'Brien, Mary, 111, 161
occupations, 132–6 passim
Old Lights/Old School, 194
O'Neill, Rev. H.H., 77, 154
Ontario Christian Conference. *See* Disciples of Christ
Orangemen, 165
organ: barrel, 54, 57, 76, 79, 92–3, 94; keyboard, 79, 80, 92; music, 100, 101
Orphan House, 121, 166
Orthodox/Hicksite schism, 27, 40–1, 86–7, 192–3, 194
Owen, Robert, 109–11 passim, 201

pacifism: among Children of Peace, 41, 171; among Quakers, 5, 36–7, 189
Paine, Tom, 166, 201
Parker, John G., 169
Passover, 95, 101
Paxson, Elizabeth, 13, 23, 149
Paxson, Howard, 9
Paxson, Isaiah, 148–9
Pegg, Eliza, 134
Penn, William, 19, 126, 145
Pennsylvania: Bethlehem, 8, 196; Catawissa, 6, 18; Columbia County, 7; Economy, 196; Ephrata, 196; Harmony, 196; Lycoming County, 7, 187; Muncy, 5; publication in, 48, 103. *See also* Bucks County, Philadelphia
Perfectionists, 196
Philadelphia, 5, 39, 40, 48, 154, 191; trip to, 46
Phillips, Isaac, 5, 15
Phillips, Rebecca, 134
Pickering, preparative meeting, 6
Pine Orchard: meeting house, 15; preparative meeting, 6
plainness: Methodist doctrines of, 25–6, 188; Quaker doctrines of, 19–23, 54, 126–9, 148, 188, 203; and republican virtue, 204; Willson's doctrines of, 57, 123–6, 129, 148
political gatherings: in Sharon, 173–5; in York, 103, 151–4. *See also* Durham Meeting
Poor House, 121. *See also* Orphan House
post office, 109
preaching: by Anglicans, 106; by Methodists, 106; by Quakers, 105; by Willson, 98, 103, 104–7, 178. *See also* ministry
predestination, 25, 202. *See also* Calvinists; New Light/New School; Old Light/Old School
Presbyterians, 9, 21, 82, 92, 156, 182, 183–4, 194; Church of Scotland, 157. *See also* Calvinists
prison confinement: during War of 1812, 37, 189; after Rebellion of 1837, 167–71
processions, 30–1, 95–6, 97, 103–4
progress, belief in, 187, 202, 204, 205
Publick Universal Friend: compared with Children of Peace, 44–6 passim; history, 43–4, 196

Puritans: meeting houses, 50–1, 75; and millennium, 42; in New England, 187, 194, 196, 200

Quakers: consensus in meetings, 15; conservative, 193; cooperative communities, 191–2; *Disciplines*, 82, 122, 126–8, 192, 203; family life, 8; and music, 93–4; opposing drunkenness, 21, 180; organization, 6, 20, 90, 188, 199; progressive, 193; and "religion of experience," 29. *See also* Barclay, Robert; Fox, George; Gurneyite Quakers; Inner Light; meetings; Orthodox/Hicksite schism; Penn, William; plainness; speech; Wilburite Quakers; women; worship
Queen Street Preparative Meeting, 12, 35, 49, 57, 89, 122, 126–7

Ramsay, Michael, 185
Rebellion Losses Bill, 176
Rebellion of 1837, 165–72, 179. *See also* Mackenzie, William Lyon, Rebellion Losses Bill
reform: through architecture, 202; movement in Upper Canada, 151–77 passim. *See also* Baldwin Act, Reform Bill, women
Reform Bill (1832), 156, 172
Regency style, 76
Reid, Hannah, 133
Reid, John, 116, 117, 133, 138
Reid, Mary, 133, 134
Reid, Sarah, 133
Reid, William: as preacher, 90; as schoolteacher,

49, 122; trip to New York and Philadelphia, 46; in 1851, 134
Reid, William, Jr, 133, 134
Reid, Willson, 133, 134–5, 138, 179
"religion of experience," 29, 106, 188, 194, 199
"religion of order," 29, 106, 188
republicanism, 156
responsible government, 157, 164, 176–7
Revelation of St John the Divine, 32, 33, 36, 42, 43, 64, 72, 87, 197, 199, 201. *See also* Apocalypse, millennium
River Brethren. *See* Tunkers
Robinson, John Beverley, 117, 166
Robinson, Peter, 166
Rogers, John, 114
Rogers, Rufus, 6, 11
Rogers, Timothy, 4–6, 15, 16, 49
Rolph, Dr Thomas, 111
Roman Catholics, 19, 50, 51, 75, 158, 196
Romanticism, 84
Rose family, 7
Rowan, Deborah, 133
Rowan, Peter, 133, 138
Russell, Ten Resolutions of Lord John, 165
Ryerson, Rev. Egerton, 163
Ryerson, Rev. George, 198

St. Alban's. *See* Holland Landing
Salem, 196
scandal: and religious movements, 45–6; over Willson and Rachel Lundy, 46, 48, 49; over Willson's "harem," 122–3
school: in Hope/Sharon, 115, 122–3, 179–80; political meetings at, 175; on Yonge Street, 49, 122, 188

Scripture. *See* Bible, Revelation
Separationists, 196
settlement: from Britain, 164–5; hindered by reserves, 157–8; of Hope, 112–15; of Quakers, 4–9, 186–9
Shakers: history, 43, 192, 196, 197; compared with Children of Peace, 43–6 passim, 98–100, 111
Sharon. *See* Hope/Sharon
Sharon Temple. *See* temple
Sharon Temple Museum Society, xii
Sheppard, Thomas, 103
Shirreff, Patrick, 74, 76, 110, 129
Sibbald, Capt. Thomas, 82, 88
Simcoe, Lt.-Gov. John Graves, 3, 5, 157, 188, 201
Sloy, Anna Savilla, 145
Small, James, 175
Smith, Joseph, 198
Society of Friends. *See* Quakers
Solomon's Temple, 39, 57, 58, 59, 64, 67, 69, 73, 88, 109
Sons of Temperance. *See* temperance movement
Southcott, Joanna: compared with Children of Peace, 43–46 passim; history, 42, 44
speech: Quaker, 18–19, 63, 105, 128; Willson's, 129
square plans, in meeting houses, 50–4, 80, 102–3
Stokes, Harriet, 184
Stokes, John, 133, 138, 182
Stokes, Martha, 133, 138
Stong, Daniel, 145
stores, 116–19, 180
Stouffville/Stoverville, 166
Strachan, John, 160
study, Willson's: "the

counting room," 76; description of, 75–6
Sullivan, Robert Baldwin, 175
Sutherland, Joseph, 141
Swan, Timothy, 92
Sydenham, Lord. *See* Thomson, Charles Poulett
synagogues, 74

Tasmania. *See* Van Dieman's Land/Tasmania
Taylor, John, 198
Teats, Jess and wife, 7
temperance movement, 180–1, 195, 204
temple: construction of, 68–70; description of, 58–60; first services in, 71–2; naming of, 74–5; plans for, 57, 60, 62; sale of, 185; symbolism of, 60–7. *See also* altar/ark; charity; Doan, Ebenezer; Solomon's temple; Willson, David; worship
Terry, Elizabeth, 133
Terry, John, 133, 138
Terry, Sarah, 133
Thomson, Charles Poulett, 173–4
Thoreau, Henry David, 85
Thorne, Dr, 166
Thorpe, Maria, 135
Titus, Austin, 11
Titus, Mary, 11
Titus, Phebe, 11, 33
Toleration Act (1689), 51
Tories, 154, 174
Toronto. *See* York/Toronto
transcendentalists, 200–1
Tunkers, 94
Tyler, Royall, 204

Universalists, 45
Upjohn, Richard, 203
Uxbridge: preparative meeting, 6; Willson's followers in, 48, 103

260 Index

Van Dieman's Land/ Tasmania, 167, 169
Vermont: Timothy Rogers from, 4; Yonge Street settlers from, 6
visions/dreams: of 1803, 108; of 1812–3, 30–46 passim, 57; of 1828, 86; of 1832, 162

War of 1812, effects on Quakers, 36–8, 47, 86, 189, 193
Ward, William and Abigail, 133
Webb family, 7, 8, 37
Webster, Miriam, 134
Welland Canal petition, 160
Wesley, Charles, 94
Wesley, John, 94
Wesleyans, 194
Whiskey Rebellion, 7–8
Wiggins, Seba and Abigail, 134
Wilburite Quakers, 193
Wilkie, D., 104–7 passim, 120, 154
Wilkinson, Jemima. *See* Publick Universal Friend
William IV, 152, 153, 154
Williams, Colin [or Orlin?], 115
Willson, Absalom, 184–5
Willson, Angeline, 134
Willson, Ann, 11
Willson, Catherine, 11, 159
Willson, Charles, 133, 138
Willson, Clinger, 134
Willson, David: appeals to Methodists, 47; appeals to Quakers, 46, 47, 48; as a carpenter, 11, 66, 70, 190; death of, 182; disownment by Quakers, 35; early life, 9–12, 156, 190; and first meeting house, 49, 52; house, 123, 131, 135, 175; household, 135; land transactions, 112; against liquor, 180; in old age, 178; personal appearance, 128–9; political involvement, 151–77; and Rachel Lundy, 35, 46; religious beliefs, 83; and school, 122–3; and temple, 57–75 passim; vision in 1813, 35–6; visions in 1812, 31–4; vision in 1828, 86
Willson, Elizabeth, 133
Willson, Hannah [?], 134
Willson, Hugh, 9
Willson, Hugh D., 112, 135, 167, 179
Willson, Israel, 11, 33, 78, 134, 135
Willson, James and Pricilla [?], 134
Willson, Job, 135
Willson, John, 11, 33, 78, 91, 134, 135, 138, 159, 166–7, 180, 182
Willson, John (David's father), 10, 11, 156
Willson, John (David's stepfather), 159
Willson, John D. and Moriah, 134
Willson, John D. and Rebecca, 134
Willson, Maria Thorpe, 135
Willson, Mary, 11
Willson, Mary, 117, 170
Willson, Mary, 134, 135
Willson, Phebe, 134, 135
Willson, Phebe Titus, 11, 33, 46, 134, 182
Willson, Rachel Syllindia, 69
Willson, Rebecca, 135
Willson, Sarah, 134, 159
Willson, Sarah, 166
Willson, William H., 115, 134

women: among Children of Peace, 98; as domestic reformers, 202, 204; among Methodists, 45; as millennial symbols, 31–3, 36, 38–9, 44, 63; among Quakers, 16–17, 20, 44–5, 188; as symbols of ancient wisdom, 87; women's rights movement, 45
worship: among Children of Peace, 72, 75, 89–90, 96–107 passim, 101–7, 200; among Methodists, 24–5, 27–8, 188, 199–200; among Quakers, 19–20, 27, 32, 188, 199

yearly meetings: of Children of Peace, 91; of Quakers, 6
Yonge Street: building of, 3–4; Durham Meeting on, 172–3; Rebellion of 1837 on, 166–7; settlement by Quakers, 4–5, 11, 186–9
Yonge Street Meeting: disownment of Willson, 35; establishment of, 4–6; library, 84; meeting house, 14–24; origin of members, 6; school, 49
York/Toronto, 103, 104, 119, 120, 151, 158, 163, 166, 169, 170, 190
York Pioneer and Historical Society, xii, xiii, 185
Young, Brigham, 198
Young, Joseph, 198
youth, discipline of, 116, 127, 176. *See also* children, dissent, schools
Youths Meeting: defined, 90; opposition from, 48